ALWAYS A WARRIOR

Books by Charles W. Sasser

Always a Warrior:
    The Memoir of a Six-War Soldier
The 100th Kill
Homicide!
One Shot—One Kill
    (with Craig Roberts)
The Walking Dead
    (with Craig Roberts)

Published by POCKET BOOKS

ALWAYS A WARRIOR

THE MEMOIR OF A SIX-WAR SOLDIER

CHARLES W. SASSER

POCKET BOOKS

New York   London   Toronto   Sydney   Tokyo   Singapore

An *Original* Publication of POCKET BOOKS

POCKET BOOKS, a division of Simon & Schuster Inc.
1230 Avenue of the Americas, New York, NY 10020

ISBN: 0-671-78931-7

Cover art by Robert Tanenbaum

Printed in the U.S.A.

This book is for my mother, Mary Sasser-Wells, my stepfather, George Wells, with love, and with great love as well for my brother Joe Sasser

Author's Note

In this book I have endeavored to render the truth as accurately and vividly as possible. This is my story, but it is also the story of hundreds of others—sailors, soldiers, Marines, and just people—who played major, or minor roles in the events narrated.

Dialogue and events are reported to the best of my recollection. While the content is accurate, naturally I cannot be certain every quote is entirely accurate word for word or that my interpretation of events will be exactly the same as someone else's. Much time has passed since many of these events occurred.

Certain names in this book are the actual names of persons. Others, however, have been changed in instances where public exposure would serve no good purpose. I have no desire to publicly embarrass individuals, no wish to needlessly harm anyone.

Occasionally in the narration, due to matters of national security, or for my own security, I cannot relate all details. I must be forgiven for those omissions if they are detected.

Charles W. Sasser

Foreword

War is insanity. Men who devote their lives and energies toward the preparation for death and destruction *cannot* be totally sane. At best, they function under illusions. Like fighting for peace. At worst, they are mad. Fighting for peace is a lot like fucking for virginity.

I know about illusions, and I know about war. At barely eighteen, a tough little hillbilly kid out of the Ozarks, I ran away from home to enlist in the U.S. Navy. Through the dehumanizing and sometimes brutal process by which kids are molded into weapons, I rose to become one of America's warrior elite in the U.S. Army Special Forces, a Green Beret soldier.

For a quarter century I trained myself and I trained others in the military art and science of warfare. I believed the illusions: God and country and Mom's apple pie; fighting and fucking for Old Glory; my country right or wrong. I endured, indeed thrived on, some of the toughest combat training in the world.

I went to war six times, from Vietnam to Desert Storm. In between, I served in the demilitarized zone in Korea, parachuted into Central America, tested the security of American foreign embassies, shot it out with Latin American guerrillas, and even slipped back into Vietnam in the 1980s when it was Soviet-occupied. I worked overt and covert operations without asking questions. I survived plane crashes and bullet wounds.

But the more time I spent in the various services, the

more difficult it became for me to hold on to the illusions. Along the way, I saw too much. . . .

The vain general who insisted common soldiers salute his parked car and his wife and their dog; the despotic division "staff wienie" whose world revolved around forcing subordinates to complete reports over and over again until every *i* was dotted and every single space the correct width; the A-Team commander who informed his Green Beret team, "I'm an officer, and therefore I'm smarter than you are"; the dogface and his squad who raped a female prisoner, then executed her; the American army officer in El Salvador who permitted the execution of civilians; the lifer so institutionalized in the military that he had nightmares about being discharged; the Marine pilot reduced to barking like a dog during survival training; the nuclear-biological-chemical instructor rationally teaching what amounted to the destruction of the earth through the use of nuclear weapons; the ambitious Desert Storm colonel willing to do virtually anything to take his men to war and win his star.

Always a Warrior is a true story about war and the men who make and fight wars, of how fighting men are created and maintained in peace and war and what happens to them along the way.

Charles W. Sasser

PART 1

Convincing people to fight, and getting them to do it well, is one of the more essential and less obvious aspects of maintaining an armed force.... Illusions must be created and maintained, often unto death.

—James F. Dunnigan

1

Martial images, particularly those from childhood, contain impact. They imprint indelible messages upon tender psyches. Plastic toy soldiers in rigid ranks. Playing combat in the woods along the creek. Memorial Day parades in small towns where swaggering veterans of past wars inspire new generations to warrior sacrifice.

One of my earliest memories, and perhaps the one that propelled me into a military life, is of the campaign cap worn by my uncle Walt when he returned from World War II, and of how cocky and heroic he looked. Another memory is of a famous photo taken at the Nuremberg trials. Although it is not widely known outside the Ozark-area community in which I grew up, Uncle Walt was an MP in that photograph.

The other MPs in their white helmets and gloves and MP brassards appear ready to reach for their .45s if one of the Nazi defendants so much as goes for his *Heil Hitler;* Uncle Walt gazes solemnly out of the photograph as though peering at the ass end of an Oklahoma mule. Still, this photo capturing for posterity his service at Nuremberg made him something of a local hero.

Uncle Walt might not have been the only member of the Sasser clan to' enlist in the military, but certainly he was of the few who ever stayed in to receive an honorable discharge. Although a contentious lot when it came to quarreling with each other, those wild and uncurried Okies living in the hills along the Arkansas border didn't much go for organized fighting—especially if it meant leaving home. They proved clever at getting themselves classified 4-F or avoiding the draft by hiding from the census takers and signing false names to receive government-surplus cheese and beans once a month. Even Uncle Walt was not a hero or a particularly brave man. Truth be known, he might not have stayed in the army either except that he found himself in Germany with a war going on and couldn'ı have gotten back home even if he'd gone AWOL.

He returned from the war a melancholy figure surrounded by an air of mystery and torment. Everyone knew he had witnessed such horrible things that he couldn't even talk about them. He lay around in the back bedroom of the old farmhouse at Maw and Paw's—my grandparents'—and read Black Hawk and Red Ryder comic books. Whenever anyone asked him about the war, his eyes fluttered like sparrows trapped in the barn. A nervous tic tapped at the corner of his mouth.

"You do what you're told," he said when I asked.

Tic! Tic! Tic! The sparrows fluttered.

"Don't talk back, do exactly what they tell you, and the army'll make a man outta you."

Like most boys, I was wildly curious about the war. "Did you ever kill anybody while you was over there, Uncle Walt?" I asked.

The sparrows fluttered. His mouth ticced. "It don't matter," he said, his voice so far away that it could still have been "over there."

"It just don't matter no more," he said.

I was too young to know, too young to let him escape with only that.

"I bet you kilt lots of them. Was they bad guys?"

He blinked at me over the top edge of Black Hawk. He tossed the comic book aside and rolled wearily off the bed. He crossed to the window and fixed his stare so hard on something outside that I had to go over to see what it was. Paw—Grandpaw—was toting a bucket of slops downhill to the pigs. That was all I saw.

I tugged on Uncle Walt's sleeve. He shook himself like a dog climbing out of the pond.

"Well?" I asked.

Tic! Tic! Tic!

"I guess most of 'em was just like me and you," he said. I stared. "Then why on earth did you kill them?"

He raked me with a disgusted look, like I should have known something that obvious. "They was the enemy."

"You hated them?"

"Mostly they did what they did because of Hitler."

"Why didn't you kill Hitler instead?"

Uncle Walt stared out the window some more. The corner of his mouth twitched like Jude's tough mule hide beneath the bite of a fly.

We watched Paw sinking down the hill until nothing remained visible except his head bobbing and the brown felt hat he had sweated in ever since I could remember.

Finally Uncle Walt muttered in defeat, "Maybe it don't make a lot of sense at your age."

After a while he said, "Sometimes it don't make a lot of sense at my age."

One time when I was about five, I caught everyone else working in the fields hoeing cotton or doing the evening milking or something. I sneaked into the dusty closet where Uncle Walt stored his campaign cap and the uniform Ike jacket with the rows of colored ribbons on it. Uniformed and armed with a broken mop handle, I pretended *I* was that silent and enigmatic figure with the exotic past.

Gallantly I defended the bunker against attack from hordes of imaginary Krauts. I fell wounded onto the worn linoleum, but I recovered in time to hold ground while my buddies fought their way clear. I dashed bravely from one gun position to another, firing my automatic mop stick. During one mission—my last mission, actually—the campaign cap slipped down over my eyes. I banged into the dresser and knocked over a bottle of aftershave. My buddies and I were forced to retreat. Uncle Walt commented on how his aftershave turned up missing and about how strong he could still smell it, but to my knowledge he never caught on to what had happened.

* * *

5

In kindergarten we sat in rows coloring Waldo the Walrus or cutting out construction-paper chains when the school siren fired off with a terrifying mechanical wailing that keened teeth and iced arteries. Like acid superheated, it flooded even nail holes and cracks in the floor. Linda Shell shrieked and flailed the air like a sheet left hanging on a clothesline during a storm.

The first time it happened I thought—I *knew*—the Holy Roller preachers' prediction had come true. It was the end of the world. Gabriel was calling the Christians home.

We sinners were going to hell.

I jumped out of my seat, flinging crayons aside, and a squirrel could not have found its hole as fast as I found the door. I was almost off the school yard before Miss Fox caught me.

"You'll be safer inside if it's the *real thing*," she said consolingly.

"What is it?" I screeched.

"It's only an air raid drill. We're practicing civil defense in case they bomb us."

"Somebody's gonna bomb us?" I yelled.

"It's the Russians." She smiled and took my hand. "They have the A-bomb. Nothing's going to hurt you. Go get underneath your desk like all the other children where you'll be safe."

I never felt safe again. I looked at pictures of Russian bombers and missiles in *Mechanics Illustrated* and *Saga*. The prints were dark and indistinct and all the more sinister for it, as if the photographers had sneaked up on man-eaters. I stared at the pictures for hours. I felt as though every bomber and missile the Russians owned was zeroed in and simply waiting to catch me out from underneath my desk. The drone of a high-flying aircraft sent me darting instinctively for cover.

Sometimes, when I was out of school and visited Uncle Walt, I caught him staring out a window the way he did. You had to touch him to bring him out of it. His eyes darted. His mouth twitched. In a strange, frightening voice he warned that there was going to be another war. The next war, he said, was going to be more terrible than World War II and Korea combined. It was going to be against the Russians—and it was going to be *hell on earth.*

"It'll be the Battle of Armageddon."

The Cold War seemed so complicated to a little hill kid. I tried, but it was hard to figure out. The Russians had been our friends against Hitler, but now they were our enemies in the Cold War. It got more confusing. The Italians had been enemies; now they were friends. At some time or another the United States had warred against just about everybody—Mexico, France, Cuba, England, Canada, Nicaragua. Germany, Japan, China—but now most of these countries were our friends and allies.

Who chose our enemies and our friends? Why did nations keep switching sides?

It was like vacant-lot baseball where the captains on each side chose players and then chose all over again for the next game.

"Politicians do it," explained Uncle Walt.

"How?"

"You ask too many questions. I don't know how. All I know is that the war's just cold now because we're getting ready for the Big War. Wait'll things start heating up. Then it's Katy, bar the door."

"Is it all right to hate the Russians even if we don't know them?" I asked Mom.

"I guess they hate us back," she said.

"Why don't we go over there and bomb them before they bomb us?"

That was the solution proposed by Dad and the other men in the family who had not been to war: "Wipe them off the face of the earth before they do it to us."

Uncle Walt stared hard into the distance. Tic! Tic! Tic!

"Even the kids and their mothers? Bomb them too?" I asked.

"It has to be done so they can't raise no more Russians," Dad decided.

I nodded wisely. I clearly saw my calling, although I was

7

only six or seven years old. I had my two younger brothers, Joe and Kenneth, and I had my mom.

"Mom, I won't let them bomb us," I promised. "I'll be a soldier like Uncle Walt when I grow up. *I'll* bomb *them.*"

2

Uncle Walt had his stories about war, most of which to my knowledge he never told. But there were more war stories that came out of WW II than just from the soldiers who were at Tarawa and North Africa and Normandy. One of those stories belonged to my mother, and to me, too, I suppose. It was many years later, after I had been to war myself, before Mom told me *her* war story.

My father—he of the big hands and big nose and small head, who had labored always at jobs no one else wanted, who was paranoid and could not read even a Stop sign—was actually my stepfather.

The name that would have been under "father" on my birth certificate, had I had a birth certificate, was Alan Stroud. Mom became pregnant with me when she was sixteen. Knowing my grandpaw, as I did later, I would have thought Alan and Mom would have had a shotgun wedding, but Alan Stroud was already married and had two kids.

Mom's dad, my grandpaw, was a big overbearing man with a mean temper. He and his Indian wife and ten kids— Uncle James was the only son, and a more rebellious one couldn't have been found in Oklahoma—operated a sheep farm alongside Big Sallisaw Creek. Grandpaw's neighbors got together once and threatened to beat him with well ropes and chains, or even to shoot him, if they ever saw his daughters out pulling plows again while mules stood in the lot; if they ever saw him thrashing his daughters again with baling wire or ropes; if they ever heard him cussing his daughters again like they were egg-sucking dogs.

Mom got pregnant just looking for somebody to love her, to touch her gently, to speak to her like a human being. Her own father ran her off from home. He beat her first, then beat her again, and he ran her away like the women did in the Bible when they stoned Sarah away from the well. She ran away with welts on her back and legs and crusted blood, and that was all she had except for underwear made out of a worn-out cotton pick sack and a threadbare feed sack dress. And me in her womb.

I was born on Drake's Prairie less than a month after the surprise Japanese attack on Pearl Harbor. I was not circumsized because no doctor attended the birth. Mom and me, we headed west as our folks had done during the Great Depression. Everyone was on the move then. Soldiers and sailors. Women following them.

My dad, Alan Stroud, I guess he ignored my birth, maybe even denied I was his. Maybe Mom never even told him. Mom managed somehow without him. But when he and his wife and two children loaded up in their old car to go to California seeking defense work, Mom and I somehow ended up going with them. We were all in the same poor condition there in the hills, all seeking a better life through war work. Alan Stroud's wife, I suppose, never discovered that I was her husband's son.

In California, Mom found work waitressing and assembly-lining in Los Angeles. She met and married a sailor. Turned out the sailor, like Alan Stroud, was already married. He was the father of my second brother, Joe. When the war ended, Mom was pregnant with Joe and trying to find a way back to Oklahoma. Returning servicemen had priority on all transportation. Everyone else went space available. Civilians sometimes waited for days trying to get a bus or a train out of a big coastal city like Los Angeles.

At midnight, Mom waited at the Los Angeles bus station holding me in her arms. We had been waiting since before breakfast. Mom was tiny and skinny and pretty. She appeared about fourteen years old and so fresh off the farm that she looked as if she was uncomfortable wearing shoes.

A black limousine, rare even around Los Angeles and Hollywood during the war, pulled up to the bus station to let off a passenger. The limousine sat there for several minutes, engine idling, while everyone stared at it. It had dark-tinted windows. Mom had never seen such a car. As she gaped at it, a young and beautiful woman got out and walked over.

"Honey, you and the baby look completely tuckered out," the beautiful lady said. "You will never get a bus out of here tonight. Let me help. Why don't you bring your baby and stay with me at my house tonight? I'll have my driver bring you back first thing in the morning."

The lady's disarming smile convinced Mom to accept. She lived in what to an Oklahoma farm girl appeared to be a mansion overlooking the lights of Los Angeles. It was the first time Mom had ever walked on carpet. She and the pretty woman talked for a long time.

The next morning the Californian said, "Mary, you've said yourself there's nothing back in Oklahoma for you and your child. Why don't you stay here and work for me? If you will, I promise your little boy shall never lack for anything the rest of his life."

That was Mom's crossroads. For some odd reason, she was driven to return to Oklahoma. Maybe it was because of her failed romance with the married sailor. Maybe it was because she was already pregnant with my brother Joe. Maybe she was just homesick. At any rate, the choice she made changed not only her life but also my life and many other lives as well. How might my life have changed, my choices altered, if Mom had stayed in Los Angeles and I had become the godson of the movie actress Shelley Winters? I always intended to write her and see if she remembered her warm act of kindness, but I never did. It was wartime. War brings out the best of the human character—as well as the worst.

3

The heart of an unsophisticated little country boy growing up in cotton fields and mountains and poverty could always be stirred to romance by the beating of the drums. On summer nights sometimes the menfolk sat in wicker chairs underneath the trees and, with the exception of Uncle Walt, discussed the bombing of Hiroshima and Nagasaki. Uncle Walt kept silent with his tap-tapping mouth. The others, who had been 4-F or something, spoke with that pride and vicarious self-assurance of fans whose AAA football team had won the state championship.

President Harry Truman, by God, they said, had balls *yeaaa big*. The Bomb shoved up the Japs' little yellow asses was exactly what they deserved. Our fine boys in uniform, by God, were goddamned heroes who made the world safe for democracy. If Ike had half the balls of ol' Harry, if he had *one-tenth* the balls, he'd send the Big Bomb to Korea and blast Russian ass and Chink ass all the way five generations back to their ancestors.

On Saturdays in Sallisaw, I watched with envy the new crop of uniformed warriors bound for Korea. They strutted around Main Street with pretty girls on their arms and bragged about how they were going to win the war singlehanded. I could hardly wait until I was old enough to join their ranks. Someday, I thought, menfolk would gather underneath trees on summer evenings and talk about *my* heroics.

To the farm people and hill people along the Oklahoma-Arkansas border, heroes were fighters. Not military men, but fighters nonetheless. That was how real men settled things—with fists and clubs, and with knives and guns if they had to. One night at the quarter-horse racetrack north of Sallisaw, a guy named Stewart and an Indian named Red Cloud Fleetwood were drinking in Red Cloud's car. They quarreled. Stewart shot the Indian. Men and boys at the track crowded around and dragged Fleetwood out of his car. His mouth opened and his eyes stared and his head lolled to one side. There was some blood smeared on his front and on his hands.

He was the first dead man I ever saw, other than old people in their caskets at the funerals Maw kept dragging me to. One minute he was alive and drinking corn mash or something. The next there was a pop and he was dead. How easy it seemed, how simple, how final.

Pop!

The argument was over.

People were always talking about fights and shootings.

"I'll never beat you for fighting," Dad vowed, "but I will beat your ass if you ever run from one. I won't have no coward or sissy in my house."

"I ain't no sissy."

I think Dad always feared I would be. He could neither read nor write, except his own name, which he could write but couldn't read. To him, *real men* worked with their muscles, and they kicked ass if they had to. It disgusted him when my aunt Ellen gave me books. The only book in our house until then was a Sears, Roebuck catalog, and that only because it had utilitarian value in the outhouse.

"Nose stuck in them goddamned book," Dad scoffed. "Ain't nothing but sissies and little girls sit around reading books."

Dad changed his mind when the bully Burdick came along.

At the McKey one-room schoolhouse, the different grade levels were broken down into a single row each. Fifth graders occupied the row nearest the window, eighth the row next to the door, with sixth and seventh graders sandwiched in between. Burdick stayed so long in each row that by the time he reached the eighth grade chairs he could barely fit into them. He swaggered about the grounds with short thick arms swinging heavy from labor at his folks' sawmill. Whoever stood where he wanted to stand simply got run over. The other kids gave him candy and first-in-line lunch and anything else he wanted.

I was deathly afraid of cottonmouth snakes, but I feared Burdick even more. It was hard to avoid him on a school yard where there were only thirty kids. It would have been easier to appease a cottonmouth than to appease Burdick.

"Fight him," the other boys encouraged me after he beat up my little brother Joe. "Beat his ass for us."

I was *half* Burdick's size. He was about thirteen while I was eight or nine and small for my age. Some of the other boys were almost his age and size, but they were afraid of him. It took me a few years to understand how nations and politicians who ran nations were a lot like the schoolboys we were. Everyone might want the bully's ass kicked, but he wanted someone else to do it.

"Fight him for us," the boys whispered behind Burdick's back. The little girls stood back and tittered and waited.

The little girls. How could you ignore all those wonderful, wide, beautiful little-girl eyes watching and waiting for the emergence of a champion? A hero in my books charged into battle with a lady's kiss on his lips or her scented hanky treasured away underneath his armor. And the ladies, they waved tearfully from shore as the warriors sailed away, and they were there waving still and weeping with joy when their brave, bloodied men returned.

"Fight Burdick for us."

"I don't start fights."

"You'll be a *hero*," they whispered into my ear while at the same time they were telling Burdick that the tough little runt Sasser was going to fight him.

"I'll *kill* him," Burdick vowed.

The fight lasted one punch. His fist hit my nose and pushed it all the way over to my cheek. After I got up off the ground my eyes started to swell so that by the end of the day I peered at the world through thin slits. The other boys fawned over the victor and strolled off with their arms cast about his powerful shoulders. The little girls thronged after them, tittering. They begged to feel the muscles of the arm that had knocked me bleeding and crying and defeated to the ground.

The lesson ran clear: To the victor indeed belonged the spoils.

I dragged my shame home to face Dad. He took one look at my battered face stained with tears of pain and humiliation. He said, "It ain't over yet."

I almost dropped to my knees in prayer. *Don't make me fight Burdick again!*

Dad and his younger brother handed me a butcher knife. It felt heavy and solid in my hand. I looked at it. I looked at the stern faces of Dad and Uncle Johnny.

"Stab him," they said. "Cut him a new navel."

They drove me to the sawmill on the highway. Burdick spotted me huddled in the backseat and swaggered over to take a look.

Uncle Johnny reached back and opened the door. "Charles, cut the grin off that piece of shit."

Burdick's grin froze dead on his face. Like it was still there, but it wasn't there. I jumped out of the car. The upraised knife picked up a glint from the afternoon sun. I was one step short of sinking the blade into the bully's chest when something inside him released about a dozen coiled springs. He squalled like a cat with its tail caught in the car door. When he lined out down the highway I could have sworn it was because half his victims in Sequoyah County were pursuing him with boiling tar and feathers.

I chased him for a mile down the road, cursing and crying in frustration because I couldn't catch him. Dad and Uncle Johnny pulled up beside me in the car. Burdick was dusting off the top of the next rise. I started off after him again.

Dad grabbed me.

"Calm down, son, and get back in the car. I think he's learned his lesson."

"I ain't giving up, Dad. I ain't no coward."

Dad smiled. "You ain't no coward, boy. You ain't that."

This lesson also rang clear. Burdick kept a respectful distance from then on; the little girls heard about it and gathered to praise me; and when the menfolk congregated underneath the trees to talk, Dad and Uncle Johnny laughed and told how I, a runt, had bested the bully of the county. What a sweet reward.

"He might read books like a sissy," Dad said, "but there ain't a sissy bone in his body."

Uncle Walt listened. "We had some guys like Charles in my unit overseas who'd tear into a buzzsaw if you ordered them to."

"Charles'd do her, by golly," whispered Uncle Johnny.

Uncle Walt nodded. "Most of them got dead," he said.

4

My mother's brother was drafted and pulled a bunch of stockade time at Fort Chaffee, Arkansas. Everyone who knew Uncle James said he was too ornery and hardheaded to adjust to military discipline. He slugged a DI, a drill instructor, shucked his army fatigues, and swam the Arkansas River to get back to Oklahoma.

Four sturdy MPs came after him. Uncle James was a scrapper, but he was no match for the four of them and their billy clubs. They dragged him back to Fort Chaffee where he was court-martialed and sent to the stockade. We visited him there sometimes, Mom and me. I was about eight or nine. The stockade was enclosed by fences and concertina wire.

"It's electric wire. I'm a prisoner of war," Uncle James insisted.

One day I climbed Wild Horse Mountain and crossed to the far end where the big cedars grew, and I looked out across the muddy Arkansas River past Fort Smith, the city, to the army training center at Fort Chaffee. I constructed a log raft and floated it Huck Finn–style across to Arkansas. I started in the morning before sunrise with nothing but a bluetick hound for company and a sackful of biscuits stuffed with homemade peach jelly. The hound and I hiked to Barling, then cut through the woods and slipped underneath the fence at a little creek.

I wanted to see what the soldiers did, and maybe I could find Uncle James and help him escape again.

We came upon some soldiers marching and singing cadence and saluting. The hound and I hid and watched. Quickly becoming bored—soldiers didn't need to do *that* in order to fight—I tied a length of baling twine around the hound's neck to keep him from jumping up a rabbit or something and giving me away. Then we followed the little creek across a golf course and a road, and soon came to a squad of soldiers congregated in a field surrounded by trees. The GIs wore helmets and combat gear. I recognized their rifles from pictures I had seen—M1 Garands.

I pulled the bluetick down with me behind a large tree. Peeking through leaves and branches, I looked over the soldiers for Uncle James's grin. In uniform all the soldiers looked as alike as pups in a litter.

There was a machine-gun bunker at the far end of the field. Some soldiers loaded a long belt of ammunition into it, then pointed it at the squad in the field and shouted. The GIs split up and yelled like Comanches as they charged the machine gun. They zigzagged, falling, rolling on the ground. The machine gun opened fire with a terrifying chatter. Its muzzle blossomed flame.

I shouldn't have said it, but I said it: "Oh, goddamn!" The hound and I hugged the ground behind the tree trunk, trembling against each other like twin fawns while the machine gun massacred the soldiers in the field. I realized then that the DIs killed you in training to get you prepared for war.

As soon as I collected my heart from the top of the nearest tree, I grabbed the dog's leash and we scuttled low through thorns and bushes. Then we jumped up and raced for the safety of the river, forgetting all about Uncle James. We ran for several miles.

I ran up to a man on the street. "Do you know what they're doing over there?" I yelled, pointing toward Fort Chaffee.

He glanced down upon a little sweating mud-caked boy leading a mangy bluetick hound.

"They're killing soldier boys!" I shrieked.

The man laughed and walked away.

I told a woman about it.

"No, they are not," she said, smiling.

Nobody cared. Uncle Walt said you had to be tough, a *survivor,* if you went to war and came back. Maybe that was what the army was doing—training survivors. If you survived training, then you survived war.

No wonder Uncle James wanted to come home.

I was afraid to ask Mom and Dad about it. They never suspected how far my hunting and fishing forays into the mountains led. Uncle Walt was my best chance.

"How many soldier boys did you see get kilt in boot camp?" I asked him.

"I heard of one, but it was an accident."

"Just *one?*"

He looked puzzled.

"They don't *shoot* you!" I cried.

"You train with blanks," he explained. "They don't use real bullets. It's to get you used to what it really feels like in war—the sound and feel of it."

"Is *that* what it's really like?" I remembered how afraid I had been, hiding behind the tree while bullets that weren't really there cut through the trees all around me.

It wasn't *that* scary, looking back on it.

I wrote Uncle James a letter: "I was going to help you get loose and come home, but I couldn't."

Uncle James behind stockade wire was like a coyote cub I found once in a den near the creek. The cub paced in his pen until he wore a trench two inches deep in the ground.

He kept trying to dig his way to freedom. I finally let him go because I couldn't stand watching him caged.

One afternoon after Uncle James escaped for the third or fourth time, I sneaked off to where he was hiding out in a shallow cave near Big Sallisaw Creek. He said the Dalton gang had used the cave for a hideout.

Uncle James was better with a slingshot than David from the Bible. "That's Goliath up here," he said, spotting a squirrel in the top of a sycamore. "That's the goddamned suck-asses in the army."

He bounced a stone off the squirrel's head. We harvested deadwood and in the evening cool at the mouth of the cave we perched on logs by the fire and roasted the squirrel. Uncle James glanced into the darkness as it closed in on us.

"They'll be coming," he said.

"The MPs?" I looked around, suddenly nervous. Uncle James still had scars from the last time.

"The whole United States Army," he said.

My voice squeaked. "They won't shoot us, will they?"

"Now, they just might."

"We ain't the enemy. We ain't Russians."

"The way the army looks at it, if you ain't *with* 'em, you're *agin* 'em. The enemy is whoever the government and the army says it is. If they say me and you is the enemy, then they got the legal right to shoot us."

He got up and tested the squirrel with his sheath knife to see if it was done. I was hungry, but I had lost interest in dinner. I was too busy trying to see into the dark. I had never thought of *our* soldier boys as the enemy.

Uncle James pointed his knife at me across the flames. Fire hollowed his eye sockets into caves at the back of which burned red coals. I shivered and edged closer to the blaze.

"Once they latch on to you," he lectured, "they don't never let go till they've broke you to the plow. Folks like them can't stand to see anybody that ain't got saddle sores and that ain't got his wings clipped. Everybody says the army'll make a man out of you, but I ain't sure I want to be that kind of man. Going around like a parrot squawking

'Yes, sir' and 'No, sir' and 'Kiss your ass for you, sir,' and 'Where would you like it, sir?'

"The army told me I'd learn to jump when they yelled 'Froggie!' or they'd kill me. Well, this ol' country frog is going to jump when and where he goddamn well pleases. Remember this, boy, just as long as your ol' uncle James lives and as long as you live: *obeying* ain't for free human beings; *obeying* is for mules and dogs and slaves."

The army never shot Uncle James, although it kept coming for him and dragging him back to the stockade at Fort Chaffee. Finally it gave up on him, as I had on the coyote, and booted him back across the Arkansas River with a dishonorable discharge. Uncle James tore it up and burned it in a campfire.

He laughed his big, deep, wild laugh and made a fist. "See them scars on my knuckles?" he said. "I'll fight them or I'll fight anybody else, but I ain't fighting folks I ain't got nothing against just because the army or anybody else tells me to."

Uncle James was a cowboy. He could ride anything with hair on it. He was born a century too late. He worked ranches from Chihuahua to Calgary. Rough, hard-laughing. Sometimes mean, always generous, occasionally larcenous. He had a wanderlust. In San Francisco he robbed a bank with a water pistol and served hard time in a cell next to Robert Stroud, the Birdman of Alcatraz. He stabbed another cowboy in Montana. I was forty years old the night he died, but I cried. He sat by a campfire until after the moon came up. Then he went inside an old pickup camper shell where he was staying, closed his eyes, and died. He had written a bad check to Safeway Stores the day before.

"The best thing you can say about this old cowboy is that he lived his life exactly the way he wanted to," his cow foreman said of him in eulogy. "He never blamed anybody for anything. He never said nothing behind your back that he wouldn't say to your face. He was his own man."

I often thought about Uncle Walt, who went and did his duty, and about Uncle James, who didn't see it as his duty. Each of them influenced me. But whatever their influences, it was clear that I was like a lot of other hill kids and country boys and poor slum kids: the military was my destiny. In the military I could be *somebody*. Besides, I had promised Mom I'd be a soldier and protect her and the other women-folk from the Russians.

In 1959 you could already hear a little rumble of distant thunder on the horizon from an obscure place called Vietnam. I turned seventeen years old and passed a U.S. Navy recruiting station in Fort Smith. I paused to study a huge panorama poster in the window. Submarines and carriers at sea and fighter aircraft streaking across the face of Mount Fuji.

"Go Navy and See the World."

I looked up and down Garrison Boulevard. It was bathed in bright sunlight. It was an omen. I strode into the recruiting station, head cocked back, and presented myself. Hero material.

"See the world," the recruiter joked, macho-like. "Visit exciting places, meet interesting people—*and kill them.*"

5

In the final chapter of Ernest Hemingway's *For Whom the Bell Tolls,* the hero Robert Jordan lies wounded behind a machine gun while he waits for the enemy to come. His guerrilla band has just blown the bridge. He must persuade Maria to leave him behind. By the time I stood at the bus terminal in Sallisaw waiting to leave for boot camp in the United States Navy, I had read the scene so many times, always with tears in my eyes, that I'd committed it to memory.

"Roberto," Maria turned and shouted. "Let me stay! Let me stay!"

"I am with thee," Robert Jordan shouted. "I am with thee now. We are both there. Go!" Then they were out of sight around the corner of the draw and he was soaking wet and looking at nothing.

Farewell scenes touched me to the bottom of an indisputable romantic's soul. I always pictured myself, lonely but free, kissing the girl before I disappeared into the sunset to rescue other maidens, slay fresh dragons. Always I died heroically with the taste of a final grateful kiss on my lips.

Even at seven or eight years old, faced with the drudgery of autumns spent in cotton fields, I had rarely complained of the weight of a cotton pick sack pulling heavy against the strap across my shoulders. Head down, sun burning on my back, I flew down the rows. I possessed something my two brothers did not have and could not understand. They grumbled incessantly. Mom in her faded blue bonnet sometimes stretched against hands placed in the middle of her back. She looked for me across the cotton.

"Charles?"

It took her three or four times calling my name.

"Charles, is everything okay?"

I had this wonderful gift. In my mind I was never in that cotton field. In my mind I could be anyone I wanted to be, go anywhere I wanted to go. I created wonderful castle-in-the-sky scenarios that played themselves out in my head—in fantastic detail. Like little movies. If I didn't like the way the world was, I changed it to be anything I wanted it to be.

Throughout the lower grades and even through high school, I remained an odd character, always dreaming about traveling to foreign and exotic lands and accomplishing heroic deeds. I avoided most ridicule because I was as handy with my fists as with my wits. I waded in with fists flying at the first suspected slight or insult.

Now, leaving for the navy, waiting for the bus, I continued my fantasies. I yearned for Sharon to be with me to play out one of the farewell scenes from my books. Sharon was the love of my young life. I had adored her from the moment I saw her playing an angel in the Christmas play when she was in the sixth grade. I experienced my first real kiss with her.

That occurred in the old Ritz Theater in Sallisaw. She sat in a row ahead of me with some other girls, tittering and whispering as young girls will. I saw nothing of the movie, not even its title; I watched Sharon. While I thought she was the most beautiful creature ever placed on earth, she barely knew I existed. If only I had the courage to occupy the vacant seat next to her, maybe she would notice me.

"How is she ever gonna know you like her?" John Garvin asked, teasing.

"She don't like me."

"You gotta show her you like her first. Get up there, Sasser. You want people to think you're chicken?"

My heart pounded harder than when I got caught in the machine-gun fire at Fort Chaffee.

"I dare you," Garvin said.

"No. No."

"I double-chicken dare you."

Taking a deep breath, I jumped out of my seat and ran down the darkened aisle and plunged into the seat next to Sharon. Startled, she turned to look at me. I pretended to watch the movie.

After a few minutes of being ignored, I said . . . nothing. I had lost my voice.

Finally I croaked, "Sharon?"

Again she turned toward me.

"I love you!" I blurted out, pecking her quickly on the lips. Then I jumped up and ran.

There had been one spin-the-bottle kiss with her since then. Around a campfire by the creek. *Let it point to her.* I closed my eyes tight, and it did. I kissed her very slowly then, a short bittersweet kiss.

"Oh!" the other teenagers hooted, laughing. "Look at his face! He's *in love!*"

Blushing furiously, speechless, I walked off into the darkness and stood alone by the creek looking at nothing. Smiling, closing my eyes so I could better remember the taste of her kiss.

Sometimes, later, I remembered the kiss in places like Vietnam and El Salvador. First loves were always the sweetest. And maybe the most tragic. They molded you.

I doubt if she even knew I had enlisted in the navy and was leaving. But maybe, I fantasized, if there was a war and my ship sank and I won medals for rescuing my shipmates from the briny sea . . . maybe she would notice me then.

Perhaps men went off to war as much for their women as for anything else. Maybe it was *because* of women that men made war.

Let there be a war.

I waited to leave the Oklahoma hills and the cotton fields and the old wood-burning cane heater whose job it was mine to stoke on cold winter mornings. Among my meager belongings, contained in one cloth hand grip, were a change of clothing, my toilet kit, and two books: *For Whom the Bell Tolls* and Cervantes's *Don Quixote.*

"You are like Don Quixote," Mr. Mullins the English teacher had said to me.

"Don Quixote?"

"I'll bring you a copy."

A bond had formed between the teacher and me. I liked the way Mr. Mullins, an old man, did one-armed push-ups and then still got tears in his eyes over *Romeo and Juliet.* He liked the essays and other writings I turned in for assignments. They showed sensitivity and talent, he said. Reading wasn't sissified, he said; it was smart. Only the stupid failed to cherish books, and they were forever trapped inside the confines of their stupidity. That was the worst kind of prison.

"Don Quixote was a Spanish idealist and dreamer who thought he was a knight," Mr. Mullins explained. "He set off on a long journey in search of adventure and to right wrongs and do battle for justice. It was all in honor of the maiden love of his life, Dulcinea.

"His illusions and reality were two separate things. In reality he was a skinny Ichabod Crane riding a worn-out bag-of-bones horse. His fat squire, Sancho, rode a jackass.

Dulcinea was a common scullery maid or something. The Don and Sancho roamed aimlessly about the countryside where the Don jousted windmills and the like, which he mistook for rival knights."

I thought I should be offended.

"Wait, let me explain," Mr. Mullins said. "Like Don Quixote, you have a tendency to fight the world to make it the way you want it to be. You're a romantic, a dreamer, an idealist, always willing to joust a windmill in the name of some higher cause. My son, the world takes advantage of its romantics. It uses them up and wastes them shamelessly. The modern world, unfortunately, needs bolt turners and parts replacers, assembly-line workers and businessmen wheeler-dealers. There is not much room in the world for romantics. They can be very lonely. We would lock up poor Don Quixote in an institution or send him to prison."

The bus was late. Dad in his khaki work clothing with his thick laborer's hands hanging, Mom in the feed sack dress she sewed herself, my two younger brothers, Joe and Kenneth, in patched jeans—they waited with me at the bus station. My farewell party. Solemn, looking around, close to tears. I was acutely aware that life was in sudden transition, but I was too young to understand the full significance of it.

Over in another corner of the bus station stood Watts and his family. If there had been flowers, it would have been a funeral. Watts had enlisted in the navy with me, buddy plan. Mom had an old photograph of him and me in a baby buggy together.

How I envied him his farewell. His girlfriend, Barbara Jean, clung to him, her eyes red and puffed from last night's crying.

I felt the loneliness, only I couldn't explain it as loneliness. I felt like that sometimes when I slept at night in the woods under the stars and listened to an owl, maybe, or a coyote on the next rise. Their mournful calls in the darkness tugged at something so deep inside me that I wanted to cry from the sheer fright of aloneness.

I wished the bus would come quickly before anyone saw me cry.

I was eighteen years old, just turned, and I had never had a real girlfriend. What girl wanted a little ragged hillbilly kid more at home in the woods with hounds and shotguns than trying to make small talk over Cokes at the malt shop? As for Watts, he had been sleeping with Barbara Jean for a time. He'd told me about the first time it happened.

"Did you take all your clothes off? Both of you?"

I tried to imagine what it might be like pressed naked against a girl.

"Not *all* of them," Watts said.

"What did it feel like? Was it hard to do?"

"You don't know?"

Like he was surprised, even though everybody knew I had never had a girlfriend.

"You're a virgin!" Watts said.

"I am not!"

"Come on. Who have you plugged? Tell me just one girl you threw the meat to."

I had the opportunity one night, but I blew it. It was a gang bang in an old car out on a country road. Four other boys and me. One of the boys drove to a party at a farm-house and picked up Jewell, a plump fourteen-year-old who kept running away from home. We drank some beers and threw the cans in the road, and Jewell started crying over something. She climbed into the backseat of the car. The boys climbed in after her one after the other.

"Sasser, it's your turn in the saddle."

The summer breeze made me tremble; I shivered from the cold stars. What they didn't know was that I *couldn't* have done it even if I'd wanted to. I was a freak. I didn't know what it was called then, but later I found out. When I was born in an old house out on Drake's Prairie, there hadn't been a doctor present. There was just Mom, and Mom was sixteen and unmarried and alone—then there was me. No birth certificate, no circumcision. I had this thick sheath encasing the working part. It hurt every time I tried to skin it back. I always tried to go to the bathroom when none of the other boys were in there to see it.

I would never make love to a girl.

25

"Jewell's waiting for you, lover boy."

The other boys thought they were real studs by this time. They swigged beer and crunched cans and giggled and exaggerated their encounters in the backseat.

"Even if it is lasts, it's better than nothing," they said. "Be a man. Get in there and slam it to that bitch."

I ambled over to the car. I tried to look nonchalant.

"She *wants* it," they said, encouraging me.

As I climbed reluctantly into the car, the musky raw odor of sex grabbed me by the throat. Jewell lay on her back with her jeans and underpants pulled off. There was a moon. I saw her shirt bunched up around her neck. I closed the door quickly and perched on the edge of the seat. My hands hung down to the floorboards. They fiddled with my knees. Finally I grabbed one with the other to keep them still.

Jewell sniffled and rubbed her eyes. "Go ahead if you want to," she said. "You might as well."

I sat there.

She wept softly. I looked at her, wanting to look at all of her, but not wanting to, either.

"Don't it hurt you?" I asked.

"It don't matter."

"You didn't have to let them do it. If I'd have known you didn't want to, I'd have fought them all to keep them from hurting you. I'm a real good fighter."

She cried into her hands.

"Oh, please stop, Jewell. I can't stand to see you cry."

Even if I *could* have done it, I wouldn't have. I sat there in the dark of the car and cried with her. We held hands.

"If you was my girlfriend," I assured her, "I wouldn't never let this happen. I'd be real good to you. I'd protect you."

"Why would you do that?"

"I don't know. 'Cause ... 'cause maybe I'd love you or something."

After we cried together long enough that the other boys wouldn't think I had chickened out, I told Jewell to put on her jeans. I got out of the car.

"Did you do it?" the boys asked.

"What do you think?"

The next day at school everyone found out I'd asked the school punch to be my girlfriend. Jewell didn't have to tell, but she did. Four boys had done it to her, then that dumb hillbilly asked her to be his girlfriend. The other boys snickered behind my back, and the girls did, too. Jewell also turned up her nose at me.

Would that damned bus never arrive so I could leave this place?

"Behave yourself in there," Mom counseled. "Don't be like your uncle James and give them trouble. And make sure you write home."

Where was that damned bus?

Finally the Trailways coach snorted into town and stopped at the little station with a release of air and exhaust. It was that time. Dad shook my hand formally. His eyes went red. Mom hugged me extra hard and started crying.

"Where did all the years go?" she wanted to know. "Oh, where?"

I didn't know where, so I couldn't answer her. I ducked my head to keep her from seeing my face. The legs of the frog in my throat had to be hanging out my mouth. I hurried onto the bus and stared straight ahead at nothing. Barbara Jean held on to Watts as long as she could. He got on the bus. I gripped his knee to reassure him because he sobbed so hard he embarrassed me in front of the other passengers.

The bus pulled out of the station. I never looked back.

6

From *The Bluejackets' Manual*, issued to each navy recruit:

Approximately half the world is communist or under communist leadership. The communists have sworn never to stop trying to take control of all the world. Wherever we chance to pull back our seapower, the communists will nose forward. . . .

The record of communism is a record of deceit, dishonesty, and tyranny. The evil of communism is not static, it is a cancer that grows ruthlessly. Unless it is checked, it expands and chokes off all other forms of government and all freedom of belief, thought, and speech. Our moral obligation to fight communism includes the necessity to maintain a strong Navy. . . .

In the case of all-out war, our easily located and exactly fixed land airbases would be liable to complete destruction by atomic bombs. But aircraft carriers are moving, not fixed, targets. A carrier can go over 600 miles in 24 hours, "losing" itself anywhere in an area of 1,500,000 square miles. A land base that has been hit by nuclear bombs may be unusable for weeks and months because of radioactive contamination. However, a carrier can "wash off" in water and thereby protect itself from radiation effects. And a carrier task force can move to another and uncontaminated part of the ocean.

To do its job the Navy is building new ships and aircraft, and perfecting new guided missiles. The important thing to know is that the Navy is moving ahead fast. All of us in the Navy are fortunate to be part of this technical revolution. From nuclear power for ship's propulsion to landing the first plane at the South Pole, the Navy is a progressive, alert, "can do" outfit that will always be the nation's first line of defense.

7

"Ask not what your country can do for you," exhorted a young newly elected president, "ask what you can do for your country."

The navy gray schoolbus crammed with shaggy-haired youngsters speaking in accents from across the nation drove through the big gates at the Naval Training Center, San Diego, California. I strained to catch a glimpse of the ocean as the bus cut down next to a dirty inlet from the sea where the whaleboats were moored, but all I saw was the inlet with gulls screeing over it.

We were deposited at a big open-air shed called R&O— Recruiting and Outfitting—where other buses lined up to disgorge still more recruits. Then it was that old bugaboo of the military everywhere: hurry up and wait. Hurry there, wait. Hurry here, wait. Then just wait.

Herded, shuttled, and shouted at. Pause, hesitate, or draw an unauthorized breath and some asshole who thought he was an ol' salt would jump down your throat and up your ass. Any minor infraction drew the standard punishment of twenty push-ups liberally punctuated in cadence by "shitbird." As in: *"Eighteen,* shitbird ... *nineteen,* shitbird ... *twenty,* shitbird ... Now give me twenty more for being a shitbird, shitbird."

In the Oklahoma hills, anyone called you shitbird or ass-hole, anyone called you *anything,* he had better be good and ready with his fists.

Watts had always possessed the cooler head. "Don't take none of it personal," he advised. "Remember that if you want to make it through boot camp without getting slammed in the brig, just say 'aye-aye' and go on."

Aye-aye.

Watts possessed the cooler head, but I possessed a nature that never let me enter anything totally blind. The philosophy behind military training, I read, was to tear down the recruit, strip him of all his old wrong civilian ways and habits, then build him up again the military way, the *right* way. Install in him fidelity, loyalty, and most of all, obedience. Beat the poor young bastards until they were so grateful when you stopped that they would do anything to keep you from beating them some more. The French Foreign Legion made its soldiers so afraid of their leaders that confronting the enemy by comparison seemed the lesser gamble.

Each of my uncles had his own perspective on it.

I glanced at Watts. We were mired elbow-deep, almost literally, in shit. He had his hand stuck into a commode, cleaning it. I was mopping. Cleaning a shithouse, even if it had a tile floor and real flushers, was not the reason I had enlisted in the U.S. Navy. The Join the Navy and See the World poster had said nothing about this.

Heroes did not clean shitters.

Watts gave me a sick grin. We looked around for someone watching. I walked over and leaned on my mop to do a little scuttlebutting. We were settling down to some real bitching when the door flew wide and a brown chief petty officer's uniform charged in as stiff as frozen shirts on a winter clothesline.

"What the hell do you two think you're doing?" the chief roared. "You get paid to work, not scuttlebutt. You pieces of hog manure. You shitbirds."

We attacked our jobs with renewed incentive. I mopped furiously. The chief swaggered close. "Don't fuck up my shoeshine, lad."

I stopped mopping. Swabbing the deck, it was called in the navy. The chief thrust his face so near mine that I smelled sour beer from the night before. He had blue eyes, paled out, and red veins that road-mapped from his eyes down the soft flesh underneath until they exploded in a bulbous nose. The guy was a drinker. My grandpaw—Paw—was a drinker.

Underneath the navy khaki bill cap in front of me was nothing but smirk and red veins. The chief walked in a complete circle to check me out. He exploded with laughter.

"My God, lad. I have never seen such big goddamned ears on a human being."

I had been given my first skinhead haircut.

"Where you from, lad?"

I cleared my throat. "Oklahoma."

"An ignorant Okie, huh? That's where they got them stump-broke cows and horses. What was your daddy—a long-eared jackass?"

Watts shook his head at me, warning. Just say aye-aye.

"You look like Mickey Mouse, lad."

The CPO stood in front of me and grabbed my ears.

"What have we got here? Handles so your buddies can hold on while they skull-fuck you?"

Was this, I wondered, the way it had begun for Uncle James?

I stepped back and in one quick motion reversed the mop in my hands like Joe DiMaggio stepping up to the plate. Watts saw it coming. He threw himself across the shitter and grabbed me before I home-runned. The chief first looked surprised, then furious. The red splotches on his nose and cheeks spread until they met at the collar line. He nodded slightly, grimly, before the smirk returned.

He about-faced and strode crisply to the door.

"This shitter had better be spotless," he said. He glared at me. "Mickey Mouse, don't start thinking this is over yet," he said. "It has just begun."

8

On the third day at Recruiting and Outfitting, we skinheads in our blue dungarees and white Dixie cup caps were herded out onto the grinder to meet the most dreaded human being ever to enter any recruit's life. Drill instructors chewed up marlin spikes for breakfast and tore apart mothballed destroyers for physical training.

We heard the training company commander's voice ripping through the air like a five-inch shell: "Fall in! Goddammit, fall in at attention!"

He charged across the grinder like a cruiser on a battle course. Watts took a look and sucked in all the air around him. I headed for the safety of a rear rank, seeking anonymity among the eighty or so other recruits of the company.

"Mickey Mouse! Freeze where' you are."

I smelled sour beer.

"Didn't you hear me say 'Fall in,' Mickey Mouse? You trying to be different or something, shitbird? Stand to attention when I talk to you."

"Aye-aye."

Aye-aye, kiss your ass for you, sir, and where would you like it, sir?

I gritted my teeth. I had a habit of grinning at the most inappropriate times.

"What the fuck you smiling at, Mickey? You think I'm funny? Is that what it is? The best part of you must have run down your mama's leg and become a stain on the mattress. I'm going to break your ass, shitbird, or you'll never leave this training center...."

On and on. Spitting and fuming. Something he said, something like "you big-eared, cocksucking bag of puke," drew a muffled snicker from the ranks. The chief's jaw locked. The rage that, until then, had centered on me unleashed a scathing broadside at the entire company.

The chief got into full steam with, "Who gave you ball-less cocksuckers permission to laugh in my formation?" He settled down to hurling around *shitbirds* and *assholes* and *scum buckets* like depth charges. While he was busy, I sneaked off to the back rank and slipped in between Watts and another recruit. I thought I had escaped until the chief suddenly noticed my absence. He fell silent and looked around.

"Where'd that shitbird Mickey Mouse go?"

I thought to turn myself into a pile of gull shit. From the front rank an eager little voice piped up. "Sir?"

"Whattaya want, shit-for-brains?"

A slope-shouldered runt turned and pointed directly at me. "Sir. Sir, I was going to tell you. Mickey Mouse, see, he's right back there."

Underneath the Dixie cap, a face like a rat's. Pimples. Puckered little red eyes like the earnest wounds from castrating a bull calf.

"Oh, you were helping me out, were you?" the chief said, smiling like he had his smile greased.

"Yes, sir."

"Well, now, I see we've got us a regular little helper here. What's your name, dick-breath?"

Dick-breath hesitated, like maybe he had second thoughts.

"Seaman Recruit Lambert, sir."

"Step right up front, Seaman Recruit Lambert. Let everybody see what a snitching, buddy-fucking, no-good piece of shit looks like. C'mon, Lambert, get up here. Git! Git!"

Lambert slunk forward. A wharf rat on a pier loaded with stevedores commanded better presence.

"Face the company, Lambert. Stand at attention. Mickey Mouse, get up here next to your brother."

That was how Lambert and I were paired like two shitbirds on a fence. I pledged to punch Lambert out the first chance I got.

"Look this garbage over while I talk," the chief directed. The company did. I felt as welcome as a snake at an old ladies' bridge party. "I'll make a promise to all of you right now. These two shitbirds are not going to make it in my navy. How many of you will join them?"

That smirk again. Of all the people I had to try to hit with a mop handle.

"In case you idiots haven't figured out who I am by now," the chief continued, "I'm Chief Petty Officer Birkes. I've been assigned to baby-sit you shitbirds through the next nine weeks of your initial military training, what may well be for some of you a brief navy career. I see I don't have much to work with. If the quality of recruits keeps going down we'll be training chimpanzees and baboons. But if you're what they give me, either I'll make fighting men out of you or I'll twist off your heads like bottle caps and let the gulls eat your brains.

"From this moment on, for the rest of your stay in *my* United States Navy, however long that may be, you will cease and desist being individuals thinking for yourselves. *I'll* do any thinking that needs to be done for you—or someone else will who has proper approval from the chief of naval operations. Is that clear?"

Mumble-mumble from the undisciplined ranks.

"I can't hear you!"

A seagull two hundred feet overhead veered abruptly off course. The company jumped in startled unison.

"I can't hear you!"

"Aye-aye, sir!"

Chief Birkes turned away. It took him a minute to clear the disgust out of his system.

"Trying to think for yourself gets you killed, or it gets the asshole next to you dead. You are now cogs in the largest, deadliest, most skilled fighting machine the world has ever known. We shout our challenge to the world: 'Don't step on us, or we kick ass!' And the slope-headed, squint-eyed, yeller-tinted, black-faced, tongue-twisted shitheads who make up the rest of the world had better listen when we fart.

"Everything you do from now on, you do *together*. You

are shit by yourself; you are nothing. Also, you are worthless to yourself and everyone else. You will march everywhere you go, and, by God, you had better be in step. If I order you to kick ass, you don't ask whose. You just start kicking ass. You'll go to chow *together,* and you'll finish *together.* You'll scrub your filthy skivvies *together* and get out of your racks *together.* You'll shit, shave, and shower *together.* If I come in some night and one man's in his rack beating his pud, I had better hear every other bed squeaking in unison. I don't want anyone trying to be different, trying to be an *individual.*"

He hawked and spat. *Individual? Filthy.*

"There are no individuals. It's just one navy. You ain't shit without each other."

He clamped his lips tight; they looked like a knife slash. His eyes burned bright and sharp like a bird of prey's as he looked the company over. Finally his gaze settled hard on his designated company shitbirds. Lambert trembled uncontrollably. I stared back.

"May God have mercy on your shitbird souls," he concluded, looking directly at me. "Because I won't."

9

Back in the hills whenever you hatched chicks and one of them was smaller and weaker than the others, or sickly and deformed, or otherwise somehow different, the healthy chicks ganged up on it like cannibals and eventually pecked it to death. It was that same kind of nature that made people look down upon those they considered inferior.

Take Lambert. Lambert was the guy muggers on the street picked to rob. Bullies looked to beat him up in bars.

My old Indian grandma—Maw—meant him when she said everyone served some useful purpose, even if only as a bad example.

Lambert and I, we were Chief Birkes's bad examples.

"You shitbirds ain't the material I want in *my* navy."

I could either grin and bear it or kick his ass and end up like Uncle James.

I grinned.

It infuriated him. "You *shitbird.*"

Lambert took it in the balls. Birkes chewed into him, and Lambert's eyes filled with tears. He fought to keep from bawling like an orphaned calf.

"Lambert, you little son of a bitch," I shouted after every encounter. "Don't let him do that to you. Hold up your head."

"I ain't like you, Mickey."

"Don't call me Mickey."

With his short legs and tiny feet, Lambert marching resembled one of those toy penguins that you wound up with a key to make walk. He managed about six pull-ups maximum during PT. He tripped going over a hurdle on the confidence course and busted his lip. Two guys boosted him into the rigging of the stationary sailing ship because he didn't have the muscles to pull himself up. He tumbled out of a whaleboat and almost drowned in the scummy inlet. After something spooked him on the firing range, he whirled around with a loaded M1 and almost gave Chief Birkes a heart attack.

The chief yelled "Shitbird" at him so often that Shitbird became his name, like mine became Mickey Mouse. A sign strung around his neck let everyone know that the pathetic runt shuffling along behind the company with his Dixie pulled down over his ears like a sack was Company Shitbird #1.

Somehow Lambert grew smaller and more silent as the days passed, as if he might eventually become invisible. The other recruits either ignored him, pushing him out of the way without seeing him, or they snapped at him like snapping at an unwanted stray dog that refused to leave off the front porch. Since Lambert clearly offered little challenge to Chief Birkes's fertile military imagination, he devoted more and more time to me.

I was supposed to be Company Shitbird #2. Too many years loping around in the mountains had given me a long, arm-swinging stride that failed to adapt to the thirty-inches-all-around cadence of the military march. Most of the time I fell into the rear of the company with Lambert. I wasn't much on protocol, either. I went to great lengths to avoid saluting officers or calling them "sir." It seemed belittling for one man to humble himself before another. Back in the Middle Ages a king would have chopped off my head sure.

If I wasn't much on military soft skills, I made up for it on hard skills. I had hunted squirrels and rabbits ever since I was six years old and Paw gave me a Long Tom 12-gauge shotgun that knocked me on my butt every time I fired it. I could outrun a mule through the woods. I led the company in shooting and running. I was always chosen first for competition in seamanship and combat skills.

I watched the resentment smoldering in Chief Birkes's red-veined blue eyes. Watts warned me that the chief had an ulterior motive when he volunteered me for the Sunday night smokers, the boxing matches.

"You've never even had a pair of boxing gloves *on*," Watts pointed out. "The chief wants to get you busted up."

If I was anything, I was stubborn. "It ain't going to happen."

Kelmer, the heavyweight—I was a middleweight, forty pounds lighter—prepared me for my first fight. He'd fought Golden Gloves before enlisting. We worked three or four rounds every night sparring in the showers. I sported a black eye for a few days, but then I learned to work a jab and feint and slip punches. I busted Kelmer's lip one night and caught him with a right hook the next night that sat him down hard on the water drain. He declared me ready.

"It's simple," he said. "Hit the other guy harder and more times than he hits you."

On Sunday afternoon before the fights that night a work party set up a ring among the barracks and surrounded it with tiered wooden bleachers. The lights went on; the recruit companies marched over. Competition ran high. Fighters chosen from each company fought against boxers from other companies. It was a means of building esprit de corps. I guessed Chief Birkes figured he could stand one loss—me— since Kelmer and three or four of the others in the company were odds-on to win. He could bask in their glory and still get his satisfaction out of seeing me busted up.

I worked up a light sheen of sweat shadowboxing, as Kelmer instructed, and sneaked a peek out the window of the shitter that served for our dressing room. As a heavyweight, Kelmer would fight the last bout on the card.

"The chief's already out there," Kelmer said.

"I see him."

Birkes sat at ringside with the other drills and the officers in their gold braid.

"Go out there and *win*," Kelmer said. He grinned. "The Virgin Sturgeon rides."

It was hard to hide anything showering with eighty other men. "Can you *use* that thing?" someone had asked in the showers.

"I can use *these*," I responded, brandishing my fists.

When the announcer called my name, I trotted down the aisle toward the ring, shadowboxing still and jumping around stiff-legged as I'd seen the pros do on TV. I stopped next to the chief.

He ignored me for a minute. Then: "Mickey Mouse, get the fuck in that ring."

"Chief, I'm gonna win. This fight's for you."

Seeing the red creep down his face and meet his collar, I laughed aloud and sprang into the ring with a mountain-boy whoop that set my company to cheering.

I was an arrogant little bastard, if nothing else.

My opponent proved to be a stocky blond middleweight with some training. He drove me into the ropes during the first round and kept me there. My nose was bleeding when the round ended. A glance in Chief Birkes's direction revealed his familiar smirk.

I called out to him. "The fight ain't over yet, Chief."

The smirk grew.

"I have to win," I cried.

Kelmer laughed. "Do it, then, Virgin. Go out there and fuck that boy up. Pretend he's Chief Birkes."

I was a street fighter, a brawler. When the bell sounded, I leaped from my corner and hurled myself across the ring. The blond boy and I collided. Fired up for the second round, I threw so many punches from so many different positions and angles that the ref gave my opponent a standing eight count. I grinned at the chief. He glared.

At the end of the round my opponent looked as though he had tangled naked with a roll of concertina wire. The ref called the fight and awarded me a TKO. I danced out of the ring. By God, I was *invincible*. Don Quixote. Chalk one down for Mickey Mouse, the Virgin Sturgeon. Hero.

"What do you think, Chief?" I shouted. "Next Sunday again?"

I was making it impossible for him to let it go on like this. Behind his back the other recruits were laughing at him.

10

Something so ugly filled the air that it was like the air around a dead cow left bloating in the sun. The other sailors whispered conspiratorially about how sailors in a sister company had risen silently in the middle of the night to drag their scrounge to the showers. They'd beaten him and scrubbed him with wire cleaning brushes until he bled from every pore. It gave conformity a new, more sinister meaning.

It reminded me of stories Maw had told about the KKK riding on moonless nights wearing sheets and hoods to hide their identities when they burned barns belonging to niggers and blanketbacks and other unwanteds. But even in the hills there weren't many guys mean enough to sic a pack of hounds on a coon once the coon was down and out. At least they saved the pelt.

During barracks and locker inspections, the displays had to be exactly right—skivvies folded precise and stacked dress-edged, socks rolled "cunt-side up and out," *The Blue-jackets' Manual* displayed, spare uniforms lined up with the towels. Each sailor's locker had to look exactly like the next. Naturally, being the example, Lambert and I expected to fail. I accepted it with a grin and a shrug. Lambert almost had a nervous breakdown.

"Mickey, Lambert's a *real* shitbird," Kelmer said. "He's bringing the entire company down."

"The boy's just fucked up. He can't help it."

"We don't want him in this company."

"Who's *we?*"

"Well ... everybody."

Everyone knew Chief Birkes's position. He called Lambert and me to attention in the middle of the barracks bay. The other recruits glared at us like we were green scum on a cold cup of coffee. When Birkes wasn't around, I was mostly accepted, because Kelmer and Watts and the others knew the situation. But Lambert. Lambert was *always* the shitbird.

The chief was at his smirking best. "These two sorry shitbirds just can't seem to get with the program," he began. "They refuse to become one of us. They are not team players like we need in the United States armed services. Shitbirds like them get their buddies killed on the battlefield. How many of you want to go to war with these pitiful excuses for human beings?"

Naturally, there were no takers. Lambert's chin dropped to his chest.

"If they don't join the machine, we're going to lose the Outstanding Company streamer. I've done everything I know to do to bring them around. I've counseled, I've punished, but patience can only go so far." He looked up and down the bay.

There was this ugly smell.

"What are we going to do?" the chief asked smoothly.

"I'm going to leave it to you, the members of the company."

He looked at Lambert and me. He looked toward the showers, just to make things clear. Then he walked off.

It was a seed skillfully sown. Lambert retreated to his bunk, where he drew a blanket around himself and sat there shivering like a kid goat surrounded by a pack of dogs. I saw him still sitting there, late, after taps, but then he went to sleep. I relaxed also and soon felt my eyes closing. It seemed the company might have survived Birkes after all.

Even later, movement in the barracks awoke me. A shadow approached. I swung upright to a fighting position.

"It's me, Mickey," Kelmer whispered. "We don't want you. We're having a GI party for Shitbird."

Kelmer reminded me of the big kid, Burdick, from the sawmill.

"Mickey?"

Everyone knew you didn't cross Kelmer. I mustered some courage. "I ain't going to no barn burnings," I said.

That left Kelmer momentarily speechless.

"Don't you care if we win the streamer, Mickey?"

"I ain't part of this thing."

Kelmer filled the silence with ominous things. I sat on the edge of my bunk, stiff, trying to control my breathing. I lay down.

"Some of the guys wanted to include you in Shitbird's party," Kelmer threatened.

I waited, nerves vibrating. After a moment, Kelmer's big shadow dissolved down bay. I retrieved my M1 rifle, gripped it across my chest ready to butt-stroke any hostile face that appeared unexpectedly.

A thick gunk-oil of excitement and anonymous danger filled the bay, mixing with the ugly smell. Shadows glided on bare feet toward Lambert's end of the barracks. Exhausted from his long vigil, he slept on, unaware that a darker reality was about to intrude upon his nightmares.

I stared into the darkness and listened because I couldn't

not listen. I felt fear like something alive curled up inside my gut. Faceless fear, soundless fear, in-the-middle-of-the-night fear—it's the worst kind.

There was almost a scream, but not quite. Something—a hand over the mouth?—stifled it. There was the excited barefoot stomping of many feet as the mob rolled Shitbird into a blanket and, en masse, dragged him across the floor to the showers. The showers were almost soundproof.

The recruits fell upon Lambert and beat him with bars of soap dropped into the toes of socks. They grunted and snarled like coyotes gnawing at a bloated carcass. Lambert's whimpering threaded its way from the showers, like blood from a shark's kill. Then he ceased whimpering and silently accepted his punishment.

I flinched every time a bar of soap struck flesh.

After it was all over, the vigilantes stole back to their bunks. Lambert sobbed as he dragged himself to bed. I lay with my M1. I felt smothered by shame. Shame for them, shame for myself. Don Quixote, that jouster of windmills, would have donned his rusty armor for combat. I had been too afraid.

Some hero. Some fucking hero.

Damn Lambert. Damn that shitbird.

Snoring filled the bay. It was as though nothing had happened. Down at the far end of the rows of bunks, Lambert, Company Shitbird No. 1, sobbed alone in the darkness.

At this end of the rows of bunks, Mickey Mouse, Company Shitbird No. 2, buried his face in his pillow in shame.

11

Chief Birkes seemed disappointed that Lambert bore the marks of his session in the showers while I had escaped a similar fate. The next time his shitbirds failed locker inspection he marched the two of us out onto the grinder at the end of the day like convicts on the way to a firing squad. He ordered us into the stationary push-up position. The sun burned through my dungaree shirt. Within five minutes the shirt turned black with sweat.

Birkes smirked. He was so good at it. "You're doing this for the company," he declared. "Just like Jesus. The company failed, but it was you two who caused it. So you're taking the punishment for their sins. If either of you drops before I give you permission, I'm going to march the entire company out here and let *them* take the punishment for *you.*"

That meant a GI party afterward for sure, for both of us.

I locked my elbows and hunched my body forward and dropped my head to relieve muscles that were already knotting with pain. The asphalt seared its way into the palms of my hands. It burned all the way to my brain.

I thought instead of Sharon and of her kisses. I had learned to fantasize in the cotton fields to relieve physical discomfort. I hung there on stiff arms above the asphalt. I even grinned.

"Mickey Mouse, you are one crazy little bastard," Chief Birkes decided before he walked off and left us there.

Puppy sounds escaped from Lambert.

"Shut the fuck up, Shitbird."

43

"I—I don't care ... Mickey. I can't stand anymore. He's never gonna let up on us. He's gonna kill us."

"Lambert ... you quit on me and you won't have to wait for the company to take you to the showers. *I'll* do it."

We endured—two figures alone and horizontal on our toes and palms in the middle of a vast parking lot next to the bay. The sun sank slowly into the Pacific Ocean that I still had not seen. A sailor who might never have an ocean.

"It's killing me," Lambert wailed after less than five minutes.

"Die, then. But don't quit. He's watching us."

Back in the hills I had a pet raccoon I called Mr. Clean. Mr. Clean insisted on washing everything he ate. If I gave him a biscuit or a slab of corn bread, he would grab it and scurry to the chickens' water. He'd chitter furiously and throw himself onto the ground in a rage when the bread dissolved in the water. But he kept washing his food anyhow.

"You can't break him from it," Dad said. "It's a coon's nature."

I had a coon's nature.

"Mickey ... ?" Lambert gasped.

"Don't think about how it hurts, Shitbird. Think about something good. Think about your girlfriend. You got a girlfriend, don't you?"

"N-no. Do you?"

"Yeah."

"What's her name, Mickey?"

I grinned. "Dulcinea."

"That's a funny name. Is—is she good-looking?"

"She's ugly."

"Your girlfriend's *ugly?*"

"An ugly girlfriend is the best kind. They don't ever leave you."

"M-Mickey, I ain't never had somebody that didn't leave me."

He panted and gasped from exertion. "M-Mickey ..."

With a long last sigh, like air escaping from a punctured

tube, he melted into the grinder and became all but a part of it. I hung above the asphalt.

"I-I am so sorry, Mickey. So sorry . . ."

Lambert lay gasping on the tarmac. A pair of spit-shined brown shoes advanced across the grinder. They halted a few inches from my face.

"Always the tough guy, aren't you, lad?" the chief said.

I hung there.

The shoes took a sidestep. "Lambert, get up from there and drag your sorry ass back to the barracks."

Birkes waited until Lambert shambled off.

A shitbird couldn't help being a shitbird. "Unsuited for military life"—that was how his discharge read. He probably ended up in Kansas or Iowa or someplace pumping gas at a filling station.

Unsuited for military life. Perhaps that was a high compliment in an underhanded way.

"You can get up too, Mickey Mouse," Birkes said.

I wanted to.

"No," I croaked.

"What did you say?"

"I ain't getting up yet."

I felt him watching me. Then he turned quickly away. My numbed limbs let him reach the far end of the grinder before they dumped me. It took me a few minutes to struggle to my feet. I massaged my legs; I pounded my arms against my body to restore circulation after the twenty-minute workout. Feeling returned with blinding bursts of pain. I dared not cry out; I wouldn't give Chief Birkes the satisfaction.

Finally I tottered off on unsteady legs, like a very old and feeble man.

The chief had stopped. He pretended to admire the last colors of the sunset. I walked past him without a word. The other recruits were outside pounding laundry on the concrete tables. When they spotted me walking, they stopped what they were doing and silently watched. I started marching. I marched into the company area with my head held high.

Like a rat in its hole, Lambert crouched upstairs on his

bunk eating a candy bar. His rheumy sad eyes shot back and forth in his skull as if they were afraid to settle. I stood on the fire escape landing and looked back toward Chief Birkes. His was a solitary figure on the grinder. He turned and walked slowly away. I lifted a clenched fist.

A victory was a victory. You took it any way you could.

12

On one of my long jaunts into the hills when I was a kid, I came upon two buck deer fighting in a forest opening. They rammed each other like goats, backed up as though astonished, shook their racks, snorted, reared, and charged each other again. Two comely females pretended not to be interested in the outcome.

When the battle ended, the more powerful buck, the victor, took possession of the does. Neck bunched into muscle by extra charges of testosterone, he was one proud, triumphant son of a bitch, high-stepping, head up and crowned with weapons. The does jumped all over themselves to please him.

I read Darwin and I read Konrad Lorenz. It occurred to me that humans weren't so different from other animals when it came to survival. Only our methods were different. Such things as prizefights, auto races, business competition, the grandest house in town, little boys displaying their muscles, bigger boys in uniform, *war*, had but one purpose— competition to win and breed with the most desirable females. An individual's entire existence was programmed toward the survival of the species by propagating the strongest, the most dominant.

We competed, dominated, selected, bred, and then, breeding completed, we deteriorated and died, leaving behind our progeny to do it all over again. The making of war marked our genes as surely as the DNA for brown eyes or a cleft chin, only it was general and marked the whole human race.

A great and suffocating sadness descended upon me. What terrible irony, I thought, that while I may have been gifted with many of the tools for successful competition, I would never complete my own personal cycle by breeding. That despised sheath of skin that encased my blade made of me a freak of nature. Each time I tried to unsheath it, excruciating pain shot out into my groin and up my spine. I was afraid to force it for fear of bleeding to death, although death might have been a kinder fate. Humiliation and embarrassment prevented my going to a doctor or someone I trusted.

"Skin it back," said the doctor at my induction physical.

My face burned. "I can't."

He looked. "Move on," he said before I gathered the courage to ask about it.

"God," I sometimes cried, "what kind of cruel prank have you played on me?"

Red Dog Warren offered some hope of remedy; I was always looking for hope. He transferred off tin cans—destroyers—into fleet school at San Diego at about the same time I made it through boot camp. Several years older than I, he had terrific red hair and a wonderful swashbuckling scar on his cheek. His dungarees were bleached out from a year at sea. Red Dog was an old salt with a rolling seagoing gait and a worldliness I immediately envied.

"You ain't never done it before?" he exclaimed, astonished. "A virgin seaman? No such thing exists."

Alas ...

"What you need for the first time is a Tijuana whore," he said.

I couldn't come right out and *tell* him, but I asked, "Will it be really wet and slippery going in? I mean, you know ... a big one?"

He roared with laughter. "We'll have to tie a two-by-four across your skinny ass to keep you from falling in."

I affected a rolling gait like Red Dog's and even smoked a couple of cigarettes without coughing too much. We swaggered from one Tijuana bar to the next, each increasingly seedier than the last. The Mexican strippers rubbed it in your face; they got right down close where the crowds of young American servicemen could smell it and touch it. Red Dog swigged some beers. I tried to match him but soon either had to give up or depend upon him to carry me. Red Dog licked the girls through their G-strings and howled. I was a hormone with feet, but I didn't lick anything and I didn't howl.

"Are you horny, man?" Red Dog demanded.

I nodded eagerly.

"Let's go get some pussy, boy."

Aye-aye.

He led me into a slum area among a badlands of gullies and arroyos. Poor, filthy little shacks and adobes perched precariously along the washouts waiting for the next flash flood or dust devil to sweep them away. Latin tempers displayed themselves on every dusty corner. Ragged brown kids rolling old tires or riding rattletrap bicycles stopped us. They glanced furtively about like movie gangsters.

"Wanna buy some pussy, *señor?* Tight pussy. Almost virgin pussy."

At least they didn't say it was their sister or their mother, like I had heard they would.

Red Dog accepted an offer. We followed the grinning boy through sobering slums where surly dark men loitered everywhere in the middle of the day. Chickens and pigs prowled about for scraps. So did the smaller children, filthy little creatures wearing ragged cutoffs or too-big trousers with the cuffs rolled up or sometimes dragging in the dirt. Young girls twelve and thirteen years old, pretty things, attempted to divert our attention.

I thought *we* had been poor growing up.

"Don't get separated," Red Dog warned. "In the Philippines I saw kids like these who hid razors in their hands.

They could slice open your pocket for your wallet or cut off your finger to get a ring and be gone before your finger fell in the dirt. You ain't in Kansas no more, Toto."

"They—they're so *poor,*" I stammered.

"Of course they're poor. They're spics," Red Dog said, enlightening me.

Poverty like this was something I had never encountered before. I soon discovered, however, that it was a common condition for most of mankind.

"The whores . . . ?" I ventured.

"What about them?"

"They do it just for the money?"

Red Dog whooped. "Why'd you think they did it? Because they love you? Look at it this way: Americans got the money, so why not pass it around a little? You get your rocks off; the whore makes a solid American greenback. Everybody's happy."

Our guide directed us to narrow, smelly places. We entered an adobe with one large room. Old curtains partitioned off the corners and sides into cribs each big enough for a bed or a mattress on the floor. The floor was packed earth. Barefoot, scantily clad young women dashed out like pigeons thrown bread crumbs. One of them grabbed Red Dog and led him away. He flashed a jaunty grin before he disappeared.

Another claimed me. There was a mattress on the floor behind her curtain. It stank of mildew and was badly stained from the loins of my countless predecessors. Stripping off her one-piece shift, the girl stood brown and skinny and naked beneath it. She smelled slightly of exotic things—fried foods and smoke and other scents I did not recognize. I took a step back and stood as stiff as any other country bumpkin his first time in a foreign whorehouse. The girl solemnly fumbled at my belt.

"Fucky?" she said, repeating like a parrot the only word she knew in English. "Fucky? Fucky?"

Red Dog was already fucky in a neighboring stall. I heard him.

I looked at the girl closely, trying to see behind the mask.

What I saw with sudden horror was Jewell and the gang bang on the country road.

"No!" I cried suddenly, grabbing my pants to keep them up.

It wasn't supposed to be like this. I didn't know what it was supposed to be like, but certainly not like this. Grunting for a few minutes over some poor unfortunate girl trying to earn an American dollar. How could she do *this* with strangers?

"No!"

It was another of those times when I *wouldn't* have even if I *could* have.

I got tangled in the curtain trying to escape. The startled Mexican girl clawed at me. I thought I might be suffocating. Blasts of gutter Spanish pursued me out the door, followed me as I bolted.

I was waiting in the nearest intersection, circling like an alley cat surrounded by dogs, when Red Dog loped out of the whorehouse wearing a satisfied smile.

"What was all the ruckus?" he asked.

"Nothing."

"You didn't screw her, did you?"

I looked elsewhere.

Red Dog laughed. His red brows banged out exclamation points. "I'm partners with a goddamned romantic!" he hooted. "You *are* a romantic, ain't you, partner? You can't fuck without love."

Yeah. Don Quixote.

"Don't worry," he assured me. "Stay in the military long enough and you'll learn you don't have to get kissed to get fucked."

13

Which young man with balls hasn't been tempted to run away to sea or to foreign lands to seek adventure, romance, his fortune? It was something in the male genes. And for the adventuring man, war and the preparation for war were the ultimate temptation. How could you keep a boy on the farm—or in the hardware store or sacking groceries or marrying the girl next door and settling down with two-point-five children and a chicken in the pot—once he'd bonded with warriors and flown fighter planes, sailed warships and parachuted onto hot landing zones? War was man's greatest adventure; its only drawback was in the way the scores were kept.

World War II was my uncle Walt's war; Korea would have been Uncle James's, except that he kept running away. I enlisted during an in-between time. Between-Wars was a historical time period. It was that time when the maimed of the previous war had passed unnoticed into the population and little remained of the war dead except faded photographs. Each generation prepared for the next war, since each generation had its own war to fight.

The preparation for war was a game made intensely compelling. Body bags—"human remains pouches"—came later when the scoring started. So young men trained and they trained, and it seemed as foolish to have a military you never used as to have a football team that kept practicing but never played a game.

War was *fun*. That was the message behind all the training. I yearned for my deflowering on the battlefield as much as I yearned to be normal and deflowered in bed. I hoped, someday, to be found capable on both counts.

"War *is* exciting,". Chief Ben Walker acknowledged.

We were piloting a C-54 transport, a four-prop, back from a night flight to Moscow. Moscow, Idaho. Back to the Whidbey Island Naval Air Station in the Pacific Northwest where I was a journalist for the base newspaper, *Prop Wash,* editor of an aviation safety bulletin, *Whidbey Approach,* and photographer for the search and rescue team. After boot camp, the navy jumped up notches in my estimation. All that reading and writing I did as a kid hadn't been wasted after all. In this *real* navy, I was nobody's shitbird.

If it flew, I was at Flight Operations wrangling a flight on it. Next to my desk in the *Prop Wash* office hung a flight suit and a helmet ready to grab on my way out the door.

"I'm going *flying!*" I shouted at the editor's door. Then I was gone.

Warplanes were beautiful machines. Fascinating in their sheer utility. Hydraulics and wires and gears all exposed like sinews and tendons. Loud, rough-flying, no frills, no luxuries. Just skin and paddings and cables and electronics and engines and guns and bombsites. Airplanes for *real men* who went to ships and flying machines while their women waited by the hearth fires for them. Men of whom heroes were made.

Commander Morgan told me Chief Walker had flown Grumman Avenger TBFs, heavy torpedo bombers, against the Japanese in the South Pacific. He had returned from some missions with his aircraft so ventilated by enemy anti-aircraft fire that the deck crews saw daylight clear through it. He'd ditched twice trying to nurse injured birds back to his carrier.

One of only a few enlisted WW II pilots still flying for the navy, Walker folded his rangy frame into a cockpit seat as if it had been GI-issued to fit. I quickly adapted a loose-jointed swagger to match Walker's, practiced his intense airman's stare.

Back in the hills, as a kid, I often hiked to the bluffs on Wild Horse Mountain overlooking the Arkansas River and

Fort Chaffee farther on. It was almost like flying if I stood with my toes stuck out over the edge. The mountain dropped down sheer for several hundred feet, leveled off, then plunged again successively until it fell into the brown river nearly a thousand feet below and several miles away. I stood as close to the edge as I could and tilted back my head until all I saw was sky and clouds and maybe a hawk riding a thermal over the river.

I *became* that hawk, trimming a wing feather, circling, hunting. I spread my wings and felt the wind tearing across them. I chandelled and dived and swooped, standing there as close as I could to the edge of the cliff. One slip would have been my last.

Standing on the edge.

No one would ever drag me back to where ragged little kids in tarpaper shacks had the imagination kicked and worked out of them by the time they were ten.

"I want to fly airplanes," I confided to Chief Walker. "I want to go to wars and win medals. Like you. Everybody will know *then* that I'm not just another hillbilly."

I was eighteen years old.

"Yes," said Chief Walker. He kind of smiled and kept flying his big airplane. "War is the ultimate aphrodisiac."

I appropriated the second pilot's seat when he went aft for a nap. Full moonlight bathed the curvature of the earth 20,000 feet below in a soft velvety glow. It was a little like what God saw when he looked down.

Walker nodded the controls over to me. He slumped in his seat, hands clasped in his lap, and gazed out the window at the nighttime earth far below. It provided me an immense feeling of power to take that big four-engine navy transport under my palm and fly, *fly*. Nevertheless, I assumed Walker's own relaxed posture and rested my wrist lightly on the yoke.

A pinpricking cluster of lights on the crust of the earth slipped beneath my wing. Suddenly in my fertile imagination I was a B-52 pilot on a combat mission of vital importance. I lined up on the lights below. *Bombs away!*

It seemed so easy.

Chief Walker keyed his head mike. "Just the thought of

war is so horrible that most men aren't honest enough to admit they might have liked it," he mused, as though to himself. "But for me, much of life afterward has been anticlimactic. We lived more intensely during those years than we ever did before or ever will again."

He paused, peering into the passing night as though back into time. I thought he might not explain himself, but the intimate red glow of the cockpit instrument panel encouraged him to continue.

"When you're faced with dying, you live so much more completely for the moment. You see and hear and feel things you never knew existed. Maybe that makes no sense now, but you'll understand when it comes your turn."

"You miss it!" I said, surprised.

Uncle Walt had never missed it.

It was, Walker admitted, the most exciting time of his life. It was only the tallying of the dead and maimed, assessing such terrible destruction as that after the A-bombs fell on Hiroshima and Nagasaki, that took something away from war.

"Maybe if I had been a ground pounder and had seen everything close up I wouldn't miss it so much now," he said, musing. "War has different perspectives. The infantryman certainly sees it differently than the airman, and the man who talks about war and misses it most is the man who went to war and survived while never actually getting real close to it."

He pointed out the cockpit window.

"What do you see down there?" he asked.

I saw the dark irregular outline of hills climbing into mountains, the bright thread of a river in the moonlight. I saw the clustered lights of a settlement alongside the stream.

"Assume that we're over enemy territory," he said, "and our target is a munitions factory surrounded by that town. Could you press the button to release bombs on the town?"

I looked. Sure I could. It was nothing but distant lights.

"On the other hand, assume that you're a combat platoon leader entering that enemy town. Now you see children sleeping with their stuffed animals, old people sitting on their front porches, young lovers walking along lanes. Is it going to be as easy to kill them once you actually see them face to face?"

I remembered hiding underneath my desk when the air raid sirens wailed.

14

Those beautiful warplanes: P2V patrol craft, low and long and dark like giant dragonflies; A3D Skywarriors, heavy attack carrier bombers with stout, angular, fast lines—airmen called them flying coffins because they were hard to escape from through the chute in the belly if they flamed out; SNB Beeches, small and maneuverable, like flying a Chevrolet; HRS choppers, popping up and down and everywhere; the lumbering C-54 and C-47 transports, workhorses.

"Do you suppose little Russian kids are shown fuzzy photos of our bombers when they hide underneath their desks during air raid drills?" I asked Ken Call. Call was a crash-fire rescueman on the red trucks next to the runway.

"So what if they do?"

If I qualified for the NAVCAD program—the Naval Aviation Cadet program—I could fly warplanes, *really* fly them. All I had to do to go to flight school was sign on the dotted line and give Uncle Sam an additional six years of my life. Golden aviator wings on my chest. An officer and a gentleman—*me!*

I would be *somebody*.

Wouldn't Chief Birkes shit his pants to see his company shitbird wearing wings and gold braid?

And why would Sharon ever want some local small town

mechanic or storekeeper for a husband when she could have a navy flier?

Choices. Funny how every crossroad meant the possible altering of a person's entire life, yet most people just went along for the ride and let circumstances make choices for them.

"Flying's for you—if you want to sign your life over to the government and be a lifer," Call said.

I thought of the lifers I knew: Marty, who worked at the base post office; Chief Cencebaugh, the commander of the search and rescue team; the low-foreheaded master-at-arms, whose job it was to stand outside the chow hall correcting sailors' appearance and behavior before permitting them to eat.

All the lifers had the "lifer look."

"Lifers and cows are the same," Call decided. "They have to have somebody take care of them, tell them what to do, where to go, when to sleep and eat and take a dump. Do you need that kind of shit for the rest of your life, Sasser?"

"It's an orderly life," Marty countered. "The navy takes care of me. I do what they tell me for twenty years, and I get a good pension for the rest of my life. The most I could expect on the outside was some job where the boss could fire me any time he got tired of me."

"In exchange for the navy being your mama," Call said, "you give up your right to make choices. Some asshole with one more stripe than you chews your ass because he thinks your shoes aren't properly shined or your scarf is on crooked or you need a haircut. You say 'sir' to cocksuckers too dumb to make it as laborers on the outside. It's socialism, just like in Russia."

"Then get out!" Marty snapped back. "We don't want you in our navy anyhow, if you're not one of us."

"Give him a GI party," I suggested, remembering. "Teach the freethinking sonofabitch to talk like that."

Call pointed toward the chain-link and barbed-wire fence that surrounded the air station. "Is that to keep *them* out or to keep *us* in?" he asked rhetorically.

"The peacetime military is so chickenshit you feel like you're living in a henhouse," Chief Walker, the pilot, said.

"Wartime is the time to be in the service. Nobody worries about chickenshit then. You just do your job like you're trained to do it."

"Do you think there'll be a war?" I asked.

"You'll get your chance if you stay in long enough. Have you decided about NAVCAD?"

"It's all the petty shit I can't stand."

"You'll like it better if there's a war."

"Let's have a war, then."

I walked the rocky beach beneath the high Deception Pass bridge that linked Whidbey Island to the Washington State mainland. Thinking about choices.

15

Trying to make up my mind about whether or not to quit navy journalism and become a NAVCAD applicant, I caught every airplane I could flying out of the Whidbey Air Station. I liked being a journalist; it was the only job I knew in the military where I could do literally anything as long as I was writing about it for my base newspaper or for the aviation safety monthly I edited. But flying! Flying. God, how I loved it.

P2V patrol flight endlessly sweeping the North Pacific, the Aleutians, nosing toward the frozen North and that narrow cold strip of salt water that separated Alaska from our deadly enemy. Searching with eyes, with electronics, finding that blip on the screen, that streak of phosphorescent ocean where a periscope sliced the seas. Airmen huddled cramped inside that long, droning tube filled with the odors of electronics and hydraulics and fuel oil and the close sweat of men.

The pilot's voice suddenly erupted over the intercom. "Take a look starboard."

I hurried forward and crouched behind the copilot's seat and looked down. The ocean stretched blue and green and white-frothed into horizons sparked by a midafternoon sun. I saw the blip of the submarine on the radar screen, and now I picked up its shadow just beneath the water's surface. Long and thick and dark and as sinister as a predator shark.

"Russian submarine," the pilot said.

There was the same kind of excitement sighting this enemy sub as there would be years later when diving with black tip sharks off Costa Rica looking for one of Sir Francis Drake's treasure ships.

The submarine plunged on. We circled it, wing dipping into a three-sixty, losing altitude. I saw the vents alongside the boat's flanks, its conning tower.

"It's a game we play," the pilot said. "They watch us, we watch them. We get as close as we can to each other to see who blinks first."

Like two boys on a school ground daring each other to fight.

"They send their subs as close as they can to our shores to test our defenses. We do the same to them. Hold on. The bastard's getting hinky. He's changing course. He'll dive in a minute."

We continued circling.

The navigator's voice came light and eager across the intercom: "Skipper, if we had just one torpedo he'd be *ours.*"

"He'd have been ours anyhow if we'd been lucky enough to catch him within national waters."

"What if he surfaces and opens up on us with his machine gun?" I asked.

"That's what we try to get them to do. We'd call in support and wax his ass to the bottom of Davy Jones's locker."

As we flew, watching the black shadow running in the ocean, the pilot told about another Russki submarine he had once tracked. Suddenly, he said, two MIGs dived in from high out of the sun. One screamed past below his patrol plane, the other above. Streaks of mottled brown and blue.

Their jet blasts stole the air, causing the American P2V to rattle and jounce in the turbulence.

He said the MIGs made two more warning passes, flying closer each time. On the last pass one of the Soviet pilots cut throttle and slow-flighted briefly alongside the slower-flying patrol Neptune. The two pilots looked at each other through glass. The commie lifted a gloved hand and gave the American the finger. The American gave it back to him.

Such confrontations between the two superpowers were commonplace around the globe. Upon such seemingly trivial encounters rested the fate of the earth. All it would have taken was one hothead and a bad day. Together, the U.S.A. and the USSR had stockpiled enough nuclear weapons to annihilate every man, woman, and child plus their dogs, cats, and canaries. Only the cockroaches would have survived.

"Fucked up," Call said. *"Fucked up."*

Big A3D Skywarriors, the carrier bombers. I sat back of the crew chief, facing aft, next to the escape hatch in the deck. Upon the wide sea below shimmering in the sun bobbed the USS *Bennington*. The carrier appeared the size of a matchbox in all that watery vastness.

I pointed. "We're going to land *this* on *that?*"

The crew chief grinned through his helmet faceplate. "Hold on to your ditty bag."

Another Skywarrior ahead on final approach sank toward the flattop. A little puff of smoke shot from each tire as it made contact with the deck. Its tail hook snagged the strung cable. The plane stopped short. Deck crewmen scurried out to clear away the aircraft to make room for the next landing.

On downwind, I watched the *Bennington* increase in size as we lost altitude. The plane banked onto crosswind, banked again, and lined up on the deck for its final approach. The jet engines cut back. The pilot rudder-walked the airplane toward the carrier that, large as it was, still appeared frighteningly small considering the size of the twin-jet bomber. The plane shifted in the air, dropped a wing, sideslipped altitude. Wind whistled against the canopy.

The carrier deck never grew quite large enough. Sailors

in blue and in blue caps waved colored flags, guiding us in. Other sailors watched the carrier qualifications from the railing below the flight deck. Some of them waved as we soared over just before the wheels smacked. On a carrier you made firm contact on landing. A full deep-throated kiss. No little pecks that missed or made you bounce over the cable and sent you into the drink.

My throat trapped my stomach. The wheels hit with impact. Momentum thrust our bodies forward into seats and harnesses as the cable stretched out and held. The airplane stopped abruptly at what seemed only inches from the end of the flight deck.

I looked around after my breath caught up with me. I grinned. The crew chief and I slapped palms.

"I hear you're going to be a pilot," he said.

"I don't know," I said. "*Six* years."

16

"We strive for realism," said the tough-looking Marine captain on the first day of Navy and Marine Corps Survival School. I had applied for admission to the school as a journalist seeking to write a story about it for the air station newspaper. It was a tough school, everyone warned. The toughest. I could quit anytime I wanted, no questions asked. But I knew I wouldn't quit. I had never quit anything.

The Marine walked with a noticeable limp as he strode ramrod-straight across the room to the podium. He held a cigarette between fingers that were scarred and mangled, the nails thick and horny and twisted.

He was introduced as the survivor of a North Korean POW camp.

"No matter what you endure during survival training," he said, his voice as crisp and clipped as rifle fire, "it is tame compared to what you'll have to suffer if the Chinks get hold of you. If your plane ever goes down behind enemy lines, remember that the enemy hates you more than you hate him because chances are you'll be fighting in *his* country, bombing *his* mother and father, raping *his* sisters. Better his than ours. Think how you'd feel if the enemy was in Nebraska or Boston doing that to us. What we'd do to him if we caught him. Think about that. Then let your fear and your hate sustain you and drive you to stay alive honorably if you ever find yourself in enemy country."

His hard eyes snapped, kept snapping. He shot out questions one after the other with the accuracy of a marksman on the range. After each question his voice rang with two words: *"I have!"*

"Did you ever see a man's tongue cut out of his head before your eyes?

"I have!

"Have you seen the skin on a man's face ripped off his skull while he's still alive and screaming?

"I have!

"Have you been forced to look while enemy interrogators cut off your buddy's dick and stuffed it into his mouth so he bled to death as he choked on his own blood and his own penis?

"I have!"

The Marine's eyes burned brightly, fiercely. These were not pretty images. The hate that sustained the fire was disturbing, all-consuming. Perhaps, I thought unexpectedly, he hadn't survived after all. Not completely. I looked around the room. Faces showed pale, rigid.

We were scared just listening to him.

"Doesn't the Geneva Convention prohibit mistreatment of POWs?" someone murmured.

The Marine barked; it was too nasty a sound to be called laughter.

"Don't you ever believe any of that horse crap they try to feed you about the Geneva Convention. It's all right to think about Geneva and The Hague and all that other political garbage if you're safe in Washington, D.C., or Paris or somewhere eating caviar off white table linen and sitting next to some cunt with her dress cut so low you can see her navel. It's okay for the sons of bitches in black coats and tails who want to soothe their consciences as they send other poor sons of bitches out to take the risks for them.

"But it's not going to be *them* out there; it's going to be *you*. The enemy never even heard of the Geneva Convention. Even if he did, he doesn't give a shit. It's dog-eat-dog survival out there. You do anything you have to do to survive. You kill the other poor bastard first, make *him* die for his country. You kill him any way you can, and if he suffers, let the bastard suffer. Cut his throat, rip out his lungs, stuff a grenade into his shorts, cut off his head and then shit in the body cavity."

A little slaver of foam caught at the corner of his mouth.

"Kill him any way you can. Kill as many of them as you can. That's how you save American lives. If I had it to do I'd wipe everybody off the face of the earth and leave nothing but Americans. Then I'd weed out the Americans . . ."

"Jesus Christ!" I didn't mean to say it. It just came out.

Afterward one of the other survival instructors drew me aside. He frowned. "You were disrespectful," he scolded. "Don't you believe him?"

"I do believe him. That's the scary part."

He looked me up and down. He wore the expression I always associated with Chief Birkes's shitbird look from boot camp.

"You can quit now," he sneered. "You won't be able to take it out there."

People often underestimated me. Even after two years in the navy I had a baby face topped by curly Shirley Temple hair, even when it was cut short—and those big ears.

I grinned. "Would you like to bet your jockstrap on it—if you wear one?"

As a kid I roamed the Cookson Hills of eastern Oklahoma and the Ozarks of Arkansas. Often alone except for a few hounds, I stayed out for days at a time, hunting and fishing and curling up nights with my dogs next to a campfire. I taught myself to be complete within. After all, I had my fantasies of adventure, and they were enough. In my fantasies I was always the hero.

"I don't understand where his head is most of the time," Dad complained. "That kid's a little odd."

Aunt Ellen, who gave me my first books, smiled. "He's a dreamer," she said. "Society needs dreamers even if it doesn't appreciate them."

She gave me more books and sometimes gave me a job tilling her garden or repairing her garage or something so I could earn money to buy more books.

So when the helicopter flew past the island in Washington's Puget Sound and kicked twelve airmen and one navy journalist—me—into the ocean drink, I knew I would adapt quickly. Each of us was equipped only with our clothing, a parachute, a helmet, and a knife. We swam to the island where we were to survive behind "enemy lines" until captured and thrown into a prisoner-of-war camp.

While one aircrewman from San Francisco occupied his long hours bitching about life and some of the others bitched just as much and grudgingly went about accomplishing the tasks to survive, I felt like Robinson Crusoe, whose tale of survival by Defoe was one of my favorites. I collected sand crabs from the beach and boiled them in seawater in my helmet. They tasted like crackers and peanut butter. I showed the others how to eat the big snails off the crusted rocks. I later learned they were called escargot and that they were considered a delicacy in the civilized world.

Forever afterward I never ate escargot without thinking of the island. Even in Paris many years later, when I was no longer young and had survived wars. I had escargot and good wine in a fine Parisian restaurant. It was the happiest I had ever been because I was on my honeymoon with the woman I loved most. I was so happy that tears came to my eyes. I had been called to another war, Desert Storm, the war against Iraq, but for the moment I was in love and I ate escargot and thought of the island.

But that was in the future. Funny how civilization can be measured in time through wars.

On that island an airman from Texas and I discovered a cherry tree ripe with fruit. It grew in a clearing in front of a shack where the "enemy" had their camp. Clayton and I hid in the woods and watched for the "enemy" to leave. At least two of them were always there.

We wanted those cherries.

I gathered a pocketful of stones and crawled across the meadow to within range of the shack. I jumped up and peppered the hut with rocks. Three "Red Chinese" scrambled out the door and popped blanks at me with their weapons. Big deal. I banged stones off their legs and arms and heads. Pissed off, they came at me with their rifles swinging like clubs.

They weren't about to catch this mountain boy. I led them on a merry loud chase into the forest and then along a steep ledge and down to the sea and back up again. In the meantime, Clayton harvested cherries. That night the two of us burrowed into a plum thicket on a cliff overlooking the sun setting at sea and enjoyed the best meal of all. We had hors d'oeuvres of sand crab and escargot boiled in salt water and seaweed. The main course was a rabbit we'd snared in a trap made of parachute shroud line. Rabbit roasted over a low, slow fire smelled and tasted delicious. And for dessert we had cherries, all we could eat.

We chuckled together over the excitement at the "enemy" camp, and we pitied the other survivors who gathered miserably in a cold, hungry camp down in the woods where the sea breezes could not reach but the mosquitoes could.

"Some people just don't know how to live," Clayton decided. He lifted one Texas leg and farted at the campfire. We laughed with contentment and rubbed our full bellies.

"Once you been poor growing up like us," I said, "everything else is pure gravy."

But after nearly two weeks like that, marooned on the island eating lizards and snails and sand crabs and dandelion greens and a few cherries, I didn't need a mirror to tell me

I had turned gaunt and scroungy, animal-like. I had dropped ten pounds.

I felt skinny as a snake as I burrowed into the thickest brush I could find. I buried my face in the moist forest floor. One eye followed the progress of an "enemy soldier" stalk-searching through the woods. He wore a Red Chinese uniform complete with red stars and a crush cap; he carried an American M14 rifle.

It was the last day of our surviving behind "enemy lines" before we were to be thrown into the POW camp. Those of us who reached a road about a half mile away before being captured would be rewarded with half a peanut butter and jelly sandwich.

I would almost have killed for peanut butter and jelly. I could taste it.

I hugged the damp earth as the "enemy soldier" approached. I smelled the forest rot. I hoped my belly would not growl and give me away. The Marine in commie garb paused in a bar of weak sunlight slanting down through the high forest canopy. His head turned slowly as he scanned for movement. BAR automatic rifle fire chattered out sentences in the near distance, punctuated by rifle-shot exclamation points. I heard shouting coming from the road.

"Yankees! Imperialistic swine! Tonight you rot in our prisons!"

Not until after I won that goddamned peanut butter and jelly sandwich.

I wondered what kind of jelly it would be.

I hoped it was strawberry.

I watched the Marine without stirring. I could take the skinny little bastard if he came close enough. Take his rifle and uniform—and *walk* right out to the road and demand my sandwich.

I waited, breathing slowly. With a last look around, the Marine turned and slipped off in another direction. I crawled forward again, working my knees and elbows in opposite tandem.

"Two of the most immediate dangers to survival are a passive attitude and the desire for comfort," the instructors had cautioned. "You have to change the way you think of comfort. When things go wrong, you have to compare present discomfort to the discomfort you'll feel if the enemy captures you."

I crawled on toward the gunfire. I remembered that day at Fort Chaffee when I thought the machine gun was firing real bullets. This was all just a game, but a deadly serious game during which kids like me learned the finer points of surviving through hate and death. I was becoming very good at it. Later, during the Vietnam War when I enlisted in the elite U.S. Army Special Forces, the Green Berets, I learned that the special units liked to recruit tough little kids like me from the more rural areas of the South and Southwest.

"When you want something *exceptional* done," a Special Forces recruiter would explain, "you want tough, independent soldiers who think for themselves and who are used to working alone or with small groups. You get them from the plains and mountains and deserts and woods, only rarely from the cities."

I crawled on toward the peanut butter and jelly sandwich. The tree line ended short of the road. I peered through bushes at more than twenty "Red Chinese" running back and forth on the road shouting in pidgin and discharging their weapons into the air. In the middle of them clustered a miserable little group of my fellow survivors. They were stripped completely naked except for canvas execution-style hoods jerked down over their heads. The POW phase about which we had heard so many horror stories was about to begin.

You had to touch the road without being seen in order to claim the sandwich. As Red Dog had said, you didn't have to get kissed to get fucked.

It was too late to react by the time I heard the combat boot whistling through the air. At least my breath reached the road, I was kicked so hard. The force of the blow flipped me over onto my back. Two or three "commies" pounced on me like I was raw meat; they pounded and pummeled me into the ground.

"Does this mean I don't get the sandwich?" I gasped.

17

The War Department or the Defense Department—it didn't matter what it was·called to the enlisted men at the bottom—had experts who spent their lives studying enemies and potential enemies and devising realistic training for American servicemen. During that era just before Vietnam, POW training reflected the real-life horrors of the World War II Japanese POW camps and the more recent Korean War torture prisons.

Back when I was a kid casting around for easier ways to earn a buck than picking cotton, I bred and hatched fighting gamecocks, tough chickens whose only purpose was to be pitted to life-and-death struggles in the ring. Before I took them to Paris, Arkansas, and the pits, I fed them well and exercised them and protected them from stray dogs and prowling coyotes and skunks.

The pit was the gamecock's only destiny.

Sometimes when there was no war, just rumors of war, false security lured soldiers into forgetting their own ultimate destiny. Years later, as a hardened army combat instructor, I growled at my young trainees: "You exist as soldiers for only one purpose. That purpose is *to make war.* To fight and die, if necessary, for your country, or for your president's pride or policy, or for oil, or because war is in your genes. When someone tells you your job is to keep the peace, he's feeding you propaganda. Your job is to go to battle after peace has already broken down. You are warriors. The bare truth is you are going to be used for war every time some general gets the opportunity."

It was so easy to forget that truth when there was no war. POW training brought back reality with a jarring shock.

During WW II, the Japanese had merely been cruel and vengeful and practical in their treatment of war prisoners. They drove wounded and diseased POWs until they fell and then casually executed them with a pistol or rifle shot through the brain pan, or they worked them until they dropped from exhaustion. Although there was some "experimentation" on the order of Hitler's, rarely were the Japanese interested in prisoners other than as a liability or a labor asset.

The communists of North Korea and China—as well as the Russians and, later, Ho Chi Minh's Vietnamese—changed all that. Korean War torture prisons introduced the first concentrated efforts at human brainwashing. For some almost incomprehensible reason, the communists felt compelled to legitimize themselves and their system of government by forcing individual prisoners of war to denounce their previous loyalties and embrace the communist ideology.

Predictably enough, while the enemy devised horror treatments "scientifically" designed to make the Yankee "confess" and renounce his country, the American military mind countered by trying to make the Yankee soldier more resistant to brainwashing. It seemed almost as important to U.S. generals and politicians that young American servicemen remain publicly loyal to their government under torture as it was to enemy generals and politicians that they renounce their government under torture. The soldier discovered himself trapped in a bizarre mind game. Damned if he did, damned if he didn't. Catch-22. If he refused to talk when captured, the enemy broke his bones and ruptured his organs with electric shock treatment. If he broke, he faced contempt and derision and possible court-martial by his own military machine. At the least, he had to live with the stigma of "collaboration" when he returned.

The American military studied the cases of returning POWs of the Korean War to determine which types of training and conditioning it could use to prevent captured soldiers in any future war from "collaborating" with the enemy's propaganda efforts. One of the cases it studied was that of Roosevelt Lunn, a black army corporal wounded and captured when his detachment ran out of ammunition after an all-night fight.

North Korean Reds had gathered seven hundred American prisoners, among them Lunn, and marched them north through the snow for many months toward the Chicom rear. Five hundred frozen corpses were left along the route of march. Many were executed when they became too weak to keep up.

Survival for the remaining two hundred at the POW camp became a living hell of punishment and interrogation, followed by demands for "confessions."

"One man would be made to stand at attention for hours, holding up an iron bar until he was totally exhausted," Lunn recalled. "Another would be stood on the Yalu River ice with his shoes off. They'd tie a man up and let him swing from a rope while they beat him with clubs. They'd stick a fellow into a hole in the ground. They'd do anything to a man. . . ."

Name, rank, and serial number. That was what the military had decided, by God. No matter how much the enemy tortured you, you kept your mouth shut. That was the Code of Conduct.

But the code meant different things to the high-ranking brass than it did to dogfaces from Watts or Possum Trot, Arkansas, or Des Moines, Iowa. During war, the military brass thought of honor and personal reputation and politics and history and another gold stripe or a star; the GI in the trenches thought of his buddies next to him and of surviving long enough to go home and sleep with his girlfriend or hug his son.

It seemed to me that the Code of Conduct explained something about the military mentality. Generals were paranoid. They were eaten up with the notion of preserving secrets that really weren't secrets and with maintaining discipline even if it meant captured soldiers would be tortured to death. Die on the rack or starve to death—but don't tell the enemy a goddamned thing.

"We must have a strong Code of Conduct," said a West Point graduate. "It's part of the disciplinary process. Wars are won by soldiers who have the will to resist instilled in them."

Even if it meant they died for nothing?

"If they die, it will be for a good cause. It creates stronger resistance in the front line."

Wars, I thought, are fought by the young, who have no concept of how very long you stay dead.

The tough-looking ex-POW Marine captain at the Navy and Marine Corps Survival School stuck with the military doctrine.

"Any American fighting man who succumbs to the enemy and collaborates in any manner should be summarily court-martialed," he declared vehemently. "Then he should be shot at sunrise, and his execution should be filmed to let every recruit know the United States armed forces will not accept weakness as an excuse.

"The enemy is tenacious and cruel. *I* know just how cruel. You must do everything in your power to avoid capture, but if he does capture you, his objective is to strip you of your pride and humanity. He will humiliate and degrade you with torture. If you are weak and succumb, you will turn on your buddies and your country to make him leave you alone. You follow his orders unquestioningly. You are brainwashed."

"A little like boot camp—only on a larger scale?" I suggested.

I thought the Marine would have me drawn and quartered.

"Military men don't question. They *obey*. It's the right thing to do. Your superiors know best. That's why they're your superiors. The minute you deviate from the wisdom and orders of your superiors and start to think for yourself is when you get into trouble."

He thrust his scarred hands above his head to make sure everyone saw and knew that *he* had not deviated.

"Name, rank, and serial number. Anyone who provides more information because he's tortured is a pussy."

He jabbed a finger hard at me. "Boy, don't question things. It'll get you into trouble."

18

Darkness fell before we began the march to the survival-course POW camp. Guards lined out the hooded little band of naked men caterpillar-style, each with his arms clasped tight around the neck of the man in front of him. Bare ass to bare belly all the way back. When one man fell, all of us fell, linked together as we were. I shivered uncontrollably, not only from the Washington night, which had turned cold, but also from fear and fatigue. Although I realized none of us would be executed or even seriously injured, reality was easily suspended after enduring days of hardship.

My bare feet and knees bled from the march and the constant falls. Guards prodded us with rifles and clubs and shouted curses. I saw nothing for the heavy hood drawn over my head and tied at the throat. Ahead in line a prisoner whimpered in short, desperate bursts. Another wheezed like an asthmatic from the pressure of bodies dragging from the arms around his neck.

"This shit is too fucking *real*," someone cried.

A guard whacked him.

The POW camp, an exact replica of those in Korea, was surrounded by forests, security fences, and dark rumors. Even its existence was declared secret by the U.S. government. After approaching it out of the woods and across a field, our progress marked by strange Oriental martial music, we were hurled inside the compound, where we took off our hoods and looked around, blinking.

It was like you went to bed one night, had a nightmare, then woke up and found you were inside your nightmare. Ten-foot-high fences, concertina wire, manned guard towers,

71

electric wire, primitive earthen bunkers, floodlights, guard dogs, and loudspeakers blaring propaganda and that awful music of reeds and brass. I wanted to cry out that someone had made a mistake, that we weren't supposed to end up in a *real* POW camp.

Some of the men cast wary glances about as they slunk off to the bunkers to hide. I stood up and looked around; so did Clayton, the Texas airman.

"It ain't for real," he said.

I managed a tight grin. "Let's find out how real."

We smiled at the guards as we ambled in the nude around the inside of the high fence. The wire appeared rusty in places. I wondered if you received a peanut butter sandwich for a successful escape.

The guards wasted no time. Two of them rushed into the enclosure and grabbed me. Being a journalist and especially a mouthy one, I suspected I might end up in the center of the instructors' focal plane. I wasn't wrong. The guards dragged me to a nearby hut outside the compound, where they tied my wrists together and tossed the end of the rope over a ceiling beam. They drew me onto my toes. An altogether unpleasant position. A few minutes later, as I hung there, an Asian wearing red stars and gold braid oozed through a side door. He selected the only chair in the room and propped himself against the wall opposite me.

We eyed each other cautiously.

It was role playing taken to extremes.

The "Chicom" got up after a moment. He carried a swagger stick. He walked around me twice. He tapped me on the balls with the stick; he looked at my sheath.

"Are you Jewish?" he asked.

I replied, "Journalist Third Class Charles W. Sasser, 350-36-71."

Name, rank, and serial number.

Bring on your fucking windmills.

The Chinese smiled as if his lips were greased. He nodded at the door. The next thing I knew, sudden stinging pain shrieked through my head like a bitter wind. I swung against the rope that bound me. I screamed. Two enemy soldiers fell upon me with what I thought were whips. I felt blood running from open wounds on my bare back.

Then I caught on. The soldiers were beating me with wet towels. The blows stung like the lashes of a whip but left no lasting damage.

They kept beating me.

The Asian laughed. He held up a hand, and the whipping ceased.

"Before night is over," he lectured smugly, "you will confess to the rotten lies and imperialistic propaganda spread like a plague by your capitalistic presses against the People's Republic."

He slapped me across the face. "You will break."

"Not before your mother ends up in a whorehouse."

I really got into it. I could take it. I was tough. *Tough.*

That was just the beginning. As the night progressed, "Chicoms" came for me again and again. The others had their share, but I was tortured constantly. I was taken directly from one torture chamber to another—tied hand and foot with my head secured so that dripping water, one maddening drip at a time for an hour or more, plopped onto my forehead between my eyes, filling my eye sockets; lowered naked into a ten-foot-deep hole in the ground that gradually filled with ice water until it reached my chin and I thought I surely must drown; beaten time and again while stretched by my thumbs to the rafters of the little shack; threatened with weapons, electricity, and razors; had a cage tied over my head into which a mouse was released; and the interrogations, the constant interrogations. The instructors played every little devious trick on me that we had learned about in our studies of the North Koreans and the Chinese.

Once, after the water barrel treatment, guards gave me my clothes and took me to the shed. They pushed me inside. Before I understood what was happening, someone shoved a plateful of fried chicken into my hands while someone else snapped a Polaroid of me holding the chicken. To anyone seeing the photo, it would appear I was having a grand meal. And the only way you received a meal like that was to cooperate with the enemy.

"You may eat it," the Chinese said with a pleasant smile. "I'm not hungry."

I was *starved*. I tossed the plate of chicken into a corner of the shack.

When the guards returned me to the compound, a navy bomber pilot had also just returned from the rats or the water barrel or another beating. Weakened physically and mentally by his two-week ordeal surviving on the island, he groveled at the feet of his guard. The guard made him pretend he was a dog. The pilot licked his captor's boots. He barked and howled, throwing back his head and opening his mouth and letting the sounds pour out.

Eerie.

Even more eerie were the other POWs. They, too, had gotten into the reality of the training. They ignored the cowering pilot. What happened to him did not concern them. Food or the lack thereof was their main concern. Something threatening in their approach made me retreat. Someone shoved a photograph at me. It was the photo of me apparently enjoying a plate of fried chicken.

I blinked. It took me a moment to catch on.

"You collaborated," a burly chopper mechanic said accusingly. "They're feeding you chicken. You're eating while the rest of us go hungry and get the shit kicked out of us."

The grim little ring of haggard men closed off all avenues of escape. It stunned me to think of the extent to which these normal young men had succumbed to an artificial environment. Think how much more astounding the behavior would be in an actual POW camp. I understood the Marine captain a little better.

I had to talk fast.

"Look, it's the oldest trick in the world: they're turning us against each other. Remember? We had classes on it. I threw the goddamn chicken on the ground. All I gave was name, rank, and serial number, just like we're ordered."

Clayton stepped forward.

"Wait a minute!" he shouted. "Sasser's right. Let's not get carried away here. Another day of this and it'll all be a bad memory."

74

That snapped everybody back into *reality* reality.

Clayton looked at the barking pilot. "Goddammit, sir, get up from there. You're not a dog."

The pilot barked on. The watching guards hurried in and marched me out of the compound again. Along the eastern sky rose a slight softening of night's curtain. The pilot continued barking, like a coyote confronted with dawn, as the guards once again stripped me of my clothing and confined me inside a wooden crate so small that my body folded nearly double. I could move only my hands.

"You are stubborn," a Chinese voice said. "But we have ways of making you confess. We have ways of discovering your greatest fear and using it to release you from your mental prison. You will break."

"Fuck off."

Someone came and opened the crate lid. I felt ropes, or something like ropes, only ropes that *moved*, dropping onto my bare skin. I detected a musky odor.

"Don't even breathe hard," a guard warned. "They're rattlesnakes."

19

I felt the belly scales contracting and releasing as the snakes sought purchase on my bare skin. I don't know how many there were. Seven or eight, maybe. Enough so that the crate suddenly became crowded. Big snakes, each two to three feet long. I knew they were not rattlesnakes—but still, I did not know.

I felt one making its way slowly up my spine toward my head. My heart stopped beating. My throat constricted. My tongue stuck to the roof of my mouth.

Another snake slithered around my drawn-up legs, against the wood of the crate with the dry sound of dead leaves blown across a pile of cow bones.

How I hated and feared snakes! The Chinese was correct; he had found my phobia.

But then, before panic had a chance to set in, I saw in my imagination the cotton fields from back home. I remembered how I'd separated body from mind to get through a long day of labor beneath the hot sun. I thought of Sharon. I must never shame her, my Dulcinea, even if she never knew about it one way or another.

I sucked in a long, calming breath.

I couldn't move my hands except for a few inches near my face. I waited.

One of the snakes, gliding thin and dark like a slice of the darkness itself, appeared in my peripheral vision. Its beaded lidless eyes surveyed me from evil inches away. Its liquid tongue slashed toward my eye.

I held my breath, steeled myself to its presence.

Either that, I thought, or start screaming and let the Chinese know he had won.

I waited.

When the snake crawled across my hand, I grabbed it. Its body whipped about, lashing my face, twisting and turning and thudding its loose end against the side of the crate. I maneuvered its head toward my other hand. With that hand I grasped the reptile's dry body just behind its head. I squeezed with all my strength. I felt bones breaking.

I squeezed the life out of the snake. I broke its bones. Then I stuffed the long body through an airhole in the box and let it fall to the ground. It was dead but still writhing, as snakes will.

I killed two more snakes like that before the guards discovered what was going on. They let me out of the box quickly before I killed all their snakes.

The Marine ex-POW lifted his brows in surprise. He came to shake my hand. "You are tough," he said. "I think I'd go to war with you."

I didn't tell him how afraid I had been.

20

We were going to crash. Dense fear. It filled the long tube of the P2V Neptune. You smelled it. I noticed how the low red sun bobbing on the Pacific tinted the rough seawater as it hosed through Deception Pass. Whidbey Island lay dark below, getting darker, except for the runway lit up like a great white way and the strobing red lights of the crash trucks lining either side.

Tankers foamed the runway. Foam would help to prevent a fire when we came in belly flopping like an albatross without legs. A puncture or some malfunction in the hydraulics system had left the airplane with its wheels jammed in its belly like a breech birth.

I had hopped the flight on a last-minute impulse. Just to be flying, although I always justified it as part of my duties as editor of the aviation safety bulletin. And now we were going to crash the damned thing. Talk about a firsthand look at aviation safety.

It was just like Chief Ben Walker had said. During times of danger your senses honed themselves so keen that common things became extraordinary—the pores in the skin of your hands, the color of the sea, red nearest the sun, darker farther off, the feel of approaching nightfall.

My knuckles whitened from gripping a fuselage cross brace. The Neptune banked sharply, circling, flaps dragging, throttles in, nose low. Slow flight to burn up fuel and reduce the chances of a fire on contact with the runway. I had seen what remained of a C-54 after it caught fire while landing with its wheels stuck. The pilot died at the controls. Someone said that burning magnesium and avgas made bright blue flames; a human burning steamed like meat on a grill. *Don't think about that.*

I unbuckled and braced myself step by step as I worked my way forward to the cockpit, past the radioman-navigator, who looked up at me, his face carefully expressionless. Weak sunlight sheened through the Plexiglas without warmth or comfort. It marbled sweat on the pilot's face.

He tried to be casual. "Hang on to your asses when we go in."

I tried to be casual too. "Got my ass, boss."

Both casuals rang stale.

I closed my eyes. Took a long, calming breath.

When I was seven or eight years old, the five of us in the family lived in a three-room shack with a tin roof and old newspapers and tarpaper nailed to the walls to keep winter from gnawing straight through. It was my job to get up first to build a fire in the wood-burning cane heater. Afterward I wrapped myself in a blanket and huddled at the desk in the kitchen to write. Mom had built the desk for me from old vegetable crates and used one-by-eights.

Sometimes Mom watched me for a few minutes from the doorway when she got up to start breakfast. There I was, seven or eight years old, and I wanted to be a famous author. It was a big joke to almost everyone.

"Let them laugh at me," I told Mom. "It don't matter. I ain't afraid of them laughing. Aunt Ellen says people laugh 'cause they're afraid to take a chance and do what *they* want to do. Well, I ain't never gonna be afraid of nothing."

Mom looked at her strange child.

"There ain't nothing to be afraid of," I said. "I've lived before."

Mom's eyes popped open wide. I thought she looked afraid.

Years later I found a word for what I meant: reincarnation.

Now, as the P2V circled the runway, expending fuel, I thought of not being afraid. Uncle Walt always said there were no atheists in foxholes, that it was easy to be brave when there was no danger. If there *was* reincarnation, I had nothing to fear.

Except there was so much in *this* life I hadn't done yet.

I held up my hand. The pilot flicked the instrument panel on red as the sun finally disappeared. Red lights made hollows in faces. I flexed my fingers, and as I did, I remembered the air crash in the mountains when an A3D jet bomber went in. Search and Rescue had scrambled, me with it as photographer. The largest piece we found of the downed crewmen after their airplane went in was a finger and a thumb that had once belonged to the copilot.

Inevitably, men practicing at war with planes and tanks and explosives were sometimes killed. "Acceptable training casualties," they were called. Somewhere in the Pentagon little military bureaucrats fiddled with numbers and war games data and came up with figures of how many men could die in training without its being unacceptable.

When the A3D crashed into the mountain on the Olympic Peninsula it left a crater, as if God had taken a skyscraper up about five thousand feet and dashed it to earth in a fit of rage. As photographer for the Search and Rescue team, I snapped shots of flesh hanging like Christmas tree ornaments from spruces and pines, grisly pictures of an eyeball and trailing nerves draped over a branch, of blood splatters dashed so hard against rocks that they became permanently embedded.

Two airmen died in the crash; the pilot bailed out. Some members of the SAR team used gasoline engines and high-powered hoses to wash the pieces of the aircraft out of the mountainside, looking for the black box that recorded flight data. The rest of us harvested all the pieces of flesh we could find and put them in a bucket.

"They took off in the plane as two whole men just like us," Cencebaugh mused. "They came back about five pounds of hamburger each. Shows just how precarious life in the service is."

Call recovered the thumb and forefinger. "Watch this,"

he said, and pulled on a long sinew that hung from the flesh. The forefinger curled, beckoning.

Young men were unlike old men whose death was imminent; young men could still laugh at death.

"War's hell even when there is no war," Cencebaugh said.

After dark and after the harvest of flesh, Call and I took a walk through the Olympic rain forest. We ended up at the seashore where the ocean battered the rocks. We stood silent, thoughtful, looking out to where sea and night blended. Something about darkness summoned fears about death and dying. Call picked up a rock and tossed it into the waves.

"What do you think happened to them after they died?" he wondered. "You know, the guys in the bucket."

I thought about it. "That wasn't *them* we put in the bucket. They were already gone."

Call studied the moonrise as though it were his first.

The men in the bucket. I looked at what was left of them for a long time. I found a stick and poked around in the flesh. Nothing happened.

"Their spirits have entered another body," I decided.

"When you're dead, you're dead," Call said. "From dust you came, and to dust you shall return. Isn't that what your Bible says?"

The Bible said that.

I decided the men in the bucket required a memorial. Someone should at least note their passage from life. The *Prop Wash* editor redlined my obituaries.

"Print those and we'll all get fired," he declared.

I didn't understand.

"We're supposed to be upbeat. Keep up the morale and brave fighting spirit of our troops."

"Nothing but propaganda?"

"It's selective publication. Everything printed in a military newspaper has to project a positive military image," he said.

I dug out old issues of military newspapers printed during the Korean War. Sure enough. No obituaries. No casualty figures. Even early in the war when we got our asses kicked all the way down the Korean peninsula, you would never have guessed, reading the military newspapers, that a lot of

men had died. It was nauseating. Like reading the hometown paper about a winning football team.

What was material was how bold and courageous Lieutenant Jones was in flying five triumphant missions against the
Chicoms to chalk up his fifth "kill." The accompanying
photo depicted him brave and smiling as he attached a MIG
sticker to the fuselage of his fighter. You half expected to
see a second photo showing him being kissed by the home-
coming queen.

Good guys never died in the military press. They grinned
like all-Americans for the photographers and posed with
their splendid war machines.

War was *fun*.

"Fucked up," Call said.

And so I flexed my fingers as the P2V continued circling,
and I wondered about the sinews in them and somebody
pulling them to make them curl, beckoning. The odor of hot
hydraulic fluid singed my nostrils. At the same time, I *felt*
the molecules in the air. I experienced an intoxicating urge
to hug the airmen trapped with me and proclaim how much
I loved them.

Life inside the airplane was that intense.

"As soon as we touch down, I'm going to feather the
props, cut the engines," the pilot said. "Get out of this coffin
quick, but wait until we've stopped moving."

The aircraft vibrated. Black wind furled loudly against itself outside. Oddly enough, as crash time drew near, I felt
more curious about it than afraid. What the hell. Sooner or
later we all ended up in the bucket. It was what you did
between cradle and bucket that counted.

I regretted most that I had never made love to a girl.

But in a short while, perhaps, it would make little difference
whether I had or had not ever made love. What difference did such things matter to a forefinger and a thumb and
a bucketful of charred flesh?

Sunlight no longer tainted even the far western sky. There
was blackness above the P2V and the great flaming white

way of the airstrip below. The pilot's voice jarred through the commo.

"We're going in. Good luck to you all."

On final, the runway approached with dizzying speed. Wings wagged, slipped, as the pilot made last-second adjustments. I tightened my seat harness, crossed my arms tight across my chest, and waited for the impact. Red lights flickering, crash trucks revved up and raced alongside the runway like dogs chasing a car.

"Brace yourselves!" the pilot barked. "We're hitting hard!"

21

"Hit it hard."

That was the way Woody had put it, whispering, as we approached Nancy's cottage in the woods near Oak Harbor.

"That's what she wants, so give it to her."

Aye-aye.

Although a wind blew, the leaves on the trees appeared sculptured in stone, compared to my insides. Woody and Gloria made it only as far as the sofa in the living room. Kittens scampered around the sofa, attacking each other and rolling.

"Pussy, pussy everywhere," Woody commented with merry drunken double entendre.

I trailed Nancy's slight form into the bedroom. The top of her head barely reached my shoulder. She flipped on the bedside light and turned down the covers. I liked the way the light picked out the brightness in her strawberry roan hair.

She turned toward me. With unconscious grace and without embarrassment, she dropped her jeans and top to the floor and stood gloriously in red bikini panties and brief bra for me to admire. My gaze locked on the little mound of hair that shadowed her bikini. My throat felt as if I'd tried to swallow one of the kittens. Maybe all of them. My hands hung clumsy like chunks of lead.

"You've never done this before, have you?" Nancy asked softly, smiling.

She was only sixteen, and married, but already separated from her husband.

I swallowed the kitten. Swallowed another one. "Sure I have," I lied.

She smiled, reaching out her hand. "You are so sweet. Come get in bed with me. I need to be held."

I swallowed some more kittens.

Nancy reached for me. I took her hand and dropped my clothing in a pile next to hers. Underneath the covers the smooth nakedness of her limbs entwined with mine. It was all there: warmth and the smell and taste of her breath, breathing with me, for me. My entire body actually ached with pleasure. It was my first time naked with a girl.

My soul filled with gratitude and with love that Nancy would do this for me.

So what if I bled to death? It would be worth it.

Her legs opened to receive, welcoming. In James Jones's *From Here to Eternity*, Prew made love to Lorene: "It was, he thought, like waters which, when dammed, create a pressure, a pressure of power that will pour out flooding, from any little channel it can find, from any little opening, flooding. . . ."

Nancy opened her legs to receive, but her open smooth female legs closed without receiving. I climaxed too soon, probably because I was so afraid. Nancy, so tiny and young but already a woman, wrapped both arms around my head and drew my burning face to her breasts. She held me and stroked my hair and back with such tenderness that tears filled my eyes. I felt her own tears scalding my cheeks and neck. We cried together and held each other against the night.

* * *

As the P2V Neptune sank rapidly toward her crippled landing, I suddenly yearned to hold Nancy again, to try once more. The mind is funny that way; it relieves pressure by shutting down or by evoking images from more normal times. There was this image of Nancy naked in my arms, and then a horrendous racket suspended all thought as the airplane dropped out of the sky and plunged into a bed of foam the color of used shaving cream.

We were thrown about inside the craft in our harnesses. A thousand impressions flickered through my thoughts with subliminal speed as the airplane skidded down the runway, dragging first one wing, then the other; flames licked past the windows; smoke filled the cabin and cockpit; metal shrieked; foam piled up on the windows, creating a total blackout inside.

The airplane bled speed. It tilted to one side, hanging me heavy in my harness. I held up my hands as the P2V came to a full stop, but I could not see them. I flexed all five fingers on each hand.

I had trained on emergency exits, but I broke all records in scrambling through the hatch above the pilot controls. The props still turned, slinging chunks of metal and of cement dug out of the runway. I ducked low and scurried aft along the fuselage. Flashing red lights circled the downed bird like predators.

A minute later crash crewmen guided us away from danger. I glanced back for a final look at the wreckage. I grinned—inappropriately, as always. Suddenly I thrust my arms into the air like when I won smokers in boot camp. *I was alive!*

If I survived *that,* surely I could survive other things.

Like sex.

22

I had to find out. No matter the cost, I had to find out.

Nancy and I parked in the night high on the island overlooking Deception Pass. It was a favorite parking spot for area teenagers and young servicemen from the base. Adrenaline from the air crash not two hours earlier still pumped through my veins. I felt ready, capable, invincible.

I also felt nervous, afraid, embarrassed, to be twenty years old and still a virgin.

Don't think about it just do it I'll bleed to death I know it. Don't think ... don't think ... don't think ...

Nancy hooked the heels of her little bare feet to the calves of my legs. She drew me down on top of her in the front seat of my Ford. With her hand she guided things toward their proper places.

"It's okay," she cooed gently, caressing me, kissing me deeply.

Don't think ...

Nancy exhaled with a slight moan. Her head flew back on the seat. She arched like a stroked cat. I exhaled too, only with sudden fear and dread.

But to my relief and surprise, everything slipped smoothly into place. Nancy drew me deep inside her. There was no pain.

I moved.

She moved.

I *moved*.

It was a first kiss all over again, only better and infinitely sweeter.

It ended quickly, that first time. Flicking on the taillights,

I jumped out of the car and ran around to the back, where I examined myself in the red taillight glow for tears and rips and bleeding. An entirely new vista suddenly presented itself. I leaped around in hopeless relief, abandoning myself to the utter joy of discovery.

"It works!" I shouted at the stars and at the water rushing below in the pass and at other cars parked at a discreet distance.

I jumped and leaped about and flung my arms like a madman.

"It works! It works!"

PART 2

Assuming, then, that we are capable of learning as much from Hiroshima as our forefathers learned from Magdeburg, we may look forward to a period, not indeed of peace, but of limited and only partially ruinous war.

—Aldous Huxley

23

GI fighting song from Vietnam:

NAPALM STICKS TO KIDS

Eighteen kids in a free-fire zone,
Books in arm going home;
Last in line goes home alone.
Napalm sticks to kids.

Vietcong woman on the run,
Struck by napalm from the sun.
When they're pregnant you get two for one.
Napalm sticks to kids.

Charlie in his boat sitting in the stern.
Thinks his goddamned boat won't burn.
Those fucking gooks will never learn.
Napalm sticks to kids.

—Author unknown

24

The Vietnam War was just a rumor, a distant rumble on the horizon, when I snatched my discharge from the navy after four years' active service and ran. But already the Air Force *Intelligence Digest* was publishing short pieces about how U.S. Army Special Forces were helping poor peasants resist communism. It published stock photos of little native kids grinning up at big smiling American warriors, thanking the Americans for keeping their country safe. The articles resembled Sears ads. Slick, commercial. How to live better by buying better.

The message was easy to buy. America prevented war, kept the peace, by maintaining a "presence" in this unknown land called Vietnam. I looked hard to find the country stuck out into the South China Sea. It looked about the size of Florida.

When LBJ escalated the war in 1965 by sending combat troops to Vietnam, I was riding a motorbike across the United States from Seattle to Miami, living in a tent. The bike was an 80cc Yamaha I dubbed the Odyssey. Maybe I should have called it Rosinante, after Don Quixote's steed. For a year I traveled, working odd jobs—fry cooking, gardening, carhopping, printing. I trained horses. I dabbled in oil painting on New Orleans's Bourbon Street.

Maybe I was America's first hippie. Except I didn't do drugs, didn't have anything to protest. I was the Happy Hippie.

"Where you goin', man?"

"Just riding."

I arrived in Miami, Florida, with virtually everything I

owned, including a large Buddha, strapped to the back of the Odyssey. I had eight dollars in my jeans, with which I rented a cubicle-sized room in a skid row tenement called the Fowler House. By that time the Vietnam War was regular dinnertime TV fare. Everyone knew the terminology: *zapped, wasted, KIA, body count, gooks, search and destroy, free-fire-zone, Puff the Magic Dragon, miniguns, air assault, frag.* . . .

The other rooms at the Fowler House were occupied by an absurd assortment of alcoholics, ex-convicts, single men, and old women scraping by on their pensions. Each evening the tenants gathered in the lobby to watch Vietnam on the news and congratulate a WW II veteran named Bill whose son had just become a helicopter pilot and been shipped to the combat zone.

Bill was so proud of him.

A month after I arrived, two army officers in dress greens came to the house looking for Bill. After they left, Bill sat upstairs on the balcony day and night for over a week, staring at nothing. He refused to talk, to eat, even to sleep. He just hunched into his chair, looking gaunt and angry and wasted, suddenly old and tired. The other residents spoke in hushed tones.

"Bill?" I ventured, pulling up a chair. "Bill . . . ?"

I was almost the same age as his son. Bill looked at me. He grabbed me and hugged me, and finally he cried in great painful sobs.

"Fuck that place!" he yelled. "Fuck the army!"

Startled people walking by on the street stopped to stare.

"They killed my son!" he shrieked. "Oh, God! They killed my son!"

I held that big man and cried with him.

"Son," he said to me, "don't you go over there. Don't you go."

But I knew I would go to Vietnam. One way or another, I knew I would go.

25

The Huey gunship worked over the clearing with rockets and machine-gun fire. It circled the target, a patch of elephant grass about the size of a backyard in suburban Los Angeles. Then it tilted and slid off sideways, down-skidding toward the target. The stuttering of its guns dotted the morning sky with little pops of trailing gun smoke. Rockets carved twin contrails in the air, followed by eruptions of flame and smoke partially absorbed by the dense jungle around the clearing.

It resembled a tiny and dangerous hornet pissed off.

From higher up, in rarefied air above the Vietnamese jungle, so intensely green it startled the eye, I watched with the eight other men of Spike Team Tiger. Chimneys of smoke formed lazily on the ground. The gunship completed its run. It hovered in the air to one side of the jungle opening, turning slowly in a three-sixty, its guns covering.

I checked the safety of my M16, checked it again a second later. I felt sweat crawling out of my armpits. My back was already wet underneath the heavy jungle ruck.

The door gunner rode his umbilical-cord safety, leaning into it out the door far out over his M60 machine gun. When he turned his head toward us, I saw us reflected in the dark wraparound shield of his helmet—nine savage faces blackened and jungle-patterned with cammie sticks. Eyes glistened, staring hard and white out of the camouflage.

Six of the faces belonged to Nung tribesmen, tiny near–Stone Age men brought into the twentieth century by U.S. Special Forces and war. War had dragged the Stone-Age into the modern age, and one day, perhaps, it would cast the modern age back to the Stone Age. The faces remained impassive. The Nungs were warriors.

Sergeant Nelson gave us a quick look. I nodded. He patted the knee of the Nung crowded next to him in the chopper. Then his gaze returned to the open door as our helicopter banked sharply and began its rapid descent, displaying a wide panorama of forest far below. Air bellowed in. Clutching our patrol caps and weapons, we stared almost straight down into Vietnam.

Or was it Laos?

This was the third clearing into which we had slicked during the last thirty minutes. Over each the gunship worked out its guns; then we slicked in fast and hovered just above the ground but did not unass. If the VC watched, they wouldn't know which if any of the three patches of elephant grass had received troops. The enemy had become so accustomed to the diversion that sometimes they didn't even bother to investigate.

We were counting on that.

The third American was the patrol leader, Sergeant Gunderson. He jabbed his thumb twice toward the ground, emphatically. Diversions were over. I felt fresh sweat. My tongue dried out and stuck to the roof of my mouth. It felt like a lizard in desert sand.

This was it.

Gunny's eyes studied me, searching for fear, panic. Seven years after navy boot camp I still had the Mickey Mouse ears. But now I looked harder, tougher, combat-ready. Army parachute training and Special Forces Qualification attracted tough men, made them tougher.

Although I had joined the police department in Miami, Florida, and even found time to get married, I still found myself drawn to the war in Vietnam. I enlisted with the U.S. Army Reserves, Special Forces, and earned my parachute wings, green beret, and flash trying to get to 'Nam. Finally, however, I gave up on the army horseshit and went to Vietnam as a civilian free-lance journalist.

I met Sergeant Gunderson in Nha Trang. When I asked to accompany him cross-border, he eyed me suspiciously.

Few journalists not connected with Special Forces knew anything about the top-secret cross-border excursions conducted by Command and Control.

"What do you know about C and C?" Gunderson snapped.

The C&C excursions had begun in 1964 under Studies and Observation Group (SOG) to check out enemy troops and supplies staging in the tri-border area where Vietnam bordered Laos and Cambodia. Networks of trails and roads known collectively as the Ho Chi Minh Trail spiderwebbed from the "neutral" countries into Vietnam, all of them swarming with enemy movement.

SOG and, later, C&C recon teams known variously during the war as Spike Teams or Snakebite Teams began working their secret forays as soon as Lyndon Johnson approved them. Composed mostly of Nung tribesmen and Montagnards led by U.S. Army Special Forces soldiers, the teams took subversion, sabotage, and psy-ops directly to the enemy's front door. They wore no markings on their uniforms, carried no dog tags or other identification. If the Special Forces of C&C got themselves captured or wasted across the borders, the U.S. government disavowed all knowledge of their existence.

"You're a journalist," Gunny said in Nha Trang. "It's my ass if you're caught with us. Politically, C&C does not exist. You won't be able to write about us. Not yet anyhow."

"Someday," I said.

He shook his head. He was about my height, not tall, but he was broader, thicker. Maybe a few years older. Special Forces were almost always older than line grunts.

"You fucking didn't have to be here in this pissy-assed country," he said. "Why did you come to this fucked-up war?"

"My wife asked me the same thing."

"What did you tell her?"

"It's not much of a war, but it's the only war we have."

The truth? I couldn't answer his question. Maybe I came for a lot of reasons—adventure, research for the big American war novel. Mostly, though, I think I wanted to discover for myself what it was about war that attracted men to it. Why was I attracted to it? If war was so horrifying, why did we perpetuate it?

I had to know *why*.

How could you rationally explain wanting to go to war?

Gunny's wide mouth divided his face into a grin. If I hadn't also been a member of the Army Special Forces Reserves, he might never have considered my request.

"You're SF all right," he decided. "You're fucking crazy like the rest of us. Okay, Mr. Journalist, meet us on the flight line at oh-dark-thirty. Maybe you had better know now, though, that if you're KIA or WIA out there, you're on your own. I can't bring you back. It'd be my ass."

Stars the next morning still shone above the flight line. They brought out in ink-sketch relief the beginning of the jungle at the bottom of the hill and the grassy flatland beyond. The Nungs dozed, propped back against their rucks. Nelson had his ruck unstrapped, endlessly rechecking its contents of ammunition and explosives. A blond man with empty blue eyes and a face that had not changed expressions in so long that it seemed permanently frozen in anger and hatred, he barely acknowledged introductions.

"A buddy of his bought the farm cross-border last month," Gunny explained, lowering his voice. "Nelson hasn't said a dozen words since then. All he thinks about is wasting gooks. We'll probably have to Section-Eight him out sooner or later."

"What happened?" I asked.

Gunny shrugged. "His team picked up VC trackers right after the insertion. If Charlie knows you're in there, he'll find you. He can *smell* you. Nelson carried Smitty out of there on his back. He was dead, but he carried him out anyhow. I went over to see the corpse. Smitty took it right here." He tapped his temple. "The bullet made mush of his brain. Poor bastard didn't know what hit him."

He looked away. He tipped his head back to look at the stars. "Nelson's okay, but he's crazy now. Maybe it takes crazy men to fight wars."

"Maybe."

He laughed, but it was not true laughter.

"Where we're going today is damned hot," he said. "Fucking slopes are everywhere, like lice. We'll poop and snoop around for a few days, see what we can find, plant a few mines on Mr. Ho's roads, then see if we can get the hell out of there with our collective ass in one piece."

Just before we boarded the helicopter, running bent low beneath the whoppering blades, Gunny disappeared. He returned in a moment with an extra M16 and a pouch of loaded clips.

"You might need it," he explained.

Yeah.

Now we dropped toward the clearing fast. My entire body puckered up like one giant asshole. The jungle rushed up at us. Thin wisps of smoke trailed skyward from the gunship's pass at the surrounding forest. No longer chimneys, they rose pencil-thin and straight in the thick air, as if the house fires were burning out.

My eyes darted, taking in the clearing, the jungle. Everything seemed so sharp, so intense, so extraordinarily *real*.

What if the gooks were waiting for us?

I puckered some more. Spike Teams traveled light, tourist class. Not even flak jackets or helmets to sit on in the chopper to keep rounds from piercing the aircraft's belly and taking your balls off.

My balls sucked up to about my navel.

There was that moment when the greenness sucked the chopper to earth like a fish taking in an insect.

Tense faces of little brown men.

Gunny's head twisting, checking.

Taut muscles bunching, waiting for the chopper to bank up short like a racehorse drawn to bit.

Expecting muzzle flashes from the tree line.

Sitting fucking ducks.

The chopper's blades whipped the surrounding trees into a hurricane's frenzy. The chopper hovered, flattening out the elephant grass below. Gunny scrambled out the door first, followed by the Nungs. I took a ragged breath and went. Nelson followed.

It was farther to the ground than I expected. I fell to my knees but scrambled up immediately, fueled by adrenaline. Elephant grass blocked out the sunlight. I fought my way through it, heart thudding, expecting to be caught in an ambush. Behind me, the Huey bounced back into the air. It rose straight aloft until it became a speck in the sky, a mote.

And the team was alone surrounded by enemy that I could feel and taste and sense but could not see or hear because the wet, dripping, hot forest consumed all sound, even that of my own rapid breathing, and it hid from view even the nearby forms of my comrades.

I lay waiting, hiding. A green snake crawled across a gnarled exposed root. Overhead were green and shadows. I felt dimness, moisture, heat, and a knot of sudden doubt that gripped my guts like a python's coils. Gunny caught my eye.

I gave him thumbs-up.

He gave the signal to move out.

26

On Saturdays back in the hills when I was a kid, we hitched the red one-eyed mule and the big black mare to the wooden-wheeled wagon and drove to town. In Sallisaw, the women sat around in the back alley gossiping and peddling cabbages or tomatoes or whatever. My brothers and I went to the movies for a dime each to see Roy Rogers or John Wayne in *The Sands of Iwo Jima*. War movies were my favorites. Paw sneaked off to Tump Kinsey's bar where he got so snockered on cheap beer that by nightfall he had to be poured into the wagon bed for the long ride home to Drake's Prairie.

I worshiped Paw even for his sour beer smell and the Garrett's snuff that always oozed brown juice out the corners of his lips and made me sneeze. I snuggled close to him nights going home in the wagon, lying there while he snored with one of his farmer-smelling arms thrown over me, gazing upward into the stars.

Life seemed so intense that it ached the way your feet ached with the pleasure of wading in a cold stream. It was as if everything that was became a part of me, and I a part of it: the clacking of hooves on gravel; the rock-jouncing and creaking and swaying of the wagon; stars burning through infinity; the scent of the creek as we crossed, it smelling all wet-rotty and rich the way creeks do after dark.

Life was intense like that sometimes when you were a kid; it was intense the first time you made love; and it was intense when you went into combat. Maybe it wasn't even original, but a U.S. Marine left his assessment of war scrawled on an empty ammo crate in Vietnam: "For those who have fought for it, Life has a special flavor the sheltered shall never know."

A special flavor. Perhaps that was what I sought.

For the first two days after the Huey slicked Spike Team Tiger into its jungle LZ—Landing Zone—we marched steadily northwest into what I was certain was Laos. Jungle closed in on us, smelly and fecund and clinging, like being wrapped in a wet-hot dirty dishrag. Communication, and only rarely, was in whispers breathed directly into each other's ears. We advanced so cautiously that a kilometer a day was a long day's hike.

"This fucking AO—Area of Operations—is crawling with dinks," Gunny whispered.

The team burrowed into jungle high on a ridgeline. Below, a red ball, an unimproved but adequate road, cut southeast around the base of the ridge. Most of the time the enemy covered his supply roads with live vegetation to conceal them from the air. Apparently the gooks weren't afraid of this one being strafed even if it was discovered.

"How far into Laos are we?" I asked Gunny, whispering. Instead of an answer, he handed me his binoculars. I glassed the road. A small convoy of bicyclists wheeled along it. I saw the strain of travel on their young faces. They wore black pajamas and cone hats. Some of them were no more than twelve years old. Kids in this war—maybe in all wars—outnumbered adults. They pumped their bicycles along the muddy ruts, pulling enormous loads on little bicycle-wheel carts or carrying equal loads lashed to handlebar baskets.

Gooks lived and even thrived with labor and diseases and intestinal parasites that would have destroyed any American.

"VC?" I mouthed.

Gunny nodded.

"Young."

"The most dangerous thing in this war is an eight-year-old with a Coke in one hand and a grenade in the other."

After a moment he shook his head in amazement and murmured, "The slant-eyes use bikes and wheelbarrows to resupply their army with rice and fish heads. We fly in cargoes of air conditioners and Sony TVs and fresh Kansas beef so the generals can have their steak dinners—and the little yellow bastards are still going to kick our ass if we keep playing politics with them."

Nelson glassed the road. His eyes narrowed. "What we need is a good body count," he said.

They were the only words I had heard him utter.

After nightfall, we first tunneled into one thicket, waited for an hour or so in case enemy trackers had seen us, then moved stealthily to another hideout for the night. A previous team had been too fatigued to use the diversion. VC fell upon them in the Vietcong night and slaughtered them all.

We lay, feet toward the center, heads out, like the spokes of a wheel, listening to the dark sounds of the night. I prayed silently to behold another sunrise; I slept only in fitful bursts, snapping awake every few minutes to make sure I still had my rifle death-gripped.

The night. Goddamned long for a man with so much imagination.

Things inhabited the night.

Somewhere nearby, no more than a twenty-minute walk away, the enemy also made night camp.

"Verily, though I enter the Valley of the Shadow of Death I shall fear no evil," I whispered to Gunny, lying next to me. Trying to overcome my fears.

"For I'm the meanest son of a bitch in the valley," he finished. He chuckled silently.

Where, I wondered, had it all gone—the glamour of ribbons and special headgear and dashing uniforms? It had all disappeared. I was dirty and tired and so scared that no matter how many times I swigged from my canteen my mouth still felt dry.

And Gunny was just as scared. I felt his lips at my ear.

"Now I lay me down to sleep," he recited. "I pray the Lord my soul to keep. If I should die before I wake, I pray the Lord my soul to take."

He tried to make it a joke, but his voice trembled slightly.

Presently I managed a muttered "Amen." The prayer I remembered from my own childhood touched me strangely here in this place of dying and killing.

One thing, in a combat zone, you never took life or each other for granted. Within a very short time Gunny and I were as close as two men were ever likely to be. War for the grunt was not some grand picture encompassing nations and corps and zones; war for the grunt was only that little part of it he saw at the time—his buddy, a bed of grass to sleep on, beans and frankfucker C's instead of ham and limas.

Such were the things men fought for. God and country and Mom's apple pie seemed so far away.

"You don't *have* to go!" Dianne cried. "I'm pregnant. We're going to have a baby."

"I'm a writer," I replied, as though that should explain everything.

"You're not a writer. You're a cop, and you're going to be a father. It's bad enough that you're a policeman. Now *this*. I don't want our son or daughter to have a dead father."

"I *have* to go," I said. "One way or another, I have to go to Vietnam."

"No! You're a husband. You have responsibilities. Get all this stuff about writing and everything out of your head. Get with the real world."

I enlisted in the U.S. Army Reserves. Special Forces. Paratroops. Snake eater. Hard as bayonet steel. Elite among the elite troopers of the world. "Take this live chicken, killer. Bite its head off. Drink the blood."

As a backup I applied with the CIA. Air America, spy stuff, and all that. By then I was a private pilot, I spoke two languages, and I had military experience in both the navy and the army.

Mom telephoned from Oklahoma. She sounded anxious. "There's some men in suits and ties and shiny shoes asking questions all over about you. Daddy wants to know what you've done. What's wrong? What's the government want you for?"

In the hills, only government men wore suits and ties and shiny shoes.

I received a telegram to call a Miami telephone number. A voice on the telephone ordered me to meet a Mr. James Wilkinson at 8:00 P.M. Tuesday at Miami's downtown Du-Pont Plaza Hotel. Mr. Wilkinson and his leather briefcase were alone in the hotel room. He was a graying, fit-looking man in an expensive suit. He locked the door behind me. I fidgeted as he darted around pulling down all the blinds.

"So you want to go to Vietnam," he said finally, apparently satisfied that we were safe from espionage and sabotage and whatever else. His hard eyes found mine and held them. "We've checked you out. Ordinarily we never accept an applicant without a college degree, but in your case, with your background in the military and in police work, we've decided to make an exception. We are prepared to make you an offer. How does a two-year contract sound, at eighteen thousand dollars a year?"

I made six thousand a year as a cop.

"I can handle it," I said.

"We think you can."

He sat down with his briefcase on his knees and snapped

it open. He took out an automatic pistol; he took out sheaves of paper with official letterheads and seals and expansive signatures.

"Anything we talk about tonight goes no farther than the walls of this room," he warned. "Don't even talk to your wife, Dianne, about it. It's classified secret. You can *never* talk about it without violating the National Security Act, whether you accept our offer or not."

Our government was serious about secrets.

"It's the politicians that are fouling up this war," Gunny said, whispering. "They tie our hands behind our backs and then tell us to go out there and fight. It'd be over tomorrow if we'd nuke Hanoi and Peking. It'll be over for us sooner than that if some slope zaps us."

"Why did you volunteer?" I asked him. All Special Forces were volunteers.

I thought he had gone to sleep there in the thickets in the Vietcong night, he remained silent so long.

He stirred.

"You're a journalist," he said. "There's something I want you to write for me when you can. I want you to let everybody know."

"Yes?"

He lay next to me, listening as much to the inside as to the outside. When he spoke again, his voice sounded harsh and came from some great, painful distance.

"War," he said. "War is a lie."

27

Who would have thought it could be so chill in a jungle in the tropics? Before dawn we nudged each other awake, shivering a little. Looking at Gunny with his hollow, thorny cheeks and eyes even more hollow, the filth ground into his face with the camouflage paint, I saw myself reflected.

"Kill the tiger," he whispered.

I looked around quickly. "What tiger?"

"The tiger that came through last night and shit in my mouth."

Falling into line silently, we ranger-filed for an hour before forming a perimeter at a different location to freshen our face paint and gobble cold patrol rations. Just another precaution. One morning we whiffed woodsmoke. A Nung slipped away and returned shortly afterward. We had halted within two hundred meters of an enemy patrol. Gunny used his hands to signal. His paleness showed even through his camouflage. The team moved away through the high hot jungle like a snake.

One glimpse of us, one suspicious sniff, and the enemy would be down on us like flies on a ripe carcass.

Wonderful thought.

Every day the narrow red balls were loaded with traffic. Sometimes we spotted small cargo trucks, sometimes motorcycles, often troops, frequently bicycles, always women and skinny boys carrying huge loads balanced on poles across their shoulders. Gunny noted everything in his notebook. It appeared the enemy might be preparing for an offensive, rumors of which had spread through South Vietnam like fleas from one cur to the next.

"I worked at a group TOC"—Tactical Operations Center—"on my first tour in the 'Nam," Gunny whispered one night. "We had all these officers there who had nothing else to do but dream up chickenshit missions to send the troops out on. All they were trying to do was impress each other and the colonels. So they'd send out a patrol to recon a road or look at a village. No reason, really. But they always made it sound like the most important thing in the world to the poor bastards who were going out on it. The patrol would go out, maybe get shot up a little, and it was all for nothing. The officers would discuss it and rationalize, and it wouldn't be long before some other officer would come up with another chickenshit mission because maybe he had heard the colonel say it was a good idea."

Grunts called officers and soldiers at the rear REMFs— Rear Echelon Motherfuckers—or Remington Raiders for the typewriters they pounded, filling out award recommendations for each other. Years later I knew a company clerk who returned from Vietnam without ever having heard a shot fired at him in anger; he wore more ribbons and garbage on his breast than did combat soldiers like Mother Norman who fought with the Fifth Special Forces and was wounded heroically in Nha Trang during Tet, and John "Mad Dog" Carson who did a year with the 173d Airborne in Vietnam.

Any officer who returned from a tour in Vietnam without at least a Bronze Star just wasn't kissing the right ass.

"And *this* mission?" I asked Gunny.

"Chickenshit. It don't mean nothin'. Any intelligence we gather on the ground has already been gathered and processed by flyovers. But let's face it: you can't have all these troops hanging around with nothing to do. Missions here are the same as picking up pinecones at Fort Bragg. Idle hands are the devil's workshop."

Gunny had this bitterness inside.

"What the hell. It don't mean nothin'. We'll plant some

C-four in the roads and blow up some of the little yellow
men and then go back and brag about how we're winning
the war to make the world safe for democracy."

Nelson planted pressure-detonated explosives—booby
traps—in the middle of the road and camouflaged them
while the rest of the team pulled security up and down the
road. We waited until the traffic slacked off near nightfall
to do it. I crouched with Gunny overlooking the road on a
little knoll that he had designated the rally point. We
watched the road, our eyes darting. Gunny kept glancing at
his watch.

"C'mon, c'mon, goddammit."

Nelson came running back. The Nung security folded in
behind him.

"Let's haul ass," Gunny commanded. "There'll be body
parts on the clouds and pissed-off slopes up our exhaust
pipe when these things go off."

I remembered the A3D crash on the Olympic Peninsula,
the two fingers, the eyeball, flesh draped in the spruces.

We marched hard until darkness forced a halt. We were
too near the road, but we had no choice. An elephant made
less noise crashing through the jungle than a patrol in a
strange forest after dark. It proved a cold camp, and a long
one. Gunny sat with his back against a tree facing the direction of the road, M16 across his legs. Only Nelson slept. I
heard him snoring lightly. The Nungs paired up and held
hands, as Asians were wont to do.

I thought about Dianne.

I wondered if she would miss her "good husband" if he
failed to come home.

I thought about Sharon.

I did not sleep.

Nelson heard a muffled explosion from the road the next
dawn. We trapped our breath collectively, listening. Then
Gunny jumped up and literally yanked the team into harness. He stepped up the pace. Every man kept looking over
his shoulders, eyes wide in dread of what he feared to see.
Even the faces of the tribesmen set themselves in solid lines

of tension. Their dark eyes darted. Gunny sent blocking teams to the rear to watch our back trail for trackers.

"If the dinks catch us," Gunny said, "they'll torture and kill the Nungs right away. They'll try to take the Americans prisoner. Save us for something better."

The stakes were much higher than half a peanut butter and jelly sandwich.

28

Gunny pushed the team to near exhaustion. He circled us to the south, then cut east toward our pickup site. Shadows thickened as the afternoon came and threatened us with evening. It surprised me when Gunny called a halt less than an hour following a previous rest break. I crouched in foliage next to the faint trail while Gunny and his radioman rushed forward to confer with point.

It was then I detected the odor. The sickly sweet cloying stench of death.

Gunny returned. An olive drab rag covered his mouth and nose. Death as thick as rotting mucus dripped from the leaves and vines of the jungle ahead.

"Ville up forward," he explained. "It looks like everybody's either *di-di*'d or is dead, but we'd better take a look-see. I don't think trackers have picked us up yet."

A two-Nung patrol checked out the village for signs of enemy. When it returned, Gunny posted security around the ville. The rest of us ventured into the open, as cautious as barn rats trying to sneak past the cat to the corn bin. Gagging, I found my own drive-on rag. It didn't help much.

There were only about ten conical hootches with banana-leaf roofs set randomly in a beaten clearing next to a small stream. I saw tiny fields—sweet potatoes or something—hacked out of the forest beyond. A black kettle rested over-turned in a long-cold fire, past which ran a bare-assed chicken. Its startled cackling added to the sense of abandonment.

The hootches were empty. Grass mats, some beads, old aluminum pots blackened from open fires, a shard of glass. Yellowed photos of an Oriental man, a woman, and a child all wearing straw hats and smiling self-consciously into the camera. Bamboo rats scurrying about, cleaning up spilled rice.

Debris. The poor trash of peasants.

The stench thickened.

Gunny crouched, rifle held at the ready. He stared, then motioned me forward without turning his head. At first, I did not comprehend what he was seeing, not expecting it. But then I did. Everything sour and vile in my soul tried to come out my throat.

There were three of them hanging upside down from a pole between two trees—two *papasans* and a boy, blackened and bloated like macabre cocoons. They had been eviscer-ated. Drawn and field-dressed the way we butchered hogs in the crisp mornings of autumn back in the hills. Hanging there, heads toward the ground, rotting. Dirty red-black ropes stretched from them where animals had pulled out their intestines, dragging them and stretching them in the dirt. Birds and rodents had been feasting. The toes were mostly gone. So were the fingers of the men whose hands trailed in the dust. So were the eyes.

I staggered to an upended log that accepted my weight. Gunny came and stood next to me.

"Old story," he said. "They refused to pay taxes to the VC, or maybe Charlie thought the village was cooperating with the government. Something. Or it could be just a warn-ing to other villages for them to supply more soldiers for the People's Army. 'Cooperate with us, or we execute.' Very effective way to govern."

"They're just peasants, farmers," I gasped. "They just want to be left alone."

* * *

Paw and Maw back in Oklahoma, they were peasants, farmers. I remembered that Maw paused one morning making breakfast. She turned from the stove, her round face reddened from the heat. Flour from rolling out biscuits was clear up to her elbows. She frowned.

"Henry?" she inquired of Paw. "Who was it won the last election anyhow?"

That had been four months ago.

Paw hated conversation before breakfast. He had already washed his face outside the door at the pitcher and basin and combed his thick hair. He waited at the table for his eggs and gravy and biscuits.

"Goddammit, Stella. I got to hitch up the team and get to working."

Maw persisted. "Who was it that got elected president?"

"Whoever it was don't plow the fields for us."

Paw. Snuff dribbling and browning the quart jar of well water we brought to him for drinking when he was down the hill in the forty. Shirt and overalls black from sweat and then caked with dust that turned to mud.

When Maw got started, she never let up. "I want to know who's president," she cried.

"What difference do it make to poor folks like us?" Paw snapped back. "The government don't do nothing for us. If it'll just stay there in Washington or wherever and leave us alone and let us go about our business, well, I figger we can't ask for anything more or better."

"*Who* is president?"

Paw frowned. He wasn't sure himself. "Goddammit to hell, Stella. You're worse than a government mule."

He scratched his head. He eyed his breakfast still on the stove. His voice softened. "Wasn't it 'I like Ike'?" he muttered.

"Who?"

"Ike. *Ike.*"

"Oh. The war hero. He was in the army with Walt."

Maw brought Paw his breakfast. All Paw ever wanted was to eat and sleep and drink beer and farm his soil. It always seemed a fair bargain to him that if the government left him alone, he'd leave the government alone.

I knew—I simply *knew*—the *papasans* hanging dead from the pole didn't know who their president was either.

Gunny looked at the ugly things.

"Sometimes in war people get in the way," he said. "They get in *their* way; they get in *our* way. War does it to all of us. I've seen things."

Yes.

They got in the way of Lieutenant William Calley at My Lai. His platoon of U.S. soldiers murdered more than 100 women, old men, and children. Calley claimed he was singled out to be punished for behavior that had become common. I was to know many American veterans whose consciences nagged them to their graves.

Years later, during another war, a black infantry grunt got drunk in a German bar. I was an MP company first sergeant; he was one of my platoon sergeants.

"I ain't never tol' nobody about it," he said, lisping from a speech impediment.

I saw the sorrow, the regret, the shame.

"She was nothin' but a slant-eyed gook," he said. He drank an entire beer, chugalugging.

His platoon in I Corps, he said, captured a suspected female VC. Every member of the platoon raped the woman, taking her in a little palm grove while everyone else cheered and catcalled and waited in line.

"Did you do it too?" I asked.

The sergeant looked away. "The lieutenant said everybody had to screw her. That way nobody could tell on nobody else. The lieutenant said it was an order. But I wasn't the first to do it."

Afterward the Americans executed the woman. Pumped one bullet through her brain pan.

"Who shot her?"

"The platoon sergeant. The lieutenant handed him his forty-five. What would *you* have done?"

I looked away. "I don't know," I said.

* * *

Now Gunny walked away from the butchered Vietnamese. His rifle hung heavy at the end of his arm.

"Shouldn't we cut them down?" I asked.

"Why?"

"They deserve some respect. They're human beings."

"We have a chopper to catch," Gunny said. "Besides, they're just hunks of spoiled meat. That's all any of us are when you come to the bottom line."

I took another look.

"It don't mean nothing," Gunny said. "None of it means shit when you end up like that."

29

The brief month I spent in Vietnam combat as a journalist, the things I experienced and witnessed, haunted me. It haunted me that my friends were dying there. I remember in particular the funeral of one friend, a slain GI.

Soldiers in dress blues solemnly marched his GI-issued coffin to its grave. The American flag draped over it fluttered around the corners in the autumn breeze. A twenty-one gun salute reverberated over the heads of mourners dressed in cheap black dresses and even cheaper blue suits, while the bugler's taps wept tears as real as those shed over the grave itself.

I only half-listened to the eulogy; the other half listened to something dark inside me. I heard phrases like: "brought down in battle ... a true American hero fighting for the cause of world freedom ... gave his life willingly that we who are left behind might enjoy the blessings of liberty ..."

I stood next to the open grave. Special Forces Airborne,

an elite American warrior, I wore army dress greens and my beret. I kept staring at the grave where it waited to receive its reward. I knew Bobby's story: Bobby wasn't brought down in battle; Bobby was on the shitter detail when it happened.

The shitter detail removed the big barrels at the bottom of the outhouses, poured diesel fuel into them, stirred up the mess, then burned it. You could smell it five miles downwind. Bobby was stirring shit and diesel and trying not to gag when an incoming VC rocket exploded everything in his face.

"Shitty way to die," Mad Dog said. "Hit by a flying turd."

"Is there an un-shitty way in war?"

"Old age. Some of the gooks started fighting in 1947. They died still fighting in 1970."

My friend Bobby died with shit splattered in what was left of his face. His son was about six. At the funeral the boy wore miniature army dress greens with a row of ribbons on the left breast. He saluted smartly at his father's gravesite while Taps played. His mother sobbed hysterically.

"His father taught him to salute like that," the proud granddad explained.

"Will he enlist when he's old enough?"

"Little Bobby will take up where his daddy left off," the grandfather said.

The little boy was looking at me after the funeral. "You're a Green Beret," he said, awed. "My daddy wanted to be a Green Beret."

I changed out of uniform. The little boy didn't look at me anymore.

"Somebody has to stand up for America," the grandfather said.

Some years later the son revenged his dad's death in Grenada. He landed on the island with the 82d Airborne Division.

"We didn't kill many of the commies," he said, "but I was there when we killed one of them. That one was for my dad."

In the footsteps of our fathers on the sands of time.

30

I returned from Vietnam to another kind of war on the streets of Miami as a police officer. Again, the violence, man's inhumanity to man, haunted me. I promised my wife, Dianne, finally that I would leave the military, leave police work. I was going to be a teacher. I was twenty-eight years old when Florida State University at Tallahassee accepted me as a student.

Three weeks before the fall semester began, three weeks before I was to resign from the police department, Miami experienced its first race riots when the Republican National Convention on Miami Beach nominated Richard Nixon for president.

Norman Mailer wrote about it: "And out in Miami, six miles from Convention Hall, the Negroes were rioting, and three had been killed and five in critical condition as Miami policemen exchanged gunfire with snipers: 'firefights like in Vietnam,' said a police lieutenant and five hundred armed National Guard were occupying one hundred square blocks."

"I caught two tours in the 'Nam," my police partner, Daniels, said. "Never even kilt anybody that I know of. I been on the police force one year and I've already shot me one. Because, you know where the *real* war is? It's right here in the good ol' red, white, and blue U.S. of A. There's a revolution going on. We are gonna be shooting us a lot more after the government breaks down."

Sometimes, if you were a cop, you thought it had already broken down.

"It's a *war* out there," Vic Butler said before he became

112

one of its casualties. Butler was a black cop; brothers killed him.

"Today's pig is tomorrow's bacon," black radicals scrawled on the ghetto walls. "Kill a cop for Mohammed. War against racist Amerika."

Some of them died; some of us died.

"I don't want you to be a policeman anymore," Dianne said. Our son David was nearly two; Dianne was pregnant with Michael when we arrived at Florida State University. "You're a family man. You have to think about security for your family."

We arrived on campus driving a red VW Beetle pulling a small trailer stuffed with everything we owned. I was an ex-cop, an ex–Green Beret paratrooper, ex-navy, Vietnam veteran, if only as a journalist. I looked years older, harder, and tougher than before. I limped my first day on campus. I was still on crutches from injuries I'd suffered in the Miami rioting. Limping into academia and into disappointment.

An academic counselor rifled through my file. "Veteran, huh? You'll have a difficult time adjusting," he decided. "You're too much a part of the establishment."

I saw him at the next antiwar rally on Landis Green. He carried a sign that said "War is not who wins or loses—but who's left."

I was finally at the university, the first of my hill clan, ever, to attend college. Dad couldn't even read "Stop," for Christ's sake, and now here I was about to learn *everything*. I hobbled all over campus my first day there. I leaned on my crutches, eyes wide with awe, surprised that I had finally made it. Surrounded by red brick buildings, silent and steady and forever, cathedrals of learning, repositories for culture, containing the best there was of what a society had created and learned and saved.

A hippie garbed out ridiculously in ragged jeans, dirty embroidered shirt, and bare feet stopped to look me over. I was older and harder-looking than most of the students.

"You're a veteran, man," he decided.

My smile slowly faded.

"The war is immoral, man. Did you napalm women and children?"

I looked at him. He took an involuntary step back.

"Just dope-smoking hippies," I said.

"Man, what's wrong with the world is you and your type."

I hobbled away on crutches. *My* type? What type was that? I believed in principles and honor and integrity and courage, didn't I? I believed in my country, and if you burned the flag in front of me you might want to put up your dukes, because there was going to be a fight. I might not like lifers much, but I went into the military, twice, because I believed in freedom and democracy and my personal obligation to help liberate the world from communism. *De oppresso libre,* the Special Forces motto, and all that. I believed that our elected leaders knew what was right for us. After all, we the people had elected them.

I believed.

Richard Nixon spoke to the great silent majority, of which I was at the heart.

"Red neck!" a yippie yelled at me, later. Anti-war and anti-establishment sloganeering and antics disgusted me. Be-ins. The snake-dancing around bonfires brandishing signs. *Baby Killer. Pigs.* Chanting: "Ho, ho, ho. Ho Chi Minh is going to win." Burn the ROTC building. Occupy adminstration offices. Weathermen. SDS. Black Panthers.

"Red neck! Red neck! You're a puppet! You believe whatever *they* say."

I scratched my head, looking around, baffled. Mr. Mullins who gave me *Don Quixote* in high school wouldn't have recognized this.

"Academia is the place for dreamers and thinkers," he said.

Mom ironed with a hand iron at a local laundry in Sallisaw ten hours a day, six days a week, for twelve dollars a week. "Poor people can't go to college," she cautioned. "You might as well forget about that. Poor people can't do nothing but work for wages. And low wages at that."

But now here I was at the place for dreamers and thinkers, and the kids, the privileged, they neither understood nor appreciated it. I thought them a bunch of spoiled brats, with professors teaching them who were little more. Most had never known a real job, never known hunger or deprivation or danger. I came to *learn,* to unlock the secrets of knowledge.

But nobody had the key.

A professor stood before the class and *proved,* he said, that social and political liberals were more intelligent than conservatives. A black sociology student confessed in class that he was a house burglar at night, robbing the rich because he had been deprived and therefore *deserved* whatever he chose to steal. The other students cheered him; the professor nodded his head with wisdom and understanding. A Vietnam veteran who had lost a leg during Tet was denied admission to an honors class because the professor said his status as a vet enraged the other students—and besides, the vet was still pro-war and therefore had nothing to contribute intellectually.

"Fucked up," Call would have said.

Everything seemed to have turned upside down. Put these dope-smoking hippies and their spoiled rich brats to pulling a pick sack in a cotton field for just a day and see what they thought about the *real* world.

"Ignore it," Dianne urged. "You're here to get an education so you can get a good job. We have a family."

I brooded.

For so long as a kid I'd lived on the outside of the American dream, picking cotton, living in shacks, so poor even poverty was a step up, that now all I wanted was the opportunity to get my part of that dream.

Only in America could a peasant family send a son to college.

Only in America could Abe Lincoln *still* become president.

Only in America.

31

I stopped going to Landis Green where protesters set up their booths to counsel draft dodgers or homosexuals, where SDS and women's rights advocates and political activists and peaceniks demonstrated nearly every day. I narrowed my world to a single goal—obtain that sheepskin and get out of this lunatic bin. I caught the gray shuttle bus that ran from married students' housing, then caught it home again. I stared out the window. The ivory towers were separate and apart from the world off-campus.

I felt the eternal outsider.

Two grad students—draft age—were talking on the shuttle bus. One had stringy brown hair and delicate, slender, effeminate, hands. The other wore his hair styled. They spoke in that pedantic way of pseudointellectuals.

"Have you seen the study done on those who seek asylum from the draft in Canada?" Delicate Hands inquired of Styled Hair.

"I know if I lost my deferment I'd be finding the next plane to Montreal," replied Hair.

"Yes," said Hands. "You fit the profile of the study. It shows that the average IQ of those who refuse to go to Vietnam is considerably higher than of those who submit to becoming cannon fodder."

I looked at my hands. Scarred from work, knotted. I saw my reflection in the window. Broken nose. More scars. Sun squint lines. Straight-looking hard hazel eyes.

Hair was saying, "Vietnam is a moral issue. It is exceedingly difficult for the less intelligent, the uneducated, to distinguish right from wrong on moral issues."

He tittered like a girl.

"Of course, war may be God's way of weeding out the undesirables," he concluded.

"That's why I never feel guilty about student deferments," Hands mused. "If we're honest enough to face it—and you and I are—we must admit that if we *have* to have wars, then they should be fought only by the lower classes. There are so many of them, most of whom drain from society with pitiful few contributions in return. The intellectuals and the educated are the ones most valuable. It is *we* who will remake society."

The men and boys I knew—they took their chances with the draft. Or they volunteered. They grew up picking cotton, hauling hay, and then they went to work at the lime kiln or the creosote plant. They sacked groceries and rode their horses in the Fourth of July parade. They stood up and took off their hats for Old Glory. Their parents kept framed pictures of them posing with the state representative or the mayor. War for them was a rite of passage. Each generation had its war.

Although my hillbilly cousins and uncles tried to avoid anything government-connected, they still would have fought if it had come right down to it. Besides, most of my hillbillies didn't have the political clout or sophistication to avoid it.

But the privileged—these two on the shuttle bus and thousands of others like them. Vietnam wasn't so much a moral issue with them as it was fear of getting their precious intellectual white hides punctured. They all had their scams to avoid the draft, especially after the lottery system took over and it became harder to obtain deferments. Draft lawyers charged five hundred dollars and found loopholes.

I knew a guy who reported for induction with peanut butter smeared in his underwear; he reached a finger inside his shorts, took a swipe, and stuck it into his mouth. And grinned.

Another guy lost down to about a hundred pounds, swallowed a near-overdose of aspirin, and staggered in for his pre-induction physical with his heart pounding. Still others reported stoned and claimed to be alcoholics or drug addicts. Many clutched folders from their anti-war shrinks or their doctors. The inductees complained of every imaginable ailment known to the human body—bad knees, backs, ankles, teeth, legs, hips, neck. Some of them went "mad" and slung urine in the orderlies' faces.

The well-educated, the middle class, often succeeded in avoiding Vietnam. Not so much so the working class. It was like the couplet I'd read in *Don Quixote:* "I'm off to the wars for want of pence; if I had more money I'd show more sense."

The two grad students on the bus continued their conversation.

"Society doesn't miss the underclasses like it would us," said Hands from the rarefied air of his superiority.

I had heard something like that before. I felt my face heating up the way it did when you came in out of the cold and stood close to the fire.

I was maybe nine or ten when our movings-about landed me briefly in school in Sallisaw, a school large and rich in comparison to the one-roomer I was accustomed to. Another country kid and I fell in together. Like me, Brian Long had patches on his knees and often needed a haircut. He also had this wonderful tubular growth on his ear. You looked at it before you looked at his eyes.

Brian and I carried sandwiches to school for lunch. They were made of bacon strips or butter and sugar, or whatever, tucked inside leftover biscuits or corn bread all wrapped in a brown paper sack or pages torn from the Sears catalog.

"What is *that?*" cried a little girl, pointing.

The others who brought their lunches had *real* bread. Light bread with a marvelous brown crust.

I turned my back on the little girl. Corn bread crumbling in my hands made embarrassing sprinkling noises falling on brown paper wrappings. My lunch that day consisted of corn bread and homemade blackberry jam. And a piece of pork.

The little girl with ruffles and shiny black pumps edged nearer. Her nose wrinkled. "Ooooo! Look at that. They're so poor they don't have bread like we do. Are you like the Dirty Dozen that lives up on the mountain in that old railroad car?"

The other kids laughed and pointed and tittered and said things other kids thought funny. My throat closed against the corn bread and jam. Brian and I slunk from the cafeteria, driven out by laughter.

"They're so poor," shouted the little girl, "that nobody will miss them."

For a while after that, Brian and I sneaked around and hid behind the hedges to eat lunch. But then we returned to the cafeteria and ate our corn bread and biscuits and *dared* anyone to comment. The first wisecrack brought swift retaliation in flying fists as soon as the offender stepped outside.

Corn bread crumbling on brown paper still embarrassed me.

The grad students on the bus—I stared at the backs of their heads.

"If I *were* to be drafted," said Hair, tittering, "I'd rather it be by the North Vietnamese People's Republic. They have the moral cause here."

Deep inside my mind, I carried with me the image of the villagers hanging from the pole, their intestines pulled out onto the ground.

"It's the killing itself," said Hands. "Have you seen it on TV? The thought of it is reprehensible. How could anyone possibly kill another person? You'd have to be the most brutish person to kill another human being. It makes you a murderer, no matter your reason for doing it."

I saw the foot, that goddamned foot. Moses's foot. Its image was also tucked away deep inside my mind.

Miami homicide detectives later located eleven bullet holes from where gunmen had opened fire on police through windows and door screens in the project on Liberty City's Sixty-second Street. It was the afternoon of the second day of the rioting that accompanied the Republican National Convention. The Democrats were also to have their problems, the "Days of Rage" in Chicago, but their rioters were white and privileged, and the riot was more like the tantrum of spoiled brats. The Republicans' rioters were ghetto blacks and poor, and they burned entire streets and shot it out with cops.

I remembered smoke choking the streets, thick and acrid, and the mobs of joyous looters who pranced through the wreckage filling grocery carts with plunder. There had been sporadic sniping since morning. A policeman in the Central Negro District shot and killed a sniper around noon. My four-man team's patrol car already displayed three bullet holes. I had fired one shot earlier, during a ten-minute stand-off when snipers opened up from behind barricades on the balconies of a high-rise project. A black man had run out of an alley and thrown a blazing Molotov cocktail. I pinged a shot at him as he ran; some gunman in the project pinged a shot at me. The bullet gouged a shiny trough in the metal of the car trunk inches from me. It whined, ricocheting into the sun.

There was shooting everywhere in the riot zone after that. Bloody gurneys bearing the injured and wounded were lined up in the hallways at Jackson Memorial Hospital. I was to join them after nightfall, injured in still another firefight that left me on crutches, but first, *first,* there was Moses.

The sun shone so brightly that the first sniper shots from the project sounded as if they flew through liquid brass. Police returned fire in a terrifying crescendo that seemed to go on forever. I threw myself behind a palm and looked around, stunned. Policemen sought cover in a long skirmish line. Most of them fired pistols and shotguns into the project that stretched back two blocks off Sixty-second Street.

Gunfire in the movies is weak-sounding, muted. In real life gunfire is resounding claps of raw energy punching holes through the cosmos.

A stocky black man in khakis was flushed out of a bush. His little pistol sparked. A cop's bullet flipped him back into the bush. He died instantly.

It was a real shooting war in the streets of an American city.

Another black man appeared, running. He wore green

work clothes and gripped a small black pistol, a Saturday night special, as he darted across an open space between retainer walls that sectioned off the project yards like a maze. Instinctively, unthinking, I picked him up in the sights of my .38 Smith & Wesson. His image froze against the rear sights and the front sighting post. I saw him framed and then frozen, as if in the camera's viewfinder.

I squeezed off a single round. The revolver bucked. My target jerked in midair but kept running on adrenaline, like a buck deer after it has been heart-shot but doesn't know it's dead yet.

After the firing ceased, an eternity later, two men were dead and a boy lay wounded by a load of buckshot. I later learned the name of the man I'd shot—Moses. Needleman and I in our police riot helmets dragged Moses's body to the nearest patrol car and shoved it into the backseat. The patrol car wouldn't start. Another cruiser pushed it speeding down the street.

The last I saw of the dead man was his bare foot sticking out stiff from an open back window. He'd lost his shoe in the street when we dragged him. From then on, every time I thought of Moses I saw his bare foot sticking out the window with the sunlight on it.

No face. Just that foot.

My stop came up. I hurried down the aisle of the shuttle bus, getting off. At the door, I turned in spite of myself. My eyes locked hard with those of the two grad students. They shifted in their seats. Their watery eyes darted for cover after a tentative look into mine.

I said nothing. I got off the bus, walking fast in the Florida sunshine. I didn't look back.

"What's wrong?" Dianne asked when I got home.

"The world," I said. "It's all wrong. Everything's turned upside down."

32

"What's wrong with you?" Dianne cried when, after college, we migrated to Oklahoma. Instead of teaching, I became a cop again with the Tulsa police department. I reenlisted in the U.S. Army Special Forces Reserves, the Twelfth Group (Airborne), first as an A-Team weapons expert, later as team medic. "You can't stay out of it, can you?"

I couldn't. Whenever Special Forces had a mission, I volunteered for it.

"I don't understand you," Dianne protested. "Why can't you be like other men?"

I didn't know. I truly didn't. It was simply that the police department, the army—that was where the action was.

"You *are* a Don Quixote. You're a fool."

Dianne should have known I wasn't like other men the first time she saw me. She and her mother were working late at their photo-art studio on Tamiami Trail in Miami when they looked out the window and laughed at what must have been a sight fully as ridiculous as that of poor Don Quixote mounted on that bag of bones Rosinante. I had just arrived in Miami riding my motorbike, Odyssey. It was over a year later that she realized the Miami cop she met and married was the same foolish youth she'd laughed at on the motorbike that night.

I had two sons with Dianne—David and Michael. Twelve years of marriage. She still couldn't understand what attracted me to exploring that dark side of human nature through the military and through police work. I couldn't explain it to her, either. I tried.

"I have to *see*," was the closest I could come, struggling. "I have to *know*."

Dianne finally left me. Twelve years of marriage, and she just left. Returned to Florida with our sons. I remained in Oklahoma where I was a homicide detective with the Tulsa police department and a career reservist in the U.S. Army. I missed her, and I missed our sons. I missed them more than I had ever missed another human being.

She was right, though, about one thing: I couldn't stay out of it.

"Fuck her. Fuck all cunts," Mad Dog Carson growled. He was my Special Forces team's assistant intelligence sergeant. Big man. Black hair growing down his back. Vietnam vet with the 173d Airborne Division. Genius-level IQ. He shot off his own left nut when he went on a domestic rampage using a .30-.30 rifle like a club. Tearing up the furniture instead of his wife. The rifle discharged and shot off his testicle.

That led to the standard team joke: "Sound off like you got a pair. Not you, Mad Dog. Not you, Mokie."

Mokie had lost a nut in kindergarten when a little girl waiting in line for the water fountain kicked him in the balls. Operations Detachment ODA-213 was the only Special Forces team in the U.S. Army with twelve men in it and only eleven sets of balls.

"There'd be a bounty on cunts," Mad Dog said, "if it wasn't for what they have between their legs."

Call always said it. Mad Dog said it, too, and he believed it. "Fucked up." Everything was fucked up. It even explained his theory of the universe, what he called the "Bigfoot Theory."

God was a Bigfoot. We were all ants. You could pray your ass off, but the Bigfoot was going to come down and squash whatever ant happened to get caught underfoot. For Mad Dog there was no order to the universe, no logic. Everything was random, unplanned. Bigfoot.

"Fucked up, Sasser. They missed me in Vietnam, but sooner or later I'm going to get my other nut shot off."

Especially if we continued conducting real-world Special Forces missions to places like Korea.

It was 120 miles across the Sea of Japan to the Republic of Korea. The MATS aircraft with its cargo of U.S. Army Special Forces hopped the sea in a half hour. The first thing I noticed about Korea was its thick pollution haze, the result of millions of oil fires used for cooking and heating. It rose thousands of feet into the air. It was so thick on the ground that you tasted it.

Korea, North and South, remained a tiny nation divided, smaller than the state of Florida. From the air I saw almost the entire peninsula. I saw Pyongyang, North Korea's capital, Manchuria, and even the USSR if I strained my eye and imagination toward the far northwest corner of the horizon.

I saw the demilitarized zone, the DMZ, 151 miles stretching from the Sea of Japan to the Yellow Sea, an ugly 2½-mile slash across mountains and valleys where troops and suspicion let nothing grow higher than grass.

The Korean Conflict did not end in 1953. Korea remained potentially one of the most explosive regions in the world.

During "isolation," Special Forces had been briefed on the military situation in Korea and our role as security for the joint war games known as Team Spirit. Over 180,000 U.S. troops and virtually the entire half-million ROK (Republic of Korea) army were involved in the games.

"Almost six hundred soldiers were killed last year in clashes along the DMZ," we were told. "You can call it a war or not, but it's a war if you're the one getting shot at and killed."

It had been a war on the streets of Miami if you were the one getting shot at and killed.

Officers were issued live ammo to distribute, just in case, since the teams would be operating along the DMZ with the Korean Special Forces "Steel Men." During one recent ten-day period, we were advised, North Koreans had infiltrated the South twenty-six times. Twenty communists had died.

One platoon-sized patrol had worked its way south to Seoul using lonely mountain trails. Somewhere along the route woodcutters had spotted the infiltrators and notified Seoul security forces. The communist commandos almost reached the presidential palace before they were intercepted.

The commies went mad. It was as if, knowing they were going to be destroyed, they wanted to wreck everything around them. A final orgy of destruction. They hurled hand grenades at city buses, killing three passengers and wounding many. Then they charged the Blue House, the president's residence. Seoul police opened fire with automatic weapons. The firefight flared fierce and bloody on the streets and on the grounds of the Blue House. When it was over, twenty-eight guerrillas lay strewn about on the battleground. Two communists escaped. One, Kim Shin Toe, surrendered.

He hung his head. He said he was a marked man. Twice he had disobeyed orders—first, by not destroying himself when he was captured; second, by turning informant. His own countrymen would kill him if they could.

"They will have executed my family by now," he said. "That is what happens when you are unsuccessful and do not do the honorable thing."

Kim and other infiltrators crossed into the South through tunnels underneath the DMZ big enough to handle tanks. U.S. forces discovered the largest of these just three months before Team Spirit. It was large enough to accommodate thousands of troops in a surprise attack.

Korea waited for war.

A month before the war games began, a party of six commie guerrillas penetrated the South, this time by boat from the Yellow Sea. Their mission was to gather intelligence on ROK military maneuvers along the DMZ. A half-hour running firefight erupted when a ROK patrol intercepted the enemy band. The guerrillas ran for their boat, which was hidden in a cove. None of the six made it. Their bodies were placed side by side on display.

"They all time do this," explained a Korean officer. "They

here now in country. They watch us. Maybe we see—how you say—commies? Maybe we kill commies."

He grinned.

"Maybe," I agreed.

"Fucked up," Mad Dog growled.

33

It was such a bitter cold morning in February that the newly planted trees on the ROK post at Bupyong crackled. Steel Men in training cheerfully shucked their black berets and blouses and turned out in T-shirts to practice karate forms. I figured they were ordered out to impress the Americans. Kicks, jabs . . . They performed in perfect mass synchronization, like dancers in a well-choreographed ballet.

One of the troops missed a cue or something. An NCO pounced on him like a cat and cuffed him to his knees. Blood flew. The NCO straightened his uniform. He spoke passable English.

"Discipline necessary," he explained. "Obedience must be required. No mistake."

"Are the troops often disciplined like that?" I asked.

"No. Sometimes we kick them."

The NCO pointed grimly toward the north. "We in combat all time. North come across DMZ, we kill. You not discipline American troops?"

The Korean blinked at my response. "You not beat soldier? How you make soldier obey orders? Beat soldier and make him strong, tough, ready die. Not beat, him lazy coward run from fight. Not beat soldier is reason Americans lose war in Vietnam."

"Soldiers didn't lose the war. Politicians did."

"Uh. One morning we will awaken to sounds of battle. If South Korea lose war, we lose homes, lives, country—everything. Perhaps Americans lose war in Vietnam because them not have so much to lose."

Maybe he was right. Certainly, war in Korea remained both imminent and personal. The mountains north of Seoul and Inchon were the most hazardous "peacetime" battle zone in the world. Ordinary life in South Korea was conducted among uniforms, barbed wire, big guns, sandbags, and all the other machines and accoutrements of war.

I walked Korea, fascinated by the nation as fortress. U.S. Pentagon planners looked upon the nation as one of those over which a nuclear war might be fought.

Taxis, like most in Asia, buzzed around like earthbound hornets menacing pedestrians, bicycles, military vehicles, and each other. Old women in the Inchon markets squatted to peddle live eels and dried squid stacked up like cords of firewood. An armed ROK officer in uniform bought a sackful of dried fish and some ginseng root. Two soldiers stepped off a broken sidewalk to urinate against a wall surrounding a military compound. A rice farmer in a little wagon drawn by some sort of rototiller passed a checkpoint manned by a soldier with a carbine.

Armed platoons of infantry were so common on the streets that an ancient woman balancing a heavy basket of produce on her head did not even glance at them when they double-timed past her. Gunners manning a .50 caliber sandbagged machine gun idly regarded the old woman. Everywhere heavily armed troops manned gun bunkers and sandbagged revetments. Concrete dragon's teeth waited to thwart armed vehicles. Big guns—105s, quad-50s, mortars, antiaircraft—stood mounted and loaded at Inchon, at Bupyong, and at other DMZ sites, their muzzles zeroed in on potential targets to the north.

Even so, the South was heavily outgunned. North Korea fielded thirty-five infantry divisions and two tank divisions to the South's seventeen infantry divisions and seven tank battalions. The Soviets armed North Korea with superior

FROG missiles, while the South had U.S. Honest Johns, Hawks, and SAMs.

But of course South Korea had America. And America had nuclear power.

North Korea had Russia and China, and they too had nuclear power.

My Korean counterpart was a lieutenant named Lee Shik. "The range of the FROG is seventy kilometers," he said. "It can hit Seoul. Seoul is only forty kilometers away. Our country is always under the FROG."

Using binoculars, I glassed the enemy along the DMZ. Their uniforms were gray-green. Red stars on the officers' tabs. Just like in the Survival POW course when I was in the navy.

"Gooks," said Mad Dog, spitting. "Chinks."

He grunted.

"But you know something. The little Chinks don't want to die either. Their government makes them die like ours makes us die."

Mad Dog had a lot of Don Quixote in him too.

One of the American team commanders, a captain, gazed toward the North. "Kill 'em all and let God sort 'em out," he suggested. He licked his lips. His eyes sharpened to bayonet points. "If we're lucky, we'll get a chance to smoke a few commies. Nuke 'em all."

"Fuck," Mad Dog muttered and walked away.

34

"Mother" Norman—Master Sergeant Roger Norman—the soft-spoken Viking team sergeant on my U.S. Special Forces team ODA-213 in Korea, shot a disgusted look at the captain who always talked about nuking the enemy.

"You weren't in Vietnam," he observed.

"I wish I had been. I was too young to go."

Norman slowly rolled up his sleeve. All that remained of the biceps of his right arm was a mass of terrible scars, a memento from the Tet offensive in Vietnam when he led a MIKE Force of Montagnards in an assault to free a captured air force commo man.

"Anybody who likes war," Norman said levelly, his gaze holding the captain's, "is a goddamned idiot."

He reminded me of my uncle Walt, whom we always caught staring out windows. Norman had volunteered for combat in Vietnam to keep his brother from going; you could sometimes request things like that. I guess Uncle Sam had a big heart and didn't want entire families wiped out.

Never, even years later when it became acceptable and even popular, did Norman denounce the war. But you could always sense something in him—a bitterness, an anger—that smoldered so deep beneath the steel-gray eyes that maybe even he didn't realize it. Sometimes he rubbed the arm where the muscle was missing, and he walked off by himself, squatted on his haunches like the Montagnards he'd commanded in II Corps, and simply stared back into time.

"Vietnam?" he said. "Vietnam."

"Mother Norman is his own man," said Mad Dog, and Mad Dog respected few men. "I'd go to hell for him if he asked."

Norman and I went back to when we were both squad leaders in a National Guard infantry scout platoon. Crazy Craig Roberts the ex-Marine was in our outfit. So was a guy named Edwards who might have been the quintessential military man: he followed orders immediately and without question.

Training in Colorado, six scout quarter-ton jeeps in a wide front charged across the plains kicking up funnels of dust, their mounted M60 machine guns chattering blanks. A scout in Edwards's jeep suddenly yelled, "Edwards! Jump, Edwards, *jump!*"

Edwards—no hesitation, not even a second breath. He sprang from the jeep, went flapping across the hardpan prairie like a rag doll tossed from an open window on the expressway. Damned near killed himself.

"If I had men that willing," observed a captain, "we could end the Vietnam War in a year."

Norman stared from those hard gray eyes.

"Don't anybody do Edwards that way again," he said.

And nobody did.

Norman had been Vietnam in-country for seven months operating with the Fifth Special Forces Group when the Tet offensive began. Charlie blasted his way into Saigon and overran provincial towns all over the South. U.S. helicopters airlifted troops to save airports at Tan Son Nhut and Bien Hoa, while airborne troops air-assaulted onto the roof of the U.S. embassy in Saigon and fought VC off the grounds and from the building itself. It was the most concentrated enemy attack of the war.

In Nha Trang, the MIKE Force (Ready Reaction Force) of some eight hundred Montagnards and Nung mercenaries commanded by Norman's twelve-man A-Team manned a stockade next door to the Fifth Group compound. Although Norman was only thirty years old, his little mountain men treated him with an affection and respect usually reserved for elder tribal leaders. Norman wore copper tribal bracelets, ate fish heads and rice with his men in the field, and had proved himself in combat.

City fighting was something new in a war which, until now, had largely been confined to the jungles and the jungle villages. After midnight, street fighting raged in most of Nha Trang. Small arms fire clattered furiously from various points. Electricity out, the city had plunged into darkness. Descending parachute flares cast eerie flickers of shadow on the streets below. Delicately carved lines of green machine-gun tracers probed for U.S. C-130s making approaches to the blacked-out airfield on the city's outskirts.

About fifty men remained in Norman's company; the rest were off-compound when the alert began in the afternoon. Advised that the ARVN radio compound had been overrun and that U.S. personnel were trapped inside, he loaded his understrength company into deuce-and-a-half trucks for the five-mile race across the city. Somehow he managed to avoid enemy contact, although firefights broke out in nearby sectors.

Arriving, he studied the ARVN radio compound from a vantage point across the street. It lay silent before him behind a six-foot-tall stone wall. Three or four square block buildings stood in uncertain silhouette against the lighter sky and the tracers from the airfield. ARVN defending it had popped off a few rounds and then hauled ass, leaving two U.S. Air Force commo advisers to fend for themselves.

As soon as dawn revealed the shapes of the mud-colored buildings in the radio compound, Norman saddled up his company and assaulted in a long skirmish line. The battle in the rest of the city gained momentum with the coming of daylight. Gunfire rattled from several quadrants.

The radio compound proved deserted except for three people. One was a dead civilian left inside some kind of steel cage behind one of the buildings. His throat had been cut. The second was a uniformed ARVN hiding in a garbage can. Something had been burning in the can when the soldier leaped into it and slammed down the lid to hide. His eyebrows, hair, and uniform were fire-scorched. He had been there all night. The third man was a black air force sergeant.

Norman pounded on his door.

"It's us," he called out. "Open up."

Silence.

"Goddammit, open the door."

The door cracked an inch, then almost closed again when the man inside spotted the Asians.

"Goddammit!" Norman said.

The airman's gaze fastened on the Montagnards' fierce-looking American leader. From then on he stayed precisely one step to the rear of his savior. Like a shadow.

"God, God, I'm glad to see you, man," he muttered.

The second American, an air force lieutenant, was gone, obviously either escaped or taken prisoner. Norman funneled his fighters into a vacant street beyond the compound.

It seemed the most obvious avenue of withdrawal for the VC who had attacked the radio compound. Many of the shop fronts along the street had been destroyed in the previous night's fighting. A little girl stood crying in one of the shops amid the broken glass.

Several other Americans eager to get into the fight joined Sergeant Norman in his advance. Two were Special Forces medics with their aid bags *and* their M16s; in Special Forces, medics were also combatants. There were also a lieutenant, a young sergeant, and a captain wearing a sarcastic grin. All were from Fifth Group headquarters.

A few weeks earlier, the captain had gotten drunk at the SF Club and laughingly commented that it was almost impossible for an American soldier to get himself killed in Vietnam.

Norman looked at him in his quiet way and said, "It is unless he goes out where Charlie is."

Now, the captain was trying to win his Combat Infantryman Badge. "Where are the chickenshit little bastards?" he asked.

Norman ignored him.

The street they followed came out to the beach and followed it a short way. Ahead squatted a huge flat-roofed building of two stories. It was enclosed by one of the stone walls that commonly marked government installations. The rising sun illuminated stark iron bars caging all the windows. The sound of fighting a few blocks beyond alerted Norman to the fact that "the chickenshit little bastards" were likely nearby.

"Do you reckon they have my lieutenant?" the air force sergeant asked Norman. "What'll they do to him?"

Suddenly a group of four or five black-pajama-clad figures carrying AK-47s darted from a side street. They did a double take, spotting the Americans and their mountain-bred troops, and broke for the government building. Their unexpected appearance likely saved Norman's force from walking into the killing zone of an ambush. Seeing their surprise lost, the enemy inside the building opened up with a heavy fusillade of rifle and machine-gun fire.

Norman swung into action.

Shouting orders in the tongue-clicking Montagnard dialect, waving his arms, the Green Beret sergeant dashed back and forth in the street directing his little warriors forward to the cover of the wall. Bullets ricocheted around him. Two or three 'Yards took hits. An SF medic dragged one of them to safety. Another 'Yard reached the wall and ran across the open walkway to fight alongside a comrade. He screamed, threw up his arms, and tumbled, his crotch shot out. He got up and hobbled to cover, clutching himself with both hands.

The air force sergeant stayed one step behind Norman. Like a second skin.

This was no ordinary hit-and-run VC tactic. Charles was going to fight it out. The ferocity of the battle meant the building was defended in force, perhaps by as many as two platoons. Norman scurried back and forth behind the wall, giving encouragement by a gentle hand on someone's shoulder, a softly spoken word. He deployed his two M60 machine guns, one at either end of the stone wall. The sound of their rapid, measured coughing suppressing incoming fire was comforting.

Listening to the battle was like standing with your head inside a barrel while a platoon of drummers beat on the barrel with steel bars. It was unlike a firefight in the jungle where foliage muffled sound and reduced the bedlam and confusion.

Norman and the lieutenant strap-hanger from headquarters crouched behind the wall to discuss strategy. While they were speaking, the headquarters captain changed his mind about an American's ability to get himself killed in Vietnam. He took a round through the belly. He crawled up next to the wall and died. A medic rushed up, shook his head, then crabbed on along the battle line, checking other casualties.

Seeing the captain die did something to the lieutenant. It was his first time under fire. He lapsed into a sudden daze and leaned back against the wall, staring at nothing. Norman shook him. Receiving no response, he moved on down the wall, followed by the black airman.

A huge pillar of stone supported the end of the stone fence on either side of the walkway leading to the building's heavy front door. Sprinting across that opening was what had gotten the one 'Yard's balls shot off. Norman flattened himself behind one of these pillars and took quick peeks around the side to get a look at the defenders.

The M60s pocked spurts of rock dust from the front of the building around the windows. The acrid haze of burned gunpowder hung over the battlefield. There was a blood smear on the closed front door. The door was riddled with bullet holes. Norman was so close he saw where the wood had splintered.

The situation looked desperate. Charlie in the top-floor windows commanded a clear field of fire. Norman's attackers had perhaps two feet close to the wall where they were protected. They were pinned down, and Charlie was picking his men off one by one. Norman counted at least four of his Montagnards lying bloodied next to the wall. Two were still moaning. Behind him, the U.S. captain was dead.

The sergeant copped another peek around the rock pillar. Charlie was waiting. A terrific shock caught his right arm and flung it snapping in the air. His M16 sailed away. The air force man stood so close to Norman's rear that he could neither fall nor back out of danger.

"Goddammit, I'm hit! Back up!" Norman snapped.

The flyboy's eyes bugged. "My God! What about me?" he gasped.

"Just back up or *I'll* shoot you."

A string of automatic fire skipped down the walkway between the pillars.

Turning away to inspect his wound, Norman glimpsed the young Special Forces sergeant fighting bravely alongside the 'Yards. The youngster popped up to fire his M16 over the top of the wall. A geyser of blood spray erupted from his face. His body slammed back against the ground and kicked feebly. The airman retched green onto the front of his already filthy fatigues.

"Go check on him," Norman ordered his shadow.

He felt blood trickling down even into his trouser leg. He

took a look inside his blouse. It shocked him to find a neat ugly bullet hole piercing his right chest. His right arm was bright with blood and mangled. He was losing blood fast. He thought he was dying, but it didn't frighten him. It was as if it were happening to someone else, a stranger.

Only a few men were able to overcome their own fears of mortality. Norman felt his mountain people staring uneasily. If his leaderless company panicked, the fortressed VC would have a field day picking off running 'Yards. In a desperate gesture of defiance and authority, the bloody Green Beret scooped his rifle off the ground and fired it one-handed at the enemy. The Montagnards looked relieved. Their leader remained with them.

A medic appeared. He had blood all over him from treating woundeds.

Norman shrugged him off. "I've got work to do," he protested.

"You're in no condition."

Norman's eyes pierced him. "You're here to take care of my men. Take care of them," he said.

"You'll bleed to death in twenty minutes."

"That's all the time I need."

The medic stared and shook his head.

Norman radioed for TacAir to drop the building down on Charlie's head. An O-1E spotter plane pilot responded: "Mary Foxtrot Two, this is Watch Dog Two. We're prohibited from using TacAir in the city."

"*What!*"

"We're prohibited—"

"I copied you. What kind of fucking idiot dreamed that up?"

"Mary, we don't like it either. Blame your politicians."

There was a pause on the radio.

"Mary, I *do* have about ten Willie Pete marking rockets. Where do you want 'em?"

The rockets of white phosphorus might do it. Norman assembled his 'Yard platoon leaders and ordered them to prepare the men for a charge as soon as the airplane finished its job.

The little propeller-driven O-1E buzzed right down on the rooftops, fast, its engine whining. It made three passes, each time drawing fire from the government building. Rockets hissed between the bars on the windows and exploded inside. White smoke belched from the windows. Completing its last run, the spotter plane climbed high aloft.

"How's that, Mary?" the pilot radioed cheerily. "Did I mark 'em for you?"

"Watch Dog Two, you did good."

Norman was growing weak from loss of blood. Not much time left. With his remaining strength, he rallied his mountain people and led the assault from the wall to the front door of the enemy stronghold. The smoke from the rockets helped conceal them. Norman burst through the shattered door with the first attackers. He fired his M16 left-handed like a pistol. His useless right arm danced like a marionette with every movement of his body, slinging blood.

The first room was huge and littered with overturned and demolished chairs and desks. Rocket smoke cut visibility to about fifteen feet. Fire crackled from somewhere upstairs.

The fight inside the building raged fierce but briefly. A VC opened fire at point-blank range. Norman returned fire, but missed. Several of his 'Yards finished the job, and the VC crashed over a desk. Another 'Yard ran over and shot him again where he was struggling on the floor.

Two other VC fell dead in the wild melee on the lower floor. Tiger-striped mountain people and black-clad Charlie intermingled in the smoke. A 'Yard kicked open a door off the hallway. The door was booby-trapped. The force of the explosion hurled the tribesman out into the hall and slammed him against the opposite wall.

For Sergeant Norman, that one room always represented Tet. It was a combination of disjointed sounds and sights and stinks—gunfire clattering in enclosed spaces; men screaming; stamping feet; the stench of fresh blood, burned cordite, and smoke; the sight of a 'Yard with his leg blown off; dead VC in black pajamas lying pooled in their own body gore.

In the midst of it all loomed the Green Beret, the tall black air force man silhouetting his every movement. Norman was everywhere at once, firing with his one good hand, looking terrible and deadly and bloody with his wasted appendage swinging. He did not shout and scream like the others. He fought instead with a silent and deadly purpose. One VC became so unnerved at the sight that he threw down his AK and fled out the back of the building. Others followed.

It was all over in seconds. Norman leaned against the banister at the foot of the stairs to regain his strength. His mission was not yet over.

Thinking of the missing air force lieutenant whose plight had helped produce all this, the wounded sergeant stepped over the bodies of the dead and maimed and climbed upstairs to search. He found the airman in one of the rooms; he had been executed with a single pistol shot to the base of the skull. Norman stood over him, staring. Then he turned without a word and radioed for his own medevac dust-off.

He insisted on waiting until his five other WIAs were loaded onto the chopper before he climbed aboard himself.

"I won't die," he growled.

Doctors at the MASH were going to amputate Norman's arm. It was the easy, fast way to do things. An arm here, a leg there. What the hell. Norman revived in time to overhear the plan.

"Take off my arm," he threatened, "and I'll kill you."

They believed him. They left his arm. He woke up in a clean hospital bed surrounded by pretty nurses. The nurses were laughing over a sign pinned to his chest.

The sign said, "Here lies a Green Beret soldier."

Underneath that, someone had added an appropriate notation: "The fightingest, baddest hard-core motherfucker in the U.S. Army."

"Vietnam," Norman said years later, rubbing his wound. "I'm not sure what it was all for."

35

From the *Nuclear Weapons* handbook prepared by the Department of Defense on how nuclear detonations affect the human body:

Due to the compression and subsequent decompression of the body and the transmission of pressure waves through the (human) organism, damage occurs mainly at junctions between tissues and air-containing organs and at areas of union between tissues of different density, such as where cartilage and bones join soft tissues. . . .

Very large doses of whole-body radiation (approximately 5,000 rems or more) result in prompt changes in the central nervous system. . . .

If the dose is in the range from 1,000 to roughly 5,000 rems it is the gastrointestinal system which exhibits the earliest severe clinical effects. There is the usual vomiting and nausea followed, in more or less rapid succession, by prostration, diarrhea, anorexia (lack of appetite and dislike for food), and fever. As observed after the nuclear detonations in Japan, the diarrhea was frequent and severe in character, being watery at first and tending to become bloody later.

36

Before the Korean mission, before any mission where there might be a chance of a nuclear confrontation, soldiers stoically endured NBC (nuclear, biological, and chemical) warfare training on how to survive and continue fighting after a nuclear holocaust. Most of the instructors by necessity were men of limited philosophical capacity, men of machines and weapons. Men who saw women and children and cities and farms instead of megatonnage and victory through strength and first-strike capability could never push the button to MAD—mutually assured destruction.

I sat in a classroom full of other soldiers while an instructor with small lifer eyes and a Hitler mustache riding his puckered mouth explained about nuclear yields and radiation damage and detonation.

"Even in the worst-case scenario," he said—there was always a worst-case scenario—"you'll still have twelve to twenty-four hours before the fallout disables you. What do you do before you're unable to fight any longer?"

I looked around and saw, for a change, rapt attention. Was I missing something here? This idiot was up there talking about destroying the world as though it were as natural as driving to the store for a loaf of bread.

A few soldiers gave tentative answers. Then I stood up.

"Sergeant Sasser, do you have an answer for that question?"

"Yes. You bend over, stick your head between your legs, and kiss your ass and the world good-bye."

Laughter. The instructor blushed, and his mouth puckered around his mustache.

"Even in the worst-case scenario," he snapped, "*every-thing* won't be gone. I suggest, Sergeant Sasser, that you pay more attention to army doctrine and learn to comply with the directives of men who are far more knowledgeable in this area than you or I. Army doctrine requires you to join with other stragglers if you are at or near ground zero. The highest-ranking man takes charge, and you continue to fight to the best of your ability."

"Even if that means fighting with sticks and stones?"

The instructor glared. "Sergeant Sasser, I don't think you understand the wisdom and importance of army doctrine in keeping the world safe for democracy."

"Oh, I *understand.*"

I had understood it as far back as during the Cuban missile crisis. CIA agents and Department of Defense officials realistically concluded that the world had veered to the brink of nuclear war and that millions of people were expected to die from blast, thermal heat, firestorms, radiation. The Joint Chiefs of Staff with their military doctrine had argued for a preemptive nuclear strike against the Soviets on the basis that if we didn't do it first, the Soviets would. It wasn't the first time the military had taken a stance which, if wrong, had the advantage of leaving no one around at the end to know.

Forbidden to divulge that Washington, D.C., would be incinerated as soon as missiles reached it, government officials ordered their own families to load station wagons with necessities and be prepared to move. If at a certain time the families did not receive phone calls, they were to drive north as fast as they could.

Armed forces around the world went on alert. At the Whidbey Island Naval Air Station, I had watched with apprehension as the fences and gates were locked down. Armed Marine sentries stalked the perimeters with weapons loaded. Combat and patrol air squadrons alike went on immediate readiness. A rumor soon circulated that the heavy attack Skywarrior A3Ds were being armed with nuclear bombs.

"Fucked up," Call grumbled. "Wouldn't you know it? I

finally got a date for this weekend, and now she might not be anything but a crispy critter."

Missile crews were ready to let fly. Troops moved into Florida and the southeastern United States. The Strategic Air Command dispersed to civilian landing fields around the country, while a secret plan was activated to save the president, key government officials, and such things as original government documents and works of art. The entire B-52 bomber fleet took to the air fully armed with nuclear weapons. When one landed to refuel, another immediately took its place.

Call and I stood on a grassy knoll at the naval airfield and watched a heavy B-52 skim in for a landing. It quickly refueled or something, then taxied out and took off again. Marines guarded it on the tarmac with machine guns. It was scary being that close to enough destructive power to wipe out several cities.

It was my childhood fears realized.

"There won't be anyplace to hide this time," Call said. He solemnly shook my hand.

President Kennedy's speech to the nation measured itself from loudspeakers posted all over the base. Uniformed sailors stood hushed and silent, waiting, listening to the calm voice with its Boston twang. It resonated in air grown as taut as nerve endings.

"Doomsday," Call said.

I thought of—I tried to think of everything. Parents, brothers, Sharon. The mountains. Sunsets. How freshly plowed land smelled after it rained. Paw and his Garrett's snuff. Clambakes on the beach. The feel of a horse's nose. Reading. Laughing. Kissing a girl.

I looked at Call. He seemed to exist in a mist. I saw tears in his eyes. He was thinking about everything too.

"Oh, *fucked up!*" he breathed.

I listened to the amplified voice of President Jack Kennedy filling the air: "My fellow citizens, let no one doubt that this is a difficult and dangerous effort on which we have set out. No one can foresee precisely what course it will take or what costs or casualties will be incurred. Many months of sacrifice and self-discipline lie ahead—months in which both our patience and our will will be tested, months in which many threats and denunciations will keep us aware of our danger. But the greatest danger of all would be to do nothing."

It was said that JFK remarked to his brother afterward that, "If anybody is around to write after this, they are going to understand that we made every effort to find peace and every effort to give our adversary room to move."

If anybody was around . . .

Standing on the little knoll watching the B-52, Call said out of a long, thoughtful silence, "What gives any government the moral right to destroy us all?"

I had no answer, so I said, "Better dead than Red?"

The world waited on the brink of destruction while a fleet of Soviet ships carrying warheads for Cuba approached the American sea blockade. The world had never come so close to annihilation before.

"What are you going to do if the missiles start going off?" Call asked me.

"I'm going home."

"You're supposed to stay and fight."

"Fight for what? There won't be anything left worth fighting for."

Call looked away. "Probably not even home," he said.

At the last possible moment the Soviet ships slowed, then went dead in the water. One by one, they turned about. The world was saved. At least temporarily.

"I've never had a better reason to go get drunk," Call said.

In Korea, nearly twenty years after Kennedy's Cuban missile crisis, the world was still poised on the brink of nuclear warfare.

37

Korean aircraft were rusted, dirty. They coughed smoke and rattled in the air. Paratroopers' teeth vibrated like castanets when the aircraft ran up their engines on preflight.

One plane displayed patched bullet holes along the fuselage. "Him fly too near DMZ," explained a Korean soldier, grinning.

American Special Forces and Korean Steel Men joined forces and parachuted onto drop zones along the DMZ. Engineer Sergeant Bodine and his joint team went out the airplane doors beneath dim starlight. Laden with eighty-pound rucks and weapons, the troopers dropped fast beneath their parachute canopies into blackness.

The drop zone was not marked, the jump being a CARP (controlled air release point). With little time for maneuvering, several jumpers missed the DZ and splashed into the Wan River. One Korean broke a leg. Bodine landed in water knee deep, Young in the river up to his shoulders. His parachute in the black current was dragging him under when a Korean soldier on a sandbar pulled him out.

The temperature was cold enough to freeze water in canteens. Fighting hypothermia, the drenched soldiers burrowed into the deep dry manure of an abandoned barn. Clasping each other like freezing puppies, they raked the loose manure over their bodies for its warmth.

"I always knew if you stayed in the army long enough you'd end up under a ton of shit," Mad Dog quipped.

I parachuted onto a sandbar in the Little Han River with my counterpart, Lieutenant Lee Shik. A daylight jump, in the afternoon. From the air with the quiet canopy swaying above, I picked out the wide swath of the DMZ. Just the year before, a U.S. soldier on guard duty had defected across it to the Reds. The commies made political hay of it, there were so few such defections. See how desirable the communist system is, they chortled in their propaganda.

Sure, and the Wall in Germany was built for aesthetic reasons; the barbed-wire Iron Curtain kept out throngs of people wanting to get *in*.

In Korea, I *felt* war, even as I had felt it in Vietnam. Koreans rose each morning accepting that the afternoon or the black night might bring war. They remembered too well the Seoul that had existed at the end of 1953. It was a ruined city with a surviving population of less than one million. The stench of death hovered over the bones of the city. Bloated bodies rotted in the torn streets. Gutter-living orphans prowled, scrounging for food scraps. An estimated one million people had died in the fierce struggle.

One million.

"But the South remains free," said Lee Shik.

Americans had not faced devastation like that on their own shores since the Civil War. Modern Americans truly failed to understand war and its consequences. War was something that happened in a distant and foreign land, brought to them only through the modern miracle of TV. Even during the Cuban missile crisis when President John Kennedy and Premier Nikita Khrushchev brought the world to the brink of nuclear annihilation, Americans stood outside with anxious faces cast toward the heavens, waiting to see if it really would happen, but never actually believing that it would.

In contrast, the Republic of Korea *expected* nuclear war. Its entire population was organized into a complicated civil defense network. It left me dumbfounded one afternoon in Seoul when air raid sirens suddenly wailed in unison like thousands of banshees. I remembered in kindergarten hiding underneath my desk. My head snapped up to face the skies. I looked for a place to hide. From Seoul to Pusan, the Republic of Korea was only 270 miles long. Missiles from the DMZ could easily strike any target.

Within one minute after the sirens began, eight million inhabitants had disappeared from the streets of Seoul, leaving only military vehicles, civilian police, and air raid wardens wearing green armbands. I couldn't imagine clearing the streets of New York within one week, much less in one minute.

I thought about the development of weapons. Stones became slingshots became catapults became bows became rifles became machine guns became bombs became rockets became nuclear missiles became . . .

"Mad Dog, help me make sense of this," I requested. "We have enough nuclear explosives to blow up the world ten times over, but still we keep stockpiling and preparing for their use. We actually train men to destroy every living thing on this planet as though that were a strategic possibility."

"Stupidity is much more common in the world than intelligence," Mad Dog answered. "One day the Bigfoot will come down on the world like it's a speck of sand."

"Yes."

"We're soldiers. We're doing our part in making the earth a barren rock in the universe."

"The end of the world is upon us!" Preacher Seaborne had shouted during the 1956 Suez Crisis. The Pentecostals and Holy Rollers back in the hills had run for their churches. "The Last Days are nigh. The Battle of Armageddon is about to be fought, and the Lord is going to call his children home. Hallelujah! Praise the Lord!"

I sat in the back pew of the old one-room schoolhouse turned church carving Sharon's initials next to mine on the back of the pew in front of me. I stopped. I looked around. Blood drained from my face. I folded my knife and stuck it into my pocket and glanced around to see how far away the door was.

It was dark outside. I saw no great fireballs. I didn't hear Gabriel's horn summoning the dead from their graves.

The Spirit attacked the congregation, faced as it was by

the Second Coming: "Hallelujah! Praise God! Take us home, Lord. *Alli my khe shun di."*

I prayed feverishly: "Oh, Jesus, don't do it now. Please? I got lots of things I ain't done yet. I'm only fourteen years old. Please, Lord, listen. I don't want the world to end when I ain't hardly seen nothing or done nothing except milk cows and pick cotton."

"Sinners!" Preacher Seaborne roared. "You ain't got much time left. The Last Days are beginning when the Lord will separate the sheep from the goats. It'll be *too late* when the battle starts."

"Oh, Jesus. Oh, Lord," I prayed.

The coal-burning stove huffed and rattled its lid. Its belly heated to a glowing red. Like the fires of hell.

"I ain't done a lot of sinning, Jesus," I mumbled, more contrite than I'd ever been in my young life.

"It's an atomic war coming!" Preacher Seaborne yodeled. Prepare to meet your Maker!"

Alli my khe shun di.

Two or three days of this while I kept looking into the cold darkness outside. Finally, I gave up listening for Gabriel's horn. I sneaked out of church. Everyone else continued shouting and praying and speaking in tongues.

"God ain't gonna do it to us," I assured my mother. "We're gonna do it to ourselves."

And we would.

38

Korea went on curfew every night from midnight until four A.M. The nation literally shut down. Police and the military blocked all thoroughfares. Only government officials and their vehicles were allowed on the streets and roads.

After the U.S. Special Forces teams returned from the DMZ and Team Spirit without significant enemy contact, Inchon's Mayor Won Byung Ui honored us with a formal party in the city's best hotel. Lovely geishas accompanied by singers and dancers in traditional costume served dish after dish on low Oriental tables. Combat boots lined the hallway outside. Sitting on pillows on the floor, I felt like Marco Polo.

"What is this?" Lieutenant Ecker asked a geisha, pointing at one of a dozen dishes.

The beautiful Asian woman pondered, searching for the English word. Finally she smiled brightly and said, "Bow-wow. Bow-wow."

Dog meat was a delicacy in much of the Orient. I laughed. "Eat your poodles and noodles, Ecker."

My team of horny Koreans and Americans slipped out of the hotel before curfew lifted and went looking for a whorehouse. Stepping into the city was like entering a science fiction movie, something like *On the Beach*, in which the entire population had been wiped out. No one walked the streets. There were no taxis, no newsstands, no late-night eateries, no weary street hookers or wandering drug addicts. Nothing. The city of Inchon had a population of over one million, but no one stirred. Footfalls echoed ominously between the darkened skyscrapers.

"What happens if the police see us?" I asked.

"Maybe they think we infiltrators and shoot us," Lee Shik said.

I heard my own breathing in this strange dark city of emptiness. Was this, I wondered, the future?

39

Another Special Forces mission.

Lightning. A bolt of raw electricity strobed, crackling in the night clouds beyond the slipstream roaring past the open paratroop doors of the C-130 Hercules. And I saw Central America for the first time. Panama below through the open doors—the black of jungle without relief, the ocean reflecting back the lightning in quick mirror return. Nothing there to explain the attraction the region would soon exert over me and would continue to exert during the next fifteen years.

An attraction, I decided, that went beyond the many little wars that made up the common war. There was something about the nations, the Latins—it went deep. Sometimes I felt as if I had lived there before, in a previous incarnation. As one of the peasants, perhaps. Maybe even a revolutionary struggling for freedom and social justice.

Rain skittered and beaded on the metal aircraft floor. The airplane bounced in the storm. During another bolt of lightning, Mother Norman cast a quick glance along the stick of paratroopers waiting for the signal. Then it was dark again, and there were the jump lights throbbing red at the doors. And Felber, the jumpmaster, leaning dangerously far out

into the wind searching for lights on the drop zone. Slipstream and darkness molded his face into his jump helmet.

It was a fourteen-second DZ, a clearing half-mooned out
of the jungle and facing the sea. Twelve paratroopers had
to go out the door over it within fourteen seconds.

"Sharks'll get you if you drop into the ocean," we were
warned during "isolation" at Fort Chaffee, in the same old
stockade, now abandoned, where Uncle James had served
so much hard time. "Don't land in the jungle, either. Jungle
trees splinter; you could get one jabbed up your ass. You
must hit the DZ, no matter what."

In a storm? On the darkest night? At three A.M.? Laden
with one hundred pounds of battle gear each? Jumping from
less than one thousand feet onto a strange DZ we couldn't
even see?

"Get fucking *real,*" Mad Dog grumbled from somewhere
in the darkness along the stick.

The entire Twelfth Special Forces Group would be para-
chuting onto DZs like this one at either end of the Panama
Canal—some kind of political "show of force" disguised as
a training mission. Some of the lessons we learned now
would be used years later in Operation Just Cause when
President George Bush sent invading American troops to
Panama to kidnap dictator Manuel Noriega and bring him
back to the United States to stand trial for drug smuggling.

Departing the continental U.S., the big C-130s carrying
parachutists flew south almost in the ocean spray to avoid
Central American radar. Jumpers rigged in-flight from piles
of gear stacked five feet high at the aircraft center lines.
Standing spread-legged to maintain their balance on the unsteady platform, hunching into the chute harnesses, snapping
on the reserves and heavy rucks and padded weapons.

Knife, utility harness, M16 rifle, ammo, flashlight, first aid
kit, strobe light, machete, rations, canteens of water, sleeping
bag, poncho, hammock, E-tool, water wings in case we
landed in the drink with the sharks ...

Fucking miserable. It took one man to pull another out
of the canvas seating to get him ready to jump. You didn't

jump, either, not rigged down like a pack mule; you tottered to the door and *fell* out.

Bodine, in the webbing next to me, was getting airsick; he always got airsick. He sat very still, trying not to barf.

"Don't barf," I shouted to be heard above the aircraft noise.

Bodine sat very still. If he barfed, it would start a chain reaction, like on the "barf jump" to Fort Bliss that time. We had flown NOE, Nap of the Earth. Low, rough flying. Brownie had started it that time, not Bodine. He'd consumed a spaghetti C-ration. He barfed, and a string of spaghetti came out his nose and hung there.

"Oh, God!" and Bodine had barfed, too.

I'd vomited into a plastic bag. It resembled cheese and scalloped potatoes from a LRRP ration. Sick as I was, I couldn't resist: "Rock?" I handed it to Rock Taylor. "Have a LRRP," I said.

"Christ!" he moaned, then barfed up his own LRRP.

We slid to the doors on a slime of barf, slipping and sliding. Tommy Hinds was on his butt, and his feet kept sliding out from underneath him when he tried to get up.

"Please don't barf this time," I said to Bodine now, as we prepared to jump over Panama. But he couldn't hear me above the aircraft noise.

I gripped his hand where it rested on his knee. He leaned back in the canvas against his main, his reserve chute in front and his ruck below that between his knees snagged to D-rings. He shifted slightly to relieve the dig of the M16 strapped to his left shoulder.

He gripped my hand in return. No matter how many times you had jumped, there always came that moment of truth before you went out the door when a friend's touch meant something. Rock Taylor never jumped without turning around in the stick and making a production of touching the man behind him.

"It's okay, Chuckie-Bear!" Bodine shouted, but he still sounded sick.

Yeah.

* * *

"It's *not* okay," Dianne had said. She begged, "Will you get out of the army and stop jumping?"

"Not yet."

And then Kathy. She was my second wife, twenty-two years old at the time we started living together. Blond, blue-eyed. Not terribly bright, but beautiful.

"Charles, please don't jump anymore," Kathy pleaded.

"He belongs to the team," Moody said. "Before the wives, we belong to the team."

The team. It lasted longer than marriages.

"Here's to ex-wives," Mad Dog toasted at a party one night. "May they all get crotch rot—or at least a yeast infection."

"Why? Why do you stay in the army?" Kathy asked me.

Mad Dog had his way of explaining it. "Fuck God and country. I been to war and it ain't shit and I ain't going back. I'm in this chickenshit outfit because that's where my buddies are. The best buddies I ever had or ever will have. Fuck a bunch of lifer motherfucking officers and the horses they rode in on. They can kiss my rosy airborne ass. And you *know* where you can stuff Mom's apple pie."

How could you explain it to an outsider? It was a male bonding with ties as close as blood.

"What if there's a war?" Kathy cried.

"Then I'll go."

"You *like* war?"

"I hate it."

"But . . . ?"

There was an inexplicable feeling you got from danger shared with brothers.

"I'm afraid for you," Kathy said. "You're always going off to wars. It's worse now than when you were a policeman. You're a writer, not a soldier."

My first novel, *No Gentle Streets,* had just been published.

"If I stop living," I said, "I stop writing."

"Charles . . . I don't understand you."

Dianne had said it, too. "I don't understand you."

* * *

Over Panama, standing in the rough-flying Hercules, attached by a static-line umbilical to the cable, I concentrated on the jump ahead. Oddly, Sharon's face flashed briefly before my eyes. My Dulcinea. A love that no real woman could replace because she existed mostly inside me now, even if she did have a name and a face.

Lightning webbed the darkened sky. Rough air threw us against each other. Below on the DZ, unknown to us in the aircraft, the jump had been scrubbed because of the storm. Too dangerous. Winds gusted seaward, toward the sharks, at forty knots. A combat jump, okay, but this was just a training jump. A Panamanian on the DZ poured the gasoline out of his marking pot. Without thinking, he struck a match to the gasoline to get rid of it.

Felber, the jumpmaster, was looking for the DZ markings. Ahead, past the wing, he spotted fire on the DZ. Thinking it meant a go, he sprang back from the door and pointed.

Stand in the door!

40

Years ago when I made my first parachute jump in training, I had stood in the door as first jumper in the stick. It took away some of the jitters to watch the countryside pass below at my feet like a detailed contour map. Watching from the door, actually seeing the ground, reduced my fear of the unknown. It was like with a firefight. Anticipating its horrors, imagining what *could* happen, was far worse than the reality of it. I was almost disappointed after my first battle. The earth did not tremble; the sun kept shining.

It was just a bunch of men shooting at each other.

The psyching up to parachute out of an airplane started

at the gates at Fort Benning, Georgia. Over them hung a bold sign: Through These Gates Pass the Toughest Paratroopers in the World. Beyond that was Hell Week, followed by another Hell Week, and then Jump Week for the survivors.

Airborne shuffle. One mile, two miles, no sweat. Four miles, five miles, not done yet.

> Two old ladies lying in bed.
> One looked over to the other and said:
> "I wanna be an Airborne Ranger.
> I wanna live a life of danger. . . ."
> Airborne! Airborne all the way!

Torture of the swingline trainers. Dangling from harnesses in the air. Practice PLFs, Parachute Landing Falls. Jumping from the 34-foot tower on a cable again and again. The 250-foot tower. More running and push-ups. Yelled at and cuffed by the Black Hats, the airborne instructors. Uniforms white-crusted with salty sweat. Wanting to kill a Black Hat, grab the arrogant little son of a bitch by his neck and hear the bone snapping.

"Billet number nine-oh-two, what are you?"

Everyone in the army was a number.

"Airborne, Sergeant Airborne. All the way!"

"Can you *kill*, Billet nine-oh-five?"

"With my bare hands, Sergeant Airborne."

"Let me hear it, paratroopers!"

"Kill! Kill! Kill!"

Men jumped out of perfectly good airplanes to do battle on the ground. Tough, reckless men with a contempt for death and danger. Warriors.

> Gory, gory, what a helluva way to die.
> Gory, gory, what a helluva way to die.
> There was blood upon the risers,
> There was brains upon the ground.
> And he ain't gonna jump no more. . . .

After all that, a few guys froze in the door and just couldn't do it, couldn't go out that terrible door into space. Some of them the Black Hats bodily threw out. Others grabbed on to the seat webbing, the center poles, hydraulic cables. It was like trying to pull the claws of a scared cat out of a screen door. These were the "chickenshits"; their billet numbers disappeared from the next morning's muster formation.

I stood in the door my first jump, and it never occurred to me that I wouldn't go. By the numbers. Tips of my fingers outside, touching the skin of the aircraft. Boot toes protruding over the edge. Slipstream screaming past just an inch from my face. I watched lazily as ponds and green fields and brown fields and cows in pastures and cars on a farm-market road drifted past precisely one thousand two hundred fifty feet below.

"*Go!*"

The jumpmaster slapped me on the ass. I stood there, smiling a little.

"*Go!*"

I went.

And I kept going, year after year.

I was going now over Panama, storm or not. It was our mission to go.

The green lights at the door came on with terrible presence. Ecker, the lieutenant, went first; I followed in the stick. Twelve men disappeared in a shuffling rush into the black wind. It always stunned me how fast and violently and furiously a stick of paratroopers exited an airplane.

I hurtled earthward through wet darkness so complete that I heard the rustling pop of Ecker's parachute opening near my head, but could not see it. My own chute ripped from its pack. Then it jerked me up hard in the wind, snapping my legs, just as an angry flash of lightning punctuated the night and blinded me momentarily. I felt rather than saw a full canopy holding air.

Hanging in the wind, feeling the slash of rain, I looked down and waited for the next blaze of lightning to reveal the

154

DZ. When it happened, I glimpsed a small grassy clearing surrounded by high black hills and jungle on three sides and abutted on the last side by ocean whitecaps. Wind howled directly from the low clouds over the jungle, pushing me tracking at full speed toward the waiting sharks.

Without a moment to lose, I toggled the Dash-One parachute against the wind and held on. Another strobe of lightning revealed the swarm of other parachutes around me, like a bed of flying mushrooms searching for a way out of the dark.

We were all tracking toward the sharks.

Desperate now, I climbed my front risers like a monkey to spill air out the canopy's back side and push me against the wind. The parachute lost lift. I seemed to hurdle through the air, coming in hot, but it was my only chance of hitting the DZ and avoiding a swim with the fish.

I sensed rather than saw ground rush. Yanking the toggles to my knees, I snapped them free at the last instant. The chute grabbed air, jerked me, then dropped me into—water.

The fucking sharks. Either that or the parachute would drown me.

My befuddled brain processed data with the speed of the best computer. It wasn't salt water, I realized, and it was shallow. Only about waist deep.

A drainage ditch that cut around the perimeter of the DZ.

Inflated with stormwinds, the parachute became a runaway horse. It dragged me spluttering and coughing down the water-filled ditch. Unable to gain my feet because of the chute at my head and the heavy ruck dragging me by its lowering line from the other end, I fumbled with wet hands for the parachute quick releases.

Just as I released the left riser to collapse the runaway parachute, a Panamanian ground crewman somehow grabbed it and held on. The strong wind dragged us both.

"Turn it loose, asshole!" I screamed.

The bastard was drowning me.

He wrapped the riser around a passing tree. It jerked me up short like a roped calf. Elsewhere, Bodine was barfing and being dragged through it. Mother Norman had blood

streaming with water down his face, and Eskridge was helping him. I sat in water up to my armpits.

"Adonde fue el pájaro?" I asked in disgusted Spanish,
giving my rescuer the pass phrase.

Lightning rippled. The guy looked at me. A howler monkey roared from the top of a jungle giant; he sounded like
a jaguar.

Mad Dog yelled from somewhere on the DZ: "I don't
need this shit."

41

Back in the Oklahoma hills before electricity finally came,
the kerosene lamp burning in Maw and Paw's living room
cast a circle of light, and the light flickered and danced and
flared up whenever a moth fell to its flaming death. Sometimes one of the farm dogs came and stood beyond the
screen door looking in. His eyes were red coals and you
couldn't see the rest of him.

As far back as I remembered, Paw was an old codger with
one of the galluses hanging loose from his overalls and
heavy socks pinned to the cuffs of the long-handled underwear he wore year-round. He always needed a shave, and
he smelled of what Maw called "ol' mule piss and ol' man
stink." When *Amos 'n' Andy* was over on the battery-
powered radio with its one dim eye glowing in the near-
dark and a wire antenna draped out the window, Paw
moaned and stretched and got ready for bed.

He took the lamp and shuffled outside to pee off the front
porch and yell "sic 'em!" at the dogs. Then he came back
inside and stomped off to bed with his face glowing in places
and his eyes kind of hollow above the lamp. He set the lamp

on the floor by his feather bed and took off his outer garments and belched and farted and scratched himself all over. Finally he climbed into bed with some more moaning and groaning and condemning the Lord and yelled that Maw could come get the lamp now.

"The ol' fart'll carry that lamp with him to light his way to the grave," Maw complained.

Later, after I'd left the hills and both the old folks had died and we'd buried them on different sunny days in the graveyard at Sallisaw, I often thought about the old man and how he carried that kerosene lamp with him to light the way. Most people, I thought, were like that about their lives. They followed a path from cradle to grave carrying a lamp and avoiding the dark corners.

I couldn't do that. I was always drawn to explore dark corners.

"The boy can't just accept something the way it is and go about his business," Mom said. "He's always got to ask 'What for?' and 'How come?' "

"Curiosity killed the tomcat," Maw clucked.

Emerging from the jungles of Panama, our field uniforms rotting at the crotch and armpits from the rains and heat and filth, we learned that President Nixon had resigned over Watergate and that there was rioting in Panama City. Mother Norman knew I wouldn't be satisfied with knowing there was rioting. I'd have to peer into the dark corners.

"You want to go *see* it?" Norman said.

"Yes."

"It could kill you."

Dressed in casual civvies, Felber and Lieutenant Ecker trailed Norman and me off the narrow-gauge isthmus train that ran between Colón and Panama City. We got off at the station behind a flat-faced San Blas Indian and his equally flat-faced wife who wore a large gold hoop dangling from her nose.

Down the darkening street beyond the tiny train station people hung out their windows and yelled and threw things while other people in the streets ran Amok. I saw a car

157

burning. Orange and blue flames cast huge gyrating people-shadows against tenement buildings. A burst of automatic-rifle fire exploded from a side street. A detail of khaki-clad militiamen wearing black riding boots and carrying .45 Thompsons and M16s ran by.

I remembered Miami and the gunfire there. And Moses.

A U.S. Army liaison officer jumped out of a staff car waiting at the curb.

"Hold up, guys," he called. "They radioed that you were on your way. I'm afraid we can't let you go down there. Americans are mighty unpopular right now."

He drove us for a drink and a steak and lobster at the American Legion Club in Balboa. A picture window overlooked the wide mouth of the Panama Canal. I watched ships steaming into the narrowing pass while others lay at anchor in the harbor. Moon on water and silver-glowing ships—and in the distance, gunfire. The canal was one of the most militarily strategic locations in the world.

The liaison officer filled us in on events. He was young, crewcut. Intelligent and, unlike so many lifers, able to shift away from military dogma to search for underlying truths. I sank into the cushions of my chair, relaxed after weeks living on the jungle floor, intensely interested in the officer's digest of current events.

"Many of the Panamanians want the United States to pack our ditty bags and leave the canal to Panamanians to operate," he said. "The catalyst came when our old friends the commie agitators urged plantation workers to go out on strike against the Chiriqui Land Company, which is American-owned and produces most of the bananas in this country. The Panamanian government then levied a one-dollar-per-box tax on all bananas exported. They're trying to drive the Americans out.

"But if we leave, the common people who think they're poor now will starve to death. The canal will close down within a year because no one knows how to repair things when they break down, and the government will run out of operating capital. Americans have always handled the technical jobs, Panamanians the menial ones.

"It's a corrupt government here," he said. Like most in Latin America and in Third World countries. "There's the government elite and the minuscule upper class who live like royalty, while the rest of the people crap on the ground behind their houses and earn about seventy dollars a year average."

He smoked. We watched the ships in the harbor.

"The American embassy was attacked and stoned today," he continued. "Some GIs downtown were beaten, mostly by the *Guardia Nacional*. You go downtown and get into a row or anything and the *Guardia* will beat your heads for you. They aren't like our police. They kill an American GI and he's paid for, as far as this government is concerned."

Years later the Panama Popular Defense Forces under Noriega shot and killed a U.S. Marine, providing President Bush with an excuse to declare Operation Just Cause. American troops nabbed Noriega and sent him to Miami where he was tried and convicted for drug trafficking. His sword, scabbard, swagger stick, cap, and uniform ended up in the Eighty-second Airborne museum at Fort Bragg.

"What the locals here see is a bunch of rich foreigners all huddling together and getting rich off the country," the liaison officer mused. "This country and a dozen others in Central and South America are ripe for revolution. When it comes to American interests, Latin America is vital. Yet we just take the little brown people south of the border for granted.

"One day," he said, "one day we'll wake up and look around and it'll be too goddamned late. We'll have war right at our doorstep, and war it will continue to be until it's war on the lawn of the White House."

42

In Mexico once, the bus on which I rode stopped near Veracruz at one of the tin-roofed inspection checkpoints. A government inspector with a .45 auto shoved into his waistband boarded the bus. He waddled down the aisle sweating and snorting like the fat man he was. The crack of his ass showed whenever he bent over to paw through a passenger's bags.

He randomly thumbed passengers to get off with their luggage. Some of them bribed him with *la mordida*—"the bite"—and he permitted them to remain in their seats. The others had to get off and empty their possessions onto the concrete floor of the shed. Local boys and men helped the inspector rummage through things. They waved brassieres and other personal items and sniggered.

A woman returned to the bus stuffing clothing back into her bag. Her expression reflected a long-suffering discontent. *"Es necesario?"* she asked of no one in particular. "Is it necessary?"

I asked that same question as I walked through the riot aftermath in Panama City, peering into dark corners where anti-American graffiti smeared tenement walls. Was it necessary that in a world so rich in resources so many people lived in poverty? I *felt* their misery as I trod narrow streets crowded by three-story tenements fading and crumbling and standing back to back with an alley or walkway in between filled with the debris of daily living.

Ringing the tenements were the shantytowns, city dumps of one-room tin huts, stretched-canvas shelters, and even packing crates in which entire families lived. It was a rat's-nest maze of old sheet iron, scrap lumber, tar paper, flattened tin cans, and cardboard, through which meandered narrow muddy trails where people stopped to relieve themselves.

Was it necessary?

Ragged children and men in britches without shirts and slender women in shapeless shifts, mostly blacks or honeybrown mulattoes or Indians, massed to loiter and stare. A woman squatted on a tin can and relieved herself while holding a baby to her breast to suckle. The baby had matchstick arms and legs and a belly like a cantaloupe.

Es necesario?

A little brown boy stopped barefoot in front of me. He was about nine. Yesterday boys like him had used razors to slice the back pocket of a soldier's trousers and relieve him of his wallet.

The youngster stared at me for a long time before he decided I was American.

"I hate you," he blurted out suddenly in Spanish.

"Porqué?" I asked. "Why?"

"Because you are American and you are rich."

"No estoy rico, I'm not rich. I'm a soldier."

"You are rich," he insisted. "Someday I will be a soldier too. I will kill your soldiers."

Although the rioting was over, mobs still swarmed to the street corners, dispersing quickly when the *Guardia* arrived brandishing Thompsons and carbines. I remained in the background, merging. Suddenly I flinched at the nearby burst of a submachine gun. Several people fell to the pavement. Others fled. I joined a small group that ran toward the alley from which the shots had originated.

A burly *Guardia* in jackboots stood spread-legged in the alley holding his Thompson with the stock resting on his hip. Smoke curled from the muzzle. At his feet sprawled a child of ten or eleven whose bare chest had been turned to bloody hamburger. The little body appeared twisted and contorted and spindly, like that of a bird dropped out of flight. His eyelids were caught wide; he stared at the sky in a kind of dazed wonder.

A new blue bicycle lay next to him. The front tire was still spinning.

The kid was a thief, the *Guardia* explained nervously.

Someone said the boy had stolen the bicycle.

I turned and walked away from the scene.

A ten-year-old killed with a submachine gun because he stole a bicycle.

Es necesario?

43

Latin America with its many little wars and revolutions seemed to attract a particular type of gringo. Get two Latins together, went an old saying, and you had a party; three together and you had a revolution. Intrigue flowed thick in the shadowy streets of the Latin capitals. Gringo soldier-of-fortune types, scoundrels, journalists, social do-gooders, the restless, adventurers—they could all be found wheeling and dealing in German, Japanese, Spanish, English, and occasionally French in places like Club El Mirador in Hotel Maya on a hill overlooking the Honduran capital of Tegucigalpa or in the club of Hotel La Ronda in the city below.

"The scum of the seven seas and all the continents, they end up washed ashore here sooner or later." Barry Sadler laughed. "If you're an adrenaline junkie and can't live an ordinary life in an ordinary place and time, then this is where the action is."

We were having drinks in the bar of Hotel La Ronda. It was during one of the many trips I made to Central America on one pretext or another. Sadler was ex–Special Forces, a Vietnam vet. In a different time and place he had become famous for writing and singing "The Ballad of the Green

Berets." Now, looking a little paunchy, a little dissipated from too much drinking, more than a little middle-aged, he wrote the Casca series of adventure paperbacks and did an on-and-off business in international gun trading.

"They're gonna kill each other anyhow," Sadler said, shrugging, "so somebody may as well sell them guns and make a little money on it. And you, Sasser? What dragged you ashore?"

It was my turn to shrug.

Tony, another Vietnam vet, a Puerto Rican with twenty years' service in the military, much of it in Special Forces and a lot of that as a military adviser and trainer in various Latin American countries, expressed a kind of bitterness.

"The U.S. does not have the patience to wage unconventional war," he said. "We want everything over and done quickly, like in Grenada. The contras are hesitant about committing themselves to fighting the Sandinistas because they know we will abandon them when the time comes. That's why they stay so close to the Honduran border—so they can bug out and save themselves when the United States changes her president and her policies toward the contra cause."

American helicopters had airlifted Honduran soldiers to the fighting along the border when the Sandinistas invaded to get at the contras, but U.S. soldiers did not participate directly. An official at the U.S. embassy in Tegucigalpa thought for a moment before cautioning me that what he said was "deep undercover" and must not be attributed.

"The United States," he declared, "in an emergency is prepared to do more than airlift Honduran soldiers. We are prepared to commit U.S. soldiers to the fighting."

"Maybe we will," Tony said. "But I still say that what we did in Vietnam, we will do again in Latin America. It's a pattern. Americans die for some cause, then the politicians change policy. The surviving Americans go home and the allies are left behind to be killed."

Sadler drank. He drank some more.

"Fuck it all," he said.

The next thing I heard about Sadler he was in Guatemala

and had been shot in the head. Something about a taxi. He and the taxi driver and a girl Sadler was with were drunk and arguing. There were three stories about the shooting: Sadler shot himself; the girl shot him; the driver shot him.

Brain-shot, he became a vegetable. Some of his old Special Forces buddies kidnapped him from the hospital and hid him when his estranged wife—his third wife, I think—tried to have him declared incompetent. But Sadler died anyhow. He died and it was like an era died with him.

What Sadler said about those who could not live ordinary lives being washed ashore in Latin America. I thought about it. I thought about it a lot. Adventure, intrigue, foreign romance with brown-skinned girls. Those were the ingredients of my boyhood dreams in the cotton fields of Oklahoma. It was addictive.

I kissed Maria long. She was my girlfriend in Tegucigalpa. A friend from the States I called Llave—Keith Laub—tapped my arm from across the table in the International Playboy Club. He nodded toward the door as two Honduran soldiers armed with M16s sauntered in. Honduras was on a war footing.

"Let's get out of here," Llave suggested. "Those boys are staring at us."

"Not us. You."

Laub was Italian-American and about the size of a door, only taller. He was a ringer done in double size for the actor John Travolta. We had been in Special Forces together. Two days ago, jobbing for an international security agency out of Ohio, we had arrived in-country to check out the U.S. embassy and make a bid for the security contract.

"Test the embassy security," Llave had instructed me.

The embassy was a square brick corner building surrounded by fence, electronic detectors, and Honduran security guards. On the other side of the street were more U.S. offices. I easily evaded embassy security and wandered around inside until a fat Honduran guard in a cheap blue uniform spotted me.

"*Alto!*" he cried. "Stop!"

I escaped out a side door into a guarded parking lot. The fat guard waddled after me. *"Alto! Alto!"* I kept going. He drew his .45 pistol.

I was agile enough to vault the fence. The guard, wheezing and puffing and yelling for help, detoured by way of the gate. I trotted easily along the street with the guard laboring behind me waving his .45. I led him in a wide circle, keeping just far enough ahead so that if he shot at me he couldn't be accurate. Once or twice, out of sheer perversity, I turned and snapped pictures of the poor fat man trying to catch me.

A few months later, mobs attacked the embassy and sacked and burned the American offices on the north side of the street.

Llave did not speak Spanish, and Maria spoke no English. Llave kept watching the soldiers, who watched him back.

"It's crazy down here," Llave worried. "They'll shoot us for nothing."

Maria was laughing and hugging and kissing me. "My funny, funny Cholla," she said. "Your friend is concerned. Let us go."

Llave studied me. "I don't know if I could live like you do," he decided.

"It's better than cotton fields."

"It'll kill you."

"There is only one destination for each of us," I said.

"Yeah?"

"The bucket."

"What?"

"We all reach the grave, just by different means."

Like Dianne. She had married again and had been living in Miami when she died of cancer. I took out our old wedding pictures. I could be as sentimental as Latins at a family funeral.

"You always seem so tough and in control," Dianne had said once. "Nobody else sees it, but I do. Inside, you'll always be that little country boy in ragged jeans going out to joust windmills."

44

In a comfortable middle-class neighborhood in Oklahoma, a Vietnamese refugee who called himself Raymond Nguyen leaned forward to view guerrillas on a videotape smuggled out of his homeland. He watched with the intensity of a man without a country who catches a glimpse of Vietnam once again, watching as though hoping to spot a familiar face, a landmark.

Many times before, I had detected that same look on the faces of Vietnamese refugees, abandoned children in Central American refugee camps, former contras hiding in New Orleans, displaced Cubans in Miami, even American Vietnam veterans who had lost buddies and other things over there.

"The United States is the greatest country in the world, a hope for freedom," said a Cuban who had fought at the Bay of Pigs. "But if you are to remain great, you must never trust your politicians and your generals. We who are without homes know what that trust can do."

"Our government is a government that abandons," Mad Dog said.

He harbored that bitterness common to so many Vietnam veterans. More than 57,000 American GIs died defending South Vietnamese independence, and then the U.S. admitted that they had died for nothing. Wars were like that. You fought for a while for a cause, and then if you weren't winning, your government practiced doublespeak and changed the definition of the cause.

"You Americans abandoned us," said Raymond Nguyen. "Now you abandon each other. It is a sad thing."

Nguyen was a former South Vietnamese air force pilot.

He had escaped Vietnam the day before the North Vietnamese Army overran Saigon on April 30, 1975, a date thereafter known to Vietnamese refugees scattered around the world as the Dark Day. Forty thousand NVA soldiers had overrun Xuanloc, thirty-five miles northeast of Saigon on the road to Bien Hoa airfield. As communists began rocketing the Saigon airport, the U.S. mission launched Option IV, Operation Frequent Wind, the largest helicopter evacuation in history. America's ignoble flight from Vietnam was like that of a cur leaving with its tail between its legs.

Over a period of eighteen hours, shuttling back and forth between the city and aircraft carriers riding at anchor offshore, a fleet of seventy U.S. Marine choppers airlifted the remaining one thousand Americans and nearly six thousand Vietnamese out of the beleaguered capital. Like other Americans, I watched on TV as hysterical Vietnamese at the American embassy grabbed chopper skids and held on as long as they could before dropping to their deaths.

It tore at my guts, watching Americans fleeing like that.

"Rats escaping a sinking ship," Mad Dog growled. He had fought hard for a year in Vietnam with the 173d Airborne. "Smoked a little dope, too," he said. "Fucked some gook pussy. Now . . ." He shrugged.

Nguyen took off from Saigon airport while mortar shells burst on the runway. He ditched his airplane in the South China Sea next to an American aircraft carrier. Helicopters were also ditching; their frightened passengers bobbed in the drink, waiting to be rescued. Deckhands on the aircraft carriers shoved other choppers off into the sea to make room for new arrivals. Everyone was trying to get out of Saigon ahead of the communist advance.

"The war did not end that day," Raymond Nguyen insisted as he watched the videotaped guerrillas, whom he called Nghia Quan—fighters for righteousness. "The struggle for Vietnamese independence from the communists goes on inside Vietnam. And it goes on in Cambodia and Laos, and it goes on as well in the United States, Canada, France, and all over the world. The war will never end until we are a free people again."

I understood his intensity. As a kid in the hills, I'd rescued a baby red-tailed hawk that had fallen from its nest. I raised the hawk free to go whenever and wherever it desired. I could never cage wild creatures. I ran across the fields with George the hawk sailing far above me, a speck. Then, on signal, he tucked his wide wings and torpedoed from the sky like a brown meteor. He flared at the last moment before plummeting to earth, and then he sailed just above my head so it was like the two of us were flying together. I felt the wind from his great wings, rejoiced in the wild *scree!* of his call. I so wanted to fly with him, *really* fly.

"Ain't you afraid he'll fly away someday?" people asked.

"If he wants to, he can go. He oughta have that right. George is free. He can go anywhere in the world he wants to. He don't even have to stop at borders. George don't worry about government and things. George is a hawk—and he's free to be a hawk."

Raymond Nguyen studied me. "They said you would do anything, go anywhere, for a story to write," he said.

"Who's *they?*"

"People in the military who know you."

I shrugged.

"The Russians are in my country," he resumed presently. "It is very dangerous there, but we need the story of the Nghia Quan told. Would you like to meet Hoang Co Minh? Would you like to return to Vietnam?"

45

After Saigon fell in 1975, organized resistance among the one million Vietnamese exiles strewn like fallen leaves across the face of the earth formed slowly. Although rumors and snatches of intelligence garnered from boat people and other sources hinted that thousands of Montagnards and ex–ARVN soldiers had refused to surrender to the communists and were carrying on the fight, Western diplomats in Bangkok estimated that there were at most two thousand of them. Those who remained banded together in cells of four or five. Ragged and hungry, they existed as little more than outlaws, permitted to survive only because they posed little threat.

Like Cubans and others who had had to flee their homelands for political reasons, the Vietnamese exiles first took care of themselves and their families, *then* looked back toward the mother country.

As the resistance movement slowly grew, infighting between the different camps and between anticommunists and communists rekindled old hostilities. Anticommunist Vietnamese gunned down a Hanoi supporter in San Francisco's Tenderloin district. Other victims of the rivalry were a Vietnamese journalist in Austin and a popular faction leader cut down on El Cajon Boulevard in Orange County, California. Harvard University's Viet historian Ngo Vinh Long survived a firebomb attack against him by a former ARVN soldier.

Orange County, California, was the home of Disneyland and of 35 percent of America's Viet exiles. I hunkered traditional-style on a grass mat with an ex–ARVN paratrooper.

"The Vietnamese are continuing the civil war in other countries outside the mother country," he said. "First we win the war in exile, then we return to Vietnam and win the war there."

Leadership was difficult to maintain among Asians. Leaders either had a charismatic quality called *uy tin* or they were replaced. Ho Chi Minh had this elusive quality. So did, I was told, Hoang Co Minh.

Hoang Co Minh's reputation had not been sullied, since he was apolitical when Vietnam fell. Born in Hanoi, he fled to the South in 1954 after the communist takeover of the North. He joined the South Vietnam Naval Academy in 1955 and rose through the ranks to become an admiral and commander of Second Region Naval Forces in central Vietnam. After Saigon collapsed, he led what remained of the navy—twenty-seven ships—to safety in the Philippines. He then sought refuge in the United States, where he owned a house-painting business in Washington, D.C. In about 1981, after more than six years in exile, he slipped back into the Asian jungles to organize what became the National United Front for the Liberation of Vietnam.

In 1983, some eight years after the Frequent Wind, I met NUFLVN guides in Bangkok for the journey back into Vietnam to link up with Hoang Co Minh and the Nghia Quan. I endured a series of short helicopter flights at treetop level and several long jungle treks with guides before I was turned over to a ragged band of Nghia Quan along an isolated stretch of Vietnam border. The guerrillas resembled bandits or heroin runners—about twenty of them clad either in leftover tiger stripes, jungle greens from the American War, or black pajamas reminiscent of the Vietcong.

There were not enough guns to go around. Every third man was armed with only a knife or machete. The others carried an assortment of weapons—U.S. M16s, Russian AKs, Swedish Ks. One man balanced an M1 Garand from World War II across his shoulder and wore a bandolier of ammo around his waist. I counted at least two Soviet RPG rocket launchers and an ancient .30 caliber machine gun.

Well armed for bandits—not so well armed for soldiers.

Ranger-filing, we advanced cautiously, as soldiers will in hostile territory, using forest trails and avoiding the occasional ville. I was unarmed except for a sheath knife. The tiger stripes I wore were soon white-crusted with body salts.

The forest remained dense, the terrain mountainous. The air sank heavy and hot and wet on top of us, making breathing difficult. I had forgotten, until now, the greenness of the jungle and how it enveloped you. The forest was so immense that after we marched all day and stopped at nightfall, it looked the same as when we'd set out that morning. For all I knew, we were going in circles.

As a member of Spike Team Tiger years before, with Gunny and Nelson and the Nungs, I had not known by location whether I was in Vietnam or Laos. It wasn't of such concern then, however, since I was with other Americans. Things were different now. It took a lot of trust, or something, for me to throw myself into the hands of these bandits, with whom I could not communicate, and to venture where only God and they knew. Presumedly we were in Vietnam, but you couldn't have proved it to me.

"We can get you into Vietnam," the ex–ARVN paratrooper in California had promised me.

"And back out?" I asked.

"Sometimes it is more difficult get out than get in."

I tried not to think about that. I shrugged deeper into the ruck I wore and followed the man ahead of me. Forest triple canopy filtered the sunlight and turned noon to twilight. The band leader ran outflank security on rest halts. Occasionally he dispatched scouts ahead to check the march route. Clearly we were in enemy country.

I didn't want to think about what might happen if the Russians caught me. It would be easy enough for them to find out I was a U.S. Army Special Forces reservist. An American Green Beret caught with antigovernment guerrillas. Great propaganda. Probably an international incident.

An official at the U.S. State Department had warned me about that.

"It's a violation of federal law to enter a country declared off-limits to American citizens," he said. "We'll confiscate your passport and send you to jail."

Better to ask for forgiveness than to ask for permission, I decided.

"If you insist on going, the U.S. government will disavow all knowledge. You're on your own," the official declared sternly.

What the hell. I had been there before.

The Russians. My own government. These bandits. If anything at all happened, there was no way I could win. Life was Asia's cheapest commodity. The way the Nghia Quan looked at me, it was as if they were already deciding the best way to bargain with me if they should run into any trouble.

I tried not to think about it.

At nightfall of the third day in-country, we burrowed into thicket and wagon-spoked for security. The leader squatted next to me, sitting flat-footed on his heels in the manner of Asian peasants. He looked at me, thinking hard.

"Di-di," he said. He made his two fingers walk like a man across his palm.

"Sun," he said. "Sun." He shaped the sun with his hands.

"Hoang Co Minh," he said.

I nodded my head. He nodded his even more vigorously.

"Tomorrow we reach Hoang Co Minh," I interpreted.

His head continued to bob. He smiled, obviously pleased that he spoke English so well.

It rained during the night. It was as if the jungle wept. I awoke shivering. I lay there in my poncho wishing I were home cradled in some pretty woman's arms, safe and warm and dry. Soldiers who went away to war always thought of home when they were miserable.

At least Americans who went away to war had homes to come home to. For other people, war *was* their home.

The poor Vietnamese. They had been at constant war for at least half a century. Peasants rarely looked up anymore from their rice paddies to watch the various armies trooping through. Life for them never changed: the Japanese burned their hootches; the French burned their hootches; the Americans burned their hootches; the Russians burned their hootches.

"House not know or care who burn," a *papasan* said to me once. "House burn all same-same."

Hoang Co Minh's base camp proved to be a concealed scattering of about twenty hootches with straw walls and banana-frond roofs. Perhaps one hundred men in the camp stared suspiciously when I entered from the jungle with the patrol, moving past the sentries. Most of the men idled about smoking husk-rolled cigarettes the size of cigars. One class, probably a political one, had attracted ten or twelve soldiers. I counted three machine guns and several 60mm mortars partially concealed with a tarp. I saw no weapons larger than these.

The camp had been there awhile. The earth was well trampled; most of the campfires contained old ashes. There were even some chickens, and I heard the grunt-squeal of pigs penned back in the jungle.

I thought it a comedown for an admiral to end up leader of a band of jungle ruffians.

The guerrillas showed me to a hut containing a sleeping mat and a pot of water. I dumped my ruck and arranged myself in the shadows opposite the door. I waited.

Presently a man as thin and stringy as beef jerky entered and blinked his eyes. I gave an involuntary start. Looking at me stood a man who could have been in his fifties, maybe even sixty, but he stood erect and proud with his head held high. He wore loose black pajamas and a checkered scarf, like a bandanna, tied around his neck. His beard hung wispy and graying from his chin.

He bore such a striking resemblance to a younger Ho Chi Minh that I thought I had been deceived and turned over to the communists.

46

Hoang Co Minh and I studied each other through a long silence. He stepped closer. We studied each other again. I stood. Then we hunkered flat-footed on our heels, like peasants, facing each other, and I looked deep into eyes as dark as a jungle pool at night. I saw sadness in those eyes, pain, and determination. The thin face remained almost smooth through its aging, as Oriental faces will, but it was the color of old parchment.

Finally Hoang spoke in English.

"The United States government tells me Americans are no longer interested in Indochina. No one wishes to hear the word 'Vietnam.' Do you think that is true?"

"Yes."

"Yet you come. *You* are interested."

"Bo Gritz came," I said. The NUFLVN had recently escorted ex–Special Forces Colonel Gritz through Laos searching for American prisoners of war.

"Yes," said Minh. "But why did you come?"

"I came to meet Hoang Co Minh who says he will liberate his country."

He studied me again. "Let us eat," he said.

The meal was rice. Rice and sun-dried fish and something that might have been meat or might have been old shoe leather. We ate out of bowls with our fingers. Minh's general staff officers joined us for the meal, but left afterward. They also wore around their necks the checkered bandannas that were Minh's trademark, his uniform.

"The admiral may have been driven in a limousine before now," one of the staff said with pride, "but now he puts on the dress of a peasant and eats rice in the forest with his men. He risks his life with us. The Nghia Quan love him for it."

"But is the hope of liberation greater than the reality?" I asked Minh when we were alone again. "Can you deliver what you promise?"

Suddenly the Vietnamese appeared thin and weary.

"We can't win militarily," he admitted, "but we can win the hearts of the people. In the war when you Americans were here, we learned that too much you can depend on airplanes and helicopters and bombs from the B-52. It was an expensive war that we fought, but of course you Americans could afford it. Ho Chi Minh fought a cheap war. He won it.

"We learned from him. We look like VC now, and we copy the strategy of the VC. We will liberate Vietnam by organizing a general uprising among the people. Our primary efforts will be in psychological warfare, not military operations. It worked for the VC; it will work for us."

He spoke for hours.

"There are many different resistance groups scattered all over South Vietnam," he said. "So we try to reunite them. So far we reunite forty different resistance groups. And the number under arms, it is greater than ten thousand. Some of them, if they are based in jungle, like here, they have a secure area from which to conduct operations. Others, they operate right outside Saigon, so they just live together, mix in with population. Fish in sea, like Mao say."

The "overseas" branch of the Front, he said, included 90 percent of the one million Viets in exile. It rallied exiles and raised money to buy much-needed supplies and arms. Chairman Hoang Co Minh, as he called himself, divided his time between his Indochina base camps and the capitals of the world, where he attempted to gain diplomatic recognition for a Vietnam government-in-exile. So far, China in its underground struggle with Russia over communist hegemony in Asia was the only nation willing to commit arms and supplies to the guerrillas. China wanted communism within its sphere of influence to be Asian-dominated. Fellow

communist or not, Russia was as much an intruder as
America had been. Hoang Co Minh, I supposed, would have
made a pact with the devil as long as it helped him free his
country. He could worry about its type of government later.

It sounded like the same old story told again. Same song,
different verse.

I recognized the fire of the committed radical smoldering
in the chairman's eyes. His were the eyes of the wonderful
fanatics of the world who saw visions and charged out to do
battle with windmills. Don Quixote had that look. The look
of the misfit, the rebel, the committed, the dreamer. Perhaps
I, too, had that look.

Maybe it was a feeling of kinship that drew me to such
men, to such places of danger.

"And maybe it's just a death wish," Crazy Craig Roberts said.

Hoang Co Minh's voice rose in an odd singsong cadence.
"We will win history," he said. "The putrid cadaver of communism will be swept aside into the blackest corner of world
history and be left to rot with the remains of today's communist leaders. We will expel those cancerous tumors and deliver them to the hell of demons and devils."

He paused. He seemed almost to fade away before my
eyes. He said, pleading, "Please tell the Americans not to
forget us."

We came down out of the mountains and across a rubber
plantation where the trees were thick-trunked and spaced
geometrically in the wan moonlight. The patrol wended its
way past a low, sprawling house where lights inside illuminated wide French windows. It was a familiar landmark to
the guerrillas; they cast only desultory glances at it as we
glided past in the night.

The patrol set up an ambush on a country road using a
claymore mine. We hid in bushes on one side of the road.
The patrol leader ran a long cord from man to man so
that it could be jerked to alert the ambush when someone
spotted prey.

A Russian patrol was supposed to come by. It passed

along this road twice a week delivering supplies to a check-point near a village thirty kilometers away. It would be a good target.

I lay belly-down in the grass, heart thumping. I thought surely the others must hear it. It thumped and thumped. My eyes strained to see down the silver thread of the roadway. The road shot out of the bushes where we hid and thinned across a wide plain.

I waited.

I heard the man next to me and down a ways snoring. My heart ceased thumping after a while. After another while—maybe an hour, maybe two hours—I laid my head on my arms.

It rained the next night—and again the Russians did not come.

On the third night we stayed in the base camp and slept. During the night someone slipped into my hootch. For a moment exhaustion fought to keep me asleep. A footfall, close. I threw myself to one side, groping for my only weapon—the sheath knife.

"Di-di. Di-di mau," a voice urged. It belonged to one of Hoang's staff officers.

"What?"

"There is danger," he said. "We go. *Di-di.* Quick."

I folded my poncho into my pack and was ready. You never fully unpacked in a combat zone. Outside, a patrol waited. The guerrillas fidgeted and cast nervous glances in all directions.

"Big communist force come this way," the staff officer explained in his limited English. "Chairman Hoang, him *di-di* quick. You *di-di* now."

The best I understood it was that the Russians might have discovered the location of the Nghia Quan base camp and were en route with a large combat force to wipe it out. The guerrillas were not equipped or prepared for face-up combat. Raids, ambushes, assassinations, okay—but not direct combat.

I cast uncertain glances in all directions. "You don't have to tell me twice."

By dawn we had placed several miles between us and the base camp, trekking west, returning to a secret chopper pad where a helicopter waited to transport me on the first leg back to Bangkok.

For a while afterward I kept up with the chairman and his quixotic efforts to liberate Vietnam. The two weeks I spent in Asia had given me enough insight to know that his was a failed cause. But he kept jousting anyhow.

NUFLVN members in the States and in Europe organized clandestine radio to broadcast political messages at Vietnam. Five Nghia Quan slipped through the shadows of My Ca Village near Cam Ranh Bay and assassinated a Soviet officer foolish enough to set a nightly pattern visiting a woman in the village. Two guerrillas kidnapped and executed a known police informant in Cu Chi. A BBC documentary reported a brief firefight between communist troops and guerrillas that left several dead and wounded.

But the general uprising Hoang Co Minh expected never occurred. His "army" never consisted of more than one thousand ragged, ill-supplied fighters at most, although he claimed ten times that many. He received little support in-country; most of the Vietnamese had had enough of war.

One summer morning in Tulsa, Raymond Nguyen called me.

"We have a report," he said through a great sadness, "that Chairman Hoang Co Minh is dead. He has been assassinated. It means the end of the resistance."

Another Don Quixote had bitten the dust.

47

A number of times during my military career I turned down offers and opportunities to become a commissioned officer. I remained an NCO, a noncommissioned officer, eventually attaining the rank of master sergeant and then first sergeant for Desert Storm, the war in the Gulf. From my perspective, enlisted men, the grunts, proved themselves in combat by putting their own lives at stake. Officers—except some of the lower-ranking ones—proved themselves by using the lives of others.

That always seemed like a significant difference.

After Vietnam and the introduction of the all-volunteer military, the breach between officer and enlisted continued to widen as the lower ranks filled up with minorities and the sons of the urban and rural poor. The result has become a kind of class warfare. Officers frequently assumed they possessed power beyond that granted to them by their position. After all, as the old saying once went in Officer Candidate School, enlisted men were crafty and cunning and could not be trusted. They had to be controlled.

Take Captain Kirchner. When he took command of my Special Forces team, his first act was to call a team meeting to introduce himself.

"I'm Captain Kirchner, your new team leader. Since I'm an officer and therefore better educated and smarter than you are ..."

That was all I heard. Among the twelve enlisted men on the team, all senior NCOs, were at least ten college degrees and four advanced degrees.

"Fuck," Mad Dog said, and he got up and walked off.

179

On Kirchner's first training mission as commander, the team parachuted into the Pisgah National Forest in the Smoky Mountains. Lieutenant Humble, the team's exec, set the pace of the march. The sun blazed so hot out of the sky that it was almost white. We were humping seventy-pound rucks, plus our weapons and other combat gear. As senior medic, I shifted up and down the file of men checking for heat problems. Harris's face had turned sunset-red. Tommy Hinds had gone pale and stopped sweating. Even Pablo Eskridge and Moody looked worn.

"L.T., better slow the pace a little," I said to Humble.

Kirchner overheard. "You don't tell an officer what to do," he snapped.

I turned on him. "I do if it involves medical problems."

He jabbed a finger in my face. "You *never* tell an officer what to do."

Humble slowed the pace. Sullen now, resentment growing, the team continued its exhausting climb into the Smokies. Mad Dog evaluated the new team commander for everyone: "Cocksucker."

Kirchner wouldn't let it lie. "I'll court-martial you!" he threatened me, looking hysterical. "You've disobeyed a direct order."

"What direct order?" I asked, genuinely surprised.

"Sir!" Kirchner corrected, still screaming. "You will call me *sir.*"

I was no longer a teenage Mickey Mouse taking shit from a boot camp tyrant.

Scarlet crept out of Kirchner's shirt collar. He looked around, too self-absorbed to recognize the hostility in the faces of the team members gathered around him deep in the forest.

"Sergeant Bodine, put this man under restriction," he ordered. "He's going to be court-martialed."

No one moved. Late shadows darkened their faces and their mood.

"With any due respect, *sir,*" Mad Dog's voice purred out, "if we were at war somebody would frag your sorry ass."

The new commander was left standing alone in the forest chomping on his rage and frustration.

"Maybe we should pay him proper respect," Mad Dog commented dryly. "He must have kissed a lot of ass to get where he is."

"Kissing ass is such an art form among officers," said Crazy Craig Roberts later, "that we had to invent a word for it. It's called 'protocol.' Tell you one thing, though: don't get in an officer's way. People wonder how Hitler's officers could have followed his orders and done the things they did. Me, I don't wonder. Most officers will do anything—*anything*—to promote and preserve their precious careers."

"The army never wants to talk about the pricks that got fragged," Mad Dog Carson grumbled. "But it was done in Vietnam as a matter of survival. I see it as an easy choice to make. If you get a prick that's about to get all of you killed, wax his ass instead. That's my vote: kill his ass. Simple."

That was the only way many enlisted men knew how to fight back. A young buck sergeant named Boling was squad leader of a security team guarding a nuclear Pershing missile in Europe. His lieutenant took a personal dislike to the sergeant and made his life miserable. One night Boling armed himself with a tent peg and lay in ambush outside the lieutenant's tent. Babe Ruth would have been proud of the home run he delivered on the lieutenant's head and Kevlar helmet.

Two other enlisted men were convicted of murdering an officer, whom they stuffed into a wall locker and dropped out of a second-story window. They went down and brought the locker back upstairs and dropped it out *again*.

I learned, however, that there was a more effective way to combat abusive, stupid, or arrogant officers—and win. While some officers tended to have little but contempt for enlisted men, whom they considered virtually their personal property to treat as they saw fit, they sometimes underestimated us.

Although I was an Army Special Forces reservist, I was also a professional free-lance journalist. I published a *Soldier of Fortune* magazine piece that apparently, the way I finally understood it, insulted the American ambassador to Liberia. The ambassador learned that I was a reserve soldier. Easy enough for him to retaliate. I received a brief form letter from my Special Forces Group commander informing me that after nearly twelve years in Special Forces Reserves I would be transferred out of the unit and possibly kicked out of the army.

"You're in deep *kimshi*," my company commander decided. "The colonel wants you out."

I zipped letters off to the State Department, the Department of Defense, and the Justice Department explaining my rights under the First Amendment as a professional writer and journalist. Something happened quickly. I received a second letter from the colonel advising me that, no, I wouldn't be transferred or kicked out after all. However, I was suspended from my team pending investigation.

I fired off more letters. They brought down a lot of heat. The colonel admitted me to his office. He had little asshole eyes behind thick-rimmed glasses. I figured him for a little asshole soul as well. With him were my company commander and the colonel's adjutant.

"Sergeant Sasser, we're sending you back to your team," the colonel said. He sounded like someone was holding a loaded gun to his head.

"Damned right. And you're sending me back *today*."

"Now, Sergeant Sasser ..." the adjutant began.

I was in no mood for it.

"This wouldn't have happened to begin with," I snapped, "if officers had balls bigger than BBs. The government would have fucked me over if I'd been some poor ignorant grunt who didn't know how to fight back. And look at all of you. Your careers, right? Your precious careers. You stood back and let this happen. Whether something is right or wrong makes no difference to any of you, does it?"

I turned abruptly and walked out. They didn't try to stop me. The next morning I was the only soldier on a C-130 Hercules bound for the Ozark Mountains of Arkansas where

Group was running an unconventional warfare training mission. I discovered my team's forest base camp marked by a huge sandstone boulder upon which was inscribed "Camp Sasser."

And the colonel, the group commander—he made general and went to the Pentagon.

"Politics." Mad Dog's lip curled. "Officers get bad backs and bumps on their heads from bending over, all of them trying to kiss the same ass."

"How do you do it?" Sergeant Rodney Gipson asked. "All these years fighting the brass and bucking the system, and you have always come out on top."

"You'd have made a hell of a knight," Colonel Judith Robson said once. "You're always mounting your charger."

" 'All that's necessary for evil to prevail is for good men to do nothing,' " I quoted from an old saying. "If you're right, you have to win."

You *have* to.

On another occasion I was class leader—like a platoon sergeant—for a U.S. Army Special Forces medical class. I was cross-training from weapons to medicine. It was a year-long course, active duty. I started out with sixty-five young SF trooper-medics. Wild, tough, crazy young bastards—Special Forces. There was never another unit like them, not with their initiative, intelligence, lust for adventure, and quick irreverent wit.

There were four phases to the medical course: initial medical specialist school, which was all regular army medics received; the much longer Special Forces medic course; the on-the-job training period at hospitals and clinics all over the United States; and the goat lab at Fort Bragg, North Carolina. I had sixteen students surviving of the original sixty-five when we assembled at a compound on a hidden corner of Fort Bragg surrounded by pines and a high, screened fence. You had to know your way there to find it. A particular musky animal odor was one of the reasons for the isolation; the other reason was to keep activities there hidden from militant animal rights activists.

"These animals are not goats, they are *patients*," explained the officer in charge, a captain in the medical corps. "They are *your* patients, and that is how you will refer to them. If your patient dies from disease due to lack of proper diagnosis and treatment, or if he dies from gunshot or knife wound, or if he dies on the operating table and it's your fault, you will be dismissed from the course. We here at the branch expect you to *live* with your patients for the next two months. They are casualties sustained in combat, and your job in combat other than killing the enemy is saving the lives of your buddies."

Unlike other medics, Special Forces medics are also combatants.

When the patients were issued, I found mine to be a huge, obnoxious billy who smelled like a long-utilized country two-holer.

"Don't get too attached to your patients," instructors warned. "They all die at the end in mass cal."

My uniform, my skin, my hair, soon reeked of the patient and of patient shit. Never had I seen such a repulsive creature with his great curving horns and the yellow piss stains on his belly, chest, and beard. But never has the illest invalid at Walter Reed received such loving and tender medical care. Even a sneeze from the patient brought out thermometer, stethoscope, BP cup, and antibiotics.

On a midnight I stopped at the barn to check on a medic and his patient who had contacted pneumonia. The patient, a young spotted female, lay on a mattress wheezing underneath an army blanket. Next to her in fitful slumber rested my youngest soldier, a kid from Kansas. His lips twitched in dream or nightmare.

I knelt by the pair. The kid's eyes popped open in alarm. "Sarge!"

He jumped up and began taking his patient's vitals.

"Sarge, I can't break her fever. She's going to die on me. I know it!"

Tears brimmed his eyes.

"I don't want her to die. They'll kick me out of the course. Sarge, I don't know what else to do."

I shucked my uniform blouse and drew on a blue hospital

top. "C'mon, son. Let's see what we can do about clearing her lungs and getting some O_2 to her."

The fever broke. She was still breathing at dawn.

"Sarge, we did it. We did it! We saved her life."

"You saved her life."

"Sarge . . . goddammit." He hugged me. "Thanks."

There would never be men like these again.

For wound therapy, patients were first anesthetized, then littered through the back door of the bulletproof shooting chamber. The patient's front or back leg or neck or shoulder or whatever was carefully aligned with a bolted-down 5.56 caliber firearm at the other end of the chamber and then strapped into position. The patient was to be wounded, not killed.

Pop!

Then off to the OR where the student emergency medical team went to work to save the patient's life. Next time, on a battlefield, the patient might be a real soldier.

All the best medical technology was available. The operating room might have been transported directly from Johns Hopkins. There we were—gowned, gloved, masked. And there the patients were, their heads out from underneath the drapes—goats with gunshot wounds from the chamber.

It was a scene from *Mad* magazine.

"Scalpel," I said, reaching.

Livestock in the barn and lot wore bandages from every imaginable wound. They bleated and hobbled and lurched about while young SF soldier-medics cried over them and compared notes and treatment.

Two final tests brought the long training ordeal to an end. The first was an exercise in mass casualties. Instructors took all the patients and shot or stabbed or doused them with gasoline and set them afire or whatever and scattered them about on the ground as though on a battlefield.

Cries of *"Medic! Medic!"* brought students rushing with their aid bags, I.V. tubes, veinous cutdowns, trachs, lung drainage poppycocks, eppy injections, tourniquets.

Evacuations, triage, secondary care at the battalion aid station . . .

Sudden bursts of tears as some gut-shot patient died quietly on the OR table and its medic experienced a sudden rush of dread that he might be at fault.

Ultimately the caretakers were graded pass or fail, and the poor animals were all overdosed and died.

The last test, the day before graduation, was on I.V.'s. A student received five minutes and two attempts to open a patent intravenous line on another student. Fail—and he was out of the course. One of my soldiers was so muscle-bound that during nearly a year of training no one had been able to find a vein in all that mass. The student who drew him failed, along with another student.

I looked at their anguished faces. One of the failures had been in the running with me for honor grad. I turned and walked away. There was nothing I could say. The standards were set; you lived with them. I stood by the patient pens, empty now after the mass casualty exercise. Some blood remained here and there; it had dried and turned black but was still attracting flies.

"If you were wounded in battle," we had heard many times, "would you want second-best working on you?'"

The next morning at graduation formation, an instructor marched out. "Sergeant Sasser, have all your men line up at the OR," he ordered. "Everyone retests on the I.V."

"What?"

I hurried to the officer in charge.

"Everyone retests," he insisted.

"Why?"

"Hobbs doesn't even have veins. It wasn't fair to test on him."

"I told you that to begin with, Captain. If you want to retest, then retest the two who failed. The others have passed. It's unfair, it's double jeopardy to put them through it again. One or two of them may even fail."

When there was a difference of opinion between an enlisted man and an officer, the officer, right or wrong, was always *right*. I came out of the OR. Every student eye in the line fixed on me. Sergeant Mansell, my assistant, waited for an answer.

"Sergeant Sasser, this is wrong," he cried, angry. "You have to do *something*."

Obviously something desperate. Which was likely to threaten my military career. A year of my life studying medicine wasted.

"What are you going to do?" Mansell persisted.

What? What? Goddammit, what?

Only one thing.

"Sergeant Mansell, have the men form up in the street."

I drew a deep breath and returned to the OR. "Captain, with any due respect, my men refuse to test."

"I'll have you court-martialed for disobeying a direct order. I'll send you to Leavenworth."

"In the meantime, my men are in formation outside."

Special Forces was a relatively small community. Ten years later a young SF trooper would mull over my name when we were introduced.

"Oh. I know who you are. The Goat Lab Revolt. That's a legend in Special Forces."

News of the revolt flashed quickly all over Fort Bragg. I explained the situation to my soldiers, including possible consequences. "But we must never," I stressed, "*never* compromise with injustice. You compromise one time, it's easier to compromise the next. Soon even the concept of justice becomes a joke."

For over two hours in the North Carolina summer sun my Green Beret soldiers stood unmoving at parade rest. I positioned myself alone in front of them. Rivulets of sweat poured down their faces and soaked their uniforms black. Their gazes fixed on a point beyond the tall screened fence. Even the two who had failed stood staring straight ahead.

"I'll have all of you kicked out of Special Forces," the captain threatened. "You'll be court-martialed. I'll have you back pounding the bush as nothing but grunt privates. I'm giving all of you a direct order. You have a choice. You can either stand there like fools and go to Leavenworth with

Sergeant Sasser or you can march back into that OR like you were ordered."

Not a soldier moved.

Colonels from the JFK Center came out and looked at us. They looked at me. They walked back inside and peeped out the windows to check our resolve. They seemed stunned that enlisted men, young enlisted men led by a grizzled reserve sergeant, dared question the authority of an officer.

It was almost noon before the captain stepped out of his office. A half dozen officers watched him from the windows. He stopped in front of me. He mumbled, "Sergeant Sasser, have your men back here at thirteen hundred hours. Everyone graduates."

I witnessed the same kind of abuse and arrogance by U.S. officers in Central America. After 1979, with the Cold War still going on, the U.S. military became involved in all the little Latin wars that sprang up like poisonous mushrooms. Supposedly U.S. troops were trainers and advisers of local government troops fighting communist insurgents, but they were also, sometimes, combatants. And more.

During the 1970s and 1980s, for more than fifteen years, I kept slipping into and out of various Central American countries at war. Sometimes, as in Panama, I went in on Army Special Forces training missions. Other times I worked for one security agency or another, all of which must remain unnamed. I also had credentials as a war correspondent, writing pieces for magazines like *Soldier of Fortune, New Breed,* and *Modern Warfare,* and for newspapers like my hometown Tulsa *Tribune.*

In El Salvador, I knew a U.S. Special Forces sergeant stationed at La Unión as a trainer for Salvadoran government troops fighting communist guerrillas. On patrol one day with a squad of *Guardia*—Salvadoran National Guard—the sergeant and a U.S. major linked up their *Guardia* patrol with a platoon of regulars to assault a village believed to be controlled by guerrillas of the communist Farabundo Martí National Liberation Front (FMLN).

It was one of those red-tiled villages where oxen stood

hitched to wooden-wheeled carts and campesinos walked with machetes at their belts.

A *Guardia* died in the raid. The surviving *Guardia* rampaged through the little town, jerking people from their homes and marching them at gunpoint to the village square. Out of the collected villagers the *Guardia* selected several men and boys. They prodded the captives to the edge of town and lined them up against a wall. The villagers' hands were tied behind their backs. A boy of about sixteen started crying.

The U.S. sergeant realized what was happening. "They're going to execute them!"

The major grabbed his NCO's arm and escorted him away. "It's their war, not ours," he warned. "We're just observers."

"But this is *murder.*"

The major's eyes narrowed. "Sergeant, you see nothing. Is that understood? *Nothing.*"

A volley of rifle fire ended the conversation. The major started to walk off. He turned. "Those men were communists," he said. "If you value your career, you'll keep your mouth shut about what happened here today."

"We should have stopped it," the sergeant agonized later, "even if they were commies. There were five of them, I think, and the *Guardia* shot and killed them against the wall. I have heard of other incidents like that down here where American advisers let the killing happen."

Muscles worked and twitched in his face.

· "My God, what are we doing? We're down here to help these people fight to keep their freedom, and we're letting *this* happen. It's ... it's like we've got another little Vietnam where officers can come and get their tickets punched for career advancement. If this happens to me again—major, colonel, I don't care who he is—I'm going to stop it even if I have to frag him."

48

I had gone to war on trains and trucks and oxcarts, but this was the first time I'd ever gone to war in a psychedelic-painted school bus. About twenty people clung to the luggage rack on top while a turkey with its legs tied lay shitting in the aisle.

The bus labored out of San Salvador, the city, up along twisting roads full of potholes, past the soldier checkpoints every few miles where *Guardia Nacional* in jackboots and gray-green Nazi-type uniforms forced everyone off the bus and facedown in the ditches. The *Guardia* frisked even women and children for weapons.

You trusted no one in this kind of war.

Babies wailed. A stout peasant woman slapped at the hands of a *Guardia* who tried to frisk her. The *Guardia* laughed. Finally he whacked the woman hard on the side of her head with his fist. After that, the woman submitted. She clenched her hands into fists, but she lay motionless with her face in the dirt. The soldier grasped and clutched her body. He said things to her that made the other *Guardia* laugh.

"*Usted es un periodista?*" the *Guardia* asked when it was my turn.

"*Sí. Soy un periodista.* I am a journalist. From the United States."

"*Me puede dar su identificación?*"

I handed him the press pass signed by Colonel Ricardo Cienfuegos who was about to be assassinated on a tennis court in the capital.

"*Adónde va, señor?*"

"I am going to El Paraíso, Fourth Brigade headquarters."

"Why do you go there?"

"I am a journalist covering the fighting."

"*Sí. Sí.*" They nodded at each other. "There is much fighting in Chalatenango Province. One could meet his God there."

They let me stand, but they still frisked me.

Guardia like these and the Salvadoran combat troops were two different breeds. I liked the combat troops; they were like grunts everywhere. The *Guardia* on the other hand took extra pains to fit into their Nazi uniforms, not wanting to appear lax and be transferred to field duty and the real fighting. Out of their ranks came many of the *escuadrillas muertas,* the feared death squads.

Two hours after the road stop, I got off the psychedelic bus at the military post outside the town of El Paraíso. Sentries inside the green-and-yellow guard shack watched suspiciously as I stood a moment beside the road in the bright sunlight. I dropped my camera bag and camouflaged backpack to the ground as the bus growled away. I tugged low the leather brim of my go-to-war cap to shade my eyes. Standing there in faded blue jeans, combat boots, and military-khaki short-sleeved shirt with epaulets, I looked around.

Fourth Brigade headquarters occupied flat country, high but still flat, with desertlike plains and jungle along the streams that flowed from the mountains. Tall barbed-wire fences reinforced by a row of razor concertina enclosed the post. Many of the guard towers standing on spindly legs along the fence appeared unoccupied. I counted a few sand-bagged machine-gun emplacements, most of them also carelessly unmanned. Farther back were rusted 105mm howitzers and the low-scale buildings of the barracks and headquarters quadrangle. Two soldiers were driving a cow uphill along a road beyond the guard shack. They shouted at the cow, laughing, and beat her bony rump with sticks.

I looked around at the compound and concluded that two detachments of crippled campesinos armed with pitchforks could overrun it. The country had grown tired; the war had no end.

"It does not matter what happens in the rest of the world," Colonel Ricardo Cienfuegos had said over dinner a few nights before. Cienfuegos was head of the Salvadoran military press section called COPREFA. We played tennis together whenever I came to San Salvador. Cienfuegos said, "We are a small nation of five million compared to your two hundred million, but already we have suffered more casualties than you did in Vietnam. The war will stop for a while, perhaps, then begin, and stop, and begin. . . . Perhaps it will change its focus or its name. But it is a thing that goes beyond the conflicting ideologies of communist and capitalist. It has a life of its own. It is a way of life in this poor, tired country. It kills off the generations."

He studied me from across the table. He was a red-haired man with freckles, born privileged into a country where almost everyone was brown and poor.

"The politicians will lose this war for us," he continued. "It is like Vietnam was for you. Always the politicians, yours and mine, who will sell the milk of their own mothers without conscience. Bah! Politicians! If we had good sense, rebels and loyalists alike, we would band together for the good of the country and attack the politicians."

The war in El Salvador had already been raging for six years and more, since 1979, when communist gunrunners out of Cuba and out of Nicaragua began arming the FMLN, the largest of the insurgent groups. It was the same old Cold War story: guerrillas representing "the people" battling the established government to win "social justice."

One night in San Salvador, the capital, I was having a pleasant patio conversation with the *dona* of the guesthouse where I was staying when I noticed Rafael, the houseboy, entering silently through the back door. After a guilty glance in my direction, he stole quickly to his room. A few days previously I had caught him listening to Radio Venceremos, the voice of revolution broadcast from Managua. Communist-backed guerrillas throughout Central America listened to the station to receive news, encouragement, and coded instructions.

Knowing that I was a journalist and somehow trusting me, Rafael admitted, *"Sí, soy un comunista."*

He was an oppressed-looking little man of about thirty with stooped shoulders and a hangdog expression.

"Come," he offered. "Let me show you why I am a communist."

Ninety percent of all Latin Americans live not just in poverty but in *abject* poverty. Rafael showed me scenes like those I remembered from Panama and elsewhere: rural refugees from the war, swept ragged like garbage into canyon slums; old and crippled people turned into beggars; children prowling the streets hustling *colones.*

In front of a private girls' school a street vendor sold *papusas* and other little cakes and candies while her ragged ten-year-old daughter slept on the sidewalk on a sheet of cardboard. On one side of the wall, within the confines of the private school, the daughters of the wealthy, all dressed in crisp blue uniforms, sang and laughed gaily. On the other side of the wall, pedestrians with hardly a glance stepped over the daughter of the poor asleep on the sidewalk.

"People have been kept illiterate and ignorant," Rafael said, "and their ignorance has kept them slaves to others' greed. But now they are finding there are better ways of living. They ask only for something *norteamericanos* take for granted. They ask only for the opportunity to do better. If it is not given, they will take it pound for pound in flesh and gallon for gallon in blood. If it is in the name of communism, they will take it. But if there is no such thing as communism, they will still take it. Revolution is revolution—the poor against the rich, the haves against those who have not. And there are so many more of us who have not."

A few minutes after Rafael slipped through the back door of the guesthouse, the house was shaken by a string of explosions detonated in various parts of the city. Power poles toppled; entire neighborhoods went dark. Underground guerrillas had struck again, sabotaging power lines to demonstrate to the government and the people how like Mao's

fish at sea they were. The underground could strike anywhere, anytime, with impunity, disappear, and then strike
again until a helpless government conceded.

Lights illuminating the guesthouse patio flickered and
dimmed. Helicopters from the Immediate Reaction Force
thumped overhead. The plump *dona* supported President
José Napoleón Duarte and his long war against the guerrillas, but she had grown discouraged. She lifted weary eyes
toward the choppers.

"They are fighting again," she said simply, then returned
to our conversation.

As a member of the FMLN, Rafael operated with a secret
terrorist, sabotage, and assassination force that also set up
escape and evasion nets, conducted psychological warfare,
and controlled an intelligence network. Rafael and his shadowy comrades collected intelligence on a government com-
munications site that occupied a mountaintop overlooking
the capital. When everything was ready, about sixty guerrillas attacked the site and its platoon of defenders. The attack
began near midnight.

I watched the fight from the lounge of the Hotel Real
where foreign newsmen lined up at the wide windows like
spectators at a cockfight. Flares, explosions, tracers, the stut-
ter of automatic weapons, occupied our total interest for the
better part of an hour before government troops rallied and
choppered to the beleaguered platoon's rescue. The guerrillas melted into the darkness when the helicopters came air-
skidding in with searchlights blazing and door guns banging.
Six defenders died at the site; the guerrillas carried off however many dead and wounded they had suffered.

"Bring me another Seven-and-Seven," the stringer for a
wire agency shouted to the bartender. He had perched on
the edge of his seat during the battle, but now he leaned
back casually and lit a cigarette, like all this was old hat.

Another stringer laughed. "That asshole has been covering the war for six years, and tonight's the closest he's
ever come to combat."

I looked at him.

He laughed again. "Everyone knows it," he explained.

"He doesn't want to get his balls shot off, so he traipses down to the American embassy for the Five O'Clock Follies"—the government news briefings—"and then files copy with the wire like he was actually on the scene."

"That's cheating," I protested.

"But he stays alive."

Always, as in my friend Cienfuego's eyes, there was the sadness when the wars were long.

"You and me, Cholla," Cienfuegos said. "Cholla," a type of cactus with sharp spikes, was his name for me. "You and me, Cholla, we are warriors in wars without end. For us there can be only one end, I fear."

Cienfuegos had arranged for me to work with Colonel Ochoa, commander of the Fourth Brigade at El Paraíso. Run a few patrols. Check out the action for some magazine pieces I planned to write. Even as the brown-skinned sentries at the El Paraíso guard shack checked my credentials, spoke into an American-supplied PRC-77 radio, and passed me through the gate, Cienfuegos was dead.

I wouldn't find out about it until I returned to the capital at the end of the month.

The colonel had been resting on a bench at the tennis courts between sets when two terrorists walked up behind him. One of them pressed the muzzle of a .32 caliber pistol to the back of his head and squeezed the trigger. Brains and blood splattered over the court. He was the highest-ranking officer to have been slain in the long civil war.

There was one other thing I wouldn't find out about until I returned to the capital. The assistant press attaché at the American embassy knew I sometimes played tennis with Cienfuegos. Through him, word reached Stateside that I was with the colonel when he was assassinated. Everyone presumed the guerrillas had kidnapped me. I was reported missing.

"Kathy'll divorce your ass," Mad Dog Carson would warn when I returned home. "Women don't like that kind of shit. How would you like to be married to you and have to try to keep up?"

In El Paraíso, unaware that Cienfuegos was dead, I followed the soldiers and the cow up the road to Colonel Ochoa's headquarters. My pack rode hot in sweat against my back.

Outside the command quadrangle in front, a patrol prepared to go out on a road sweep in a waiting deuce-and-a-half truck. Something was wrong with the blooper gunner's M-79 grenade launcher. He pounded on it with the palm of his hand. The weapon discharged and spewed a missile between two other members of the patrol. The grenade arced above a 105 emplacement and exploded harmlessly next to an unoccupied guard tower.

Welcome to El Paraíso—Paradise.

The soldiers exchanged sheepish grins. They were all just kids. The blooper gunner appeared no older than fifteen or sixteen. Babies. All wars were fought by babies.

"Hola, guerreramos," I chided them. "Hello, warriors."

The kids grinned and shuffled their feet.

49

The Chalatenango. It was a high rugged country where a wonderful gentle mountain wind carried with it the scents of great pines and palms oddly juxtaposed. On the truck, the Salvadoran machine gunner legged his M60 and its belt of gold-copper ammunition onto the cab top. Lieutenant Camino, the patrol leader, wanted me to ride inside the cab with him, but instead I clambered into the bed with the rest of the patrol. If I had to, I wanted to unass quickly. Drivers and seat passengers died first in an ambush.

The road doubled back on itself constantly as it climbed out of the flats of El Paraíso. Truck patrols from Fourth

Brigade ran the roads near the border to keep them clear. The Soccer War between El Salvador and Honduras that had begun with a brawl at a soccer game had left a thin strip of disputed mountains along the border that both countries claimed but that neither entered. It was there in the no-man's-land, a refuge for revolutionaries and bandits and other misfits, that the FMLN guerrillas had their base camps.

The machine gunner's head ratcheted from side to side as the truck climbed the road at full speed, leaving a rooster tail of dust in its wake. Alert, obviously nervous, the other members of the patrol fingered the triggers of U.S.-supplied M16s at every switchback.

Only a few days before, peasants had reported seeing strange gringos in the mountains running weapons to the People's Liberation Front. The gringos had come from the direction of the Corridor, that narrow strip of Honduras separating El Salvador from Nicaragua. It was through communist-ruled Nicaragua that the FMLN received most of its arms. The gringos had brought with them two large wooden crates believed to contain Soviet rocket-propelled grenade launchers.

They came in a jeep in the late afternoon and took the crates into the mountains, then apparently slipped back across the border into Honduras.

"They are Russians," Colonel Ochoa decided, "or they are American adventurers doing it for money."

The gunner with his M60 tripoded on the roof of the truck cab proved trigger-happy. As the truck cut sharp around a curve, something exploded from bushes to the right. A burst from the machine gun chewed up the road ahead. A scrap of paper caught by the wind continued across the road. Air devils carried it high off the side of the mountain.

The driver goosed the truck. It swerved dangerously. Lieutenant Camino stuck his head out the window and yelled at his gunner. After a while, nerves settled. The gunner turned and shrugged, grinned, embarrassed.

We raced on.

I sipped water from my canteen to soothe a throat suddenly so dry I couldn't swallow.

When we came to the villages we detrucked and patrolled them on foot. There was something strangely melancholy about Lieutenant Camino, short and dark and as solid and broad-chested as an Angus bull, posing with a basket of flowers from a little carnival in one of the villages. He refused to have his picture taken showing him with weapons.

"El rifle no es mi amigo," he declared. "The rifle is not my friend."

The soldiers in his platoon jumped to obey even a slightly raised eyebrow. Camino was very brave, they said, but he also had much in the way of common sense. Once, they said, he closed with an enemy soldier during a fight and choked him and broke his neck, using only his hands.

"It is something in which I have little pride," he said. "Killing is not a grand thing."

There was that familiar sadness in his eyes from having been at war for seven years.

"Sometimes I have questions," he confessed after we were *amigos.* "We in this country are brothers who kill each other off. You Americans send us arms and tell us we must fight to preserve our freedom. The Russians send the liberation forces weapons and tell them *they* must fight for freedom. So we fight each other while the Americans and the Russians watch us. Why don't the Russians and the Americans fight each other instead?"

Back in the hills when I was raising gamecocks, I remembered, there was a dispute in the pit between two cockers, both of whose cocks lay mortally wounded. One man slugged the other, knocking him to the ground. The man jumped up with a knife in his fist. The other handler grabbed a club. They squared off against each other in the same pit in which their little feathered proxies had fought and were now dying.

Other cockers jumped into the ring and separated the two. "Hey, hey," they cried. "It don't do any good for us to fight each other. You can get hurt. Let the roosters do the fighting."

Yes. If the United States and Russia fought, they would

go for their big knives and clubs and annihilate the world with nuclear weapons.

"I have questions," Lieutenant Camino said.

"Yes?"

"The longer we fight, the worse things are. Whoever wins, nothing will change for the people, except for the worst. They will still be poor."

In most of the villages, townspeople sat in their doorways or loitered on corners, chatting. One village, however, appeared deserted. The patrol unassed the truck outside the town where the dirt road that cut high and snaking through the mountains became a cobblestone street in the village. Red-tiled roofs tiered precipitously off the side of the mountain, stair-stepping down toward a jungle stream at the bottom of a canyon.

Camino looked around, his gaze searching, before he staggered the foot patrol to either side of the narrow street. The silence that greeted our arrival became ominous. I heard the safety lever on Camino's rifle click. I heard other clicks.

Danger was something you sensed after a while, a tangible something that you almost tasted in the air. I felt the brown fronts of the baked-mud buildings closing in on me. I had difficulty breathing.

Camino slowly lifted his palm. I saw him take a deep breath.

His hand moved forward. The patrol advanced into the town.

50

The trigger-happy machine gunner who took point could have been walking barefoot on hot coals, he seemed so jumpy. The snout of his machine gun, which he carried by its strap across his shoulders, nosed suspiciously toward every door, every recess in the street. After every few slow steps, he halted, crouching, to look and listen. I flattened myself against the fronts of buildings.

The only thing ahead that moved was a flock of chickens pecking and scratching for food. The cobblestone street made a Y at the chickens and divided into two separate streets. A low stone wall ran between the streets at the Y. Camino chose the right fork. It led slightly uphill between solid walls of brown houses with red roofs.

Going into combat when you expected it was bad enough, but this, not knowing when or where or even *if*, took the nerves and stretched them until they whined; then a demon came in to torture the stretched nerves with fire.

It was like being dropped into a totally black cage and told a tiger was in there with you.

It was like walking into a snake pit in the dark.

It so frayed the nerves that it was a relief when something *did* happen. When the point man yelled, I felt like a clock wound too tight whose innards suddenly gave way.

A yell blended instantly into gunfire. The machine gun pounded out a long burst that echoed and reverberated through the streets, like raw sound trapped. Thank God for the nervous gunner; one less alert might not have spotted the ambush. Another fifty meters and the patrol would have walked into the kill zone bull's-eye.

Everyone was firing, running, shouting. I felt as if I had been tossed into a huge tin can rattled by a giant. Tracers—the red of friends, the blue-green of enemy—webbed the street like laser tag. The web was thick enough to catch flies. Ricochets screamed and whined. Camino threw himself prone on the cobblestones and opened up downstreet with his M16.

I remembered thinking that no one could survive such a fusillade.

I grabbed my butt with both hands, as it were, and sent it hurtling over the low rock wall. I would have liked to brag later about how I snapped great combat photos of the fight. Instead, what I got were pictures of red-tiled roofs, clouds, and soldiers running in blurs from cover to cover. It was tough getting shots when someone else was taking real shots at you.

Two of the ambushers took off down a side street and out of town. They ran so fast they left little puffs of dust kicking up behind them. They scurried up a steep bare knoll at the end of the street. Machine-gun bullets geysered, adding impetus to their flight. They disappeared over the rise.

Then it was over as quickly as it had begun. The silence that followed seemed as deep and profound as that moment in church immediately following congregational prayer. It was that moment when you realized you were still alive, before the jitters set in and you began talking and laughing for no other reason than that you were still alive.

Lieutenant Camino radioed for a ready reaction force. A half hour passed before a single helicopter full of troops whoppered in and landed on the outskirts of town. By that time the villagers were reappearing to gawk, and the guerrillas had melted back into the mountains. They left a spoor of blood, but no bodies.

Camino checked his own men. By some miracle, none had been hit. It was harder to kill a man in battle than most people supposed. The men stood up from hiding one by one, looking around, blinking as though amazed by it all. I heard nervous laughter.

"Mire," a soldier called, pointing. "Look."

Hundreds of shots had been fired over a matter of a few seconds—and the only apparent casualty was one fat black hen lying dead on the cobblestones.

"The battle of the One Dead Chicken," the laughing soldier said. But he sounded relieved.

He picked up what was left of the chicken by its legs.

"La comida," he said. "Dinner."

At sunset, Lieutenant Camino and I ate dinner together at a village café that also served as a barbershop. We washed our hands out back at a well, then occupied the long wooden table at one end of the single room. In the opposite corner sat an ancient barber's chair. The wonderful mountain wind eddied around the high tiled roof. While a hen strolled in to peck up crumbs, we drank dark local beer and talked of the war.

"Es muy triste," Camino decided. "It is very sad."

"Yes."

I recalled another sunset as lovely as this. It was when we were coming home from the cotton fields that time, up and out of the Webber Falls bottoms along the Arkansas River. I huddled at the tailgate of Peatree's old tarped truck in which he hauled hands to the fields. The weariness drained away as I watched the display on the horizon beyond the flats. I glanced up once at Mom in her old blue bonnet and work shirt and the overalls caked on the knees with dirt. Mom watched the sunset too.

For the first time, I think, I realized consciously how beautiful she was. For that time of the sunset, at least, the sadness that was always a part of her was not there.

"Mom, the sunsets belong to me," I whispered. "But I'll share with you."

It was that kind of sunset that Camino and I watched through the open door of the café. It brought out the red in the tiled roofs; it deepened the greens; it backlighted an armed soldier on a rooftop keeping guard while the platoon commander ate. It was a time of peace after the war had come so near.

Perhaps peace could only be known as a result of its contrast with war.

51

The recon patrol was wasted, punched out, climbing the high country of the Chalatenango along El Salvador's border with Honduras, trying to scare up some intelligence on the guerrillas who occupied this no-man's-land. Camera equipment bag riding heavy in my pack, I had joined the government's patrol in La Palma to gather material for magazine articles and maybe, someday, a novel on the Salvadoran civil war. And just *experiencing* it, too, looking at this thing of war.

The FMLN guerrillas hid out in the mountains to lick their wounds and bide their time before coming out to strike again at government troops. It was an isolated empty land of black granite and tufts of stunted gray shrubbery clinging to the higher slopes like hair. Winds crept among the stark rock pinnacles. Four days climbing around in the mountains and the patrol had spotted nothing more threatening than a late-night thunderstorm.

Lieutenant Vasconcelos, the patrol leader, paused and pointed deep across the valley that opened below onto a wide green plain. Far in the distance, just before the afternoon haze took over the horizon, the village of El Paraíso could be seen clinging to the bank of a stream. Vasconcelos took a pair of binoculars from his pack and scanned the open valley. He handed the glasses to me. I quickly picked out Colonel Ochoa's Fourth Brigade headquarters on the flats outside of town.

"It is beautiful country," I said.

"Our motherland."

I had seen land like this before, in Guatemala near the Mexican border. Another valley remarkably similar to this one. Instead of with government troops that time, however, I had been with rebels fighting against the Guatemalan government. I had gone there to see for myself.

The rebels' base camp was a scattering of grass-thatched huts low on the side of an extinct volcano. A skinny kid of about fourteen with an AK-47 and no shirt manned a checkpoint. Other kids trained in the dust using sticks for rifles and tin cans for grenades. In addition to the kids, there were maybe seven or eight men in the camp. Dark-skinned, ragged. One of them was armed with a WW I Springfield '03.

The rebels seemed as poor as the lone ox tied to a tree in the square, its rib cage pushed out against its hide like slats. A guerrilla with the placid face and callused hands of a campesino pointed at the valley.

"Look," he said in Spanish. "There. I will have land when the revolution succeeds."

"To whom does the land belong now?" I asked.

"Does it matter? It will be mine after the revolution. The *jefes* have promised it to me."

There were so many promises in war.

Now, in El Salvador, the rebels were also looking at the land and wanting their share for the poor. And government troops had driven the rebels off the land and into the mountains of the Chalatenango. Vasconcelos took out a dirty rag and wiped sweat from his face.

"The war continues," he said.

The twelve-man patrol pushed on with heads lowered and weapons hanging at the ends of arms. Altitude and heat and four days' boredom patrolling the bush had beaten them. Even the point man focused his dull eyes just ahead of his feet.

We cut down off the side of a mountain and entered a jungle at the bottom of a draw. A cattle trail or goat path or whatever followed the floor of the draw. The draw became a canyon that gradually narrowed between high sheer walls. The patrol waded into a clear stream. We splashed our hot faces and dunked our heads before saddling up again and moving on.

I glanced at the walls towering above on either side, forbidding ramparts. I noticed Vasconcelos watching them as well.

The canyon narrowed some more.

Fuck it.

We had gone too far to turn back now. It was an effort simply to place one foot in front of the other. The pack rode heavy on my back. What I needed was a shave, a bath, and a good night's sleep. How fine it would be in the guesthouse in the capital where the *dona* and I could sit in the little courtyard sipping drinks and watching Rafael sneak in after plotting with his underground friends.

I must be getting soft.

Like sheep to the slaughter we blundered onward.

Funny. It happened just as it happens in an auto accident. One minute you're doing sixty down the expressway and the next a Peterbilt crosses the centerline roaring directly toward you. The canyon simply exploded with automatic rifle and machine-gun fire. I recall thinking how the *bark-bark!* of the Soviet Kalashnikovs was deeper-throated, more guttural, than the tinny *bang! bang!* of the American M16s.

I thought the world had blown up in my face.

Then it slowed down to quarter speed. It almost stopped. The scream that pierced the first thick rumble-rattle of gunfire seemed to come out of the center of the cosmos, the primal scream, and it pierced through eternity. An eternity was how long it took the radioman to fall to earth. A bullet from the first bursts had caught him in the eye. Pink mist and the scream exploded from his skull. Vasconcelos's dark face, written exaggerated with terror, turned toward him; and the pink mist sprayed his face like paint from a high-pressure can. Vasconcelos's own scream shredded the wind. He sounded like a gull in a hurricane whose cry had been ripped from its throat.

The soldier in front of Vasconcelos also went down—hard and on his back. His feet drummed against the trail and his spine arch-spasmed his body high as he died.

I didn't notice the third man down until later. He crawled across the ground whimpering and dragging his leg and leaving a blood trail like a slug crawling.

There is a flat sound, something like a bolt of raw energy, that accompanies a bullet passing through the air. Those flat sounds filled the air around me. Green tracers plunged from the top of the cliff on our right flank. During that first mad minute, automatic fire chewed into the trail, ripped through trees and shrubbery, ricocheted off rocks and boulders. Men yelled and screamed and bolted.

Everything happened in slow motion, but every detail seared itself into my brain. Options raced through my mind. As an army combat instructor, I immediately recognized the hopelessness of the situation. The ambushers were high on the cliff, immune from a counterattack, and they had us trapped in the kill zone between the two walls of the canyon. The expression *Like shooting fish in a barrel* occurred to me.

Our only hope lay in returning such a heated volley of fire that the ambushers would be driven back. From the intensity of the fire, I guessed the enemy to be our equal in force, maybe greater. But they had the advantage of surprise, and they had the high ground. At such times, thoughts of survival replaced all other thoughts. There could be no bystanders, no observers. Journalist or not, either I fought and survived with the patrol—or I died with it.

My eyes focused on the fallen radioman's rifle lying next to him. I sprinted toward it, scooped it off the ground, and combat-rolled to cover behind a boulder perched on the bank of the little stream.

I yelled in English, Vasconcelos in Spanish: "Return fire! Goddammit, open up! *Fire! Fire! Fire!*"

We were all going to die.

I sprayed the top edge of the cliff over which crept a thin veil of gun smoke punctuated by sparkling muzzle flashes. A second later I heard our own machine gun pounding, *pounding,* and I said a little prayer, or maybe I only thought it. The crescendo of the battle doubled in volume as the patrol returned fire bullet for bullet. Tracers crisscrossed in space.

I yelled at the cliff: *"Cocksuckers!"*

Combat quickly became personal.

With the M16 on full auto, I emptied a thirty-round banana clip into the muzzle flashes above us. The bolt stayed open after the last round. A second clip had been taped upside down to the bottom of the first. An old combat trick. I rolled behind the boulder where I shucked my ruck and quickly switched clips and released the bolt to slam in a fresh cartridge.

With my back pressed hard against the boulder, I took a second to draw a breath that felt like my first since the action had started. I breathed deeply and assessed the situation.

Fortunately, boulders, some of which were half the height of a man, littered the ground between the trail and the stream. Two men lay obviously dead while a wounded third had crawled behind a boulder and fainted from shock and loss of blood. The rest of the patrol was fighting savagely from behind other boulders, rock piles, and flood drifts.

Maybe we weren't going to die after all. Not all of us, at any rate.

I rolled over, ready to fire, and popped three-round automatic bursts at muzzle flashes until I'd expended the second clip.

I was out of ammo.

I made myself small behind the boulder and debated my chances of reaching the downed radioman in order to relieve him of his ammo pouches. I hesitated. Gradually, it seemed, the volume of fire toned down. I chanced a quick look at the cliff top.

No muzzles were sparking.

The enemy had pulled out, hit and run.

I felt the rough texture of stone through the back of my khaki shirt. I noticed the worn toes of my combat boots. I held my hand before my eyes, moved my fingers. I held up the other hand. I laughed aloud with relief. Elsewhere, another soldier also realized that the enemy was gone. He cheered roundly, like at a football game for a winning touchdown.

Firing ceased. Profound silence. But just for an instant. Then came that great immediate surge of high when men were talking and shouting and some were laughing and others were crying. Then that ceased, too, because someone noticed the dead men and the wounded one.

This had been no Battle of the One Dead Chicken.

"We killed the enemy too," Vasconcelos said; his face still wore the red-paint blood of his dead radioman.

Of course there were no bodies left on the cliff's edge, and of course the guerrillas had vanished into the pines and palms of the Chalatenango. The ready reaction force, when it arrived in helicopters, found only scattering pools of blood.

"I think you must have killed some men, the way you were firing," Vasconcelos said to me. "You were savage."

"And you as well," I said.

"*Sí.* I report that we killed six of them. Are there not six puddles of blood?"

52

I remembered from when I was a kid that Maw had this thing about death. She attended every funeral in the county. It didn't matter if she knew the deceased or not. She donned her only black dress, shiny on the broad seat from having been worn so much, put on her hat with the black veil, grabbed me by the hand, and we set off.

"Payin' proper respects," she called it.

I huddled as small as I could next to Maw in the pew and

tried not to suffocate in the overpowering odor of cut flowers and the mournful weeping of organ music so thick it felt
like sorghum molasses. When it came time to view the remains, as that part of the ritual was called, I clutched Maw's
dress hem and held on. In spite of my fears, I tiptoed forward to peer into the casket.

I stared wide-eyed, expecting maybe the eyes to open, the
nose to twitch. *Something.*

Nothing.

"Where do they go?" I asked.

"They go to heaven to be with their loved ones."

"*Everybody* goes to heaven?"

"Of course not."

"Where do the others go?"

That was before the tent revivals and *Alli my khe shun
di* and all that.

"Why do you always ask so many questions?" Maw
fussed.

"Where *do* the others go?"

"They go to the bad place."

"God really *burns* them?" I asked.

I looked at the corpse in the casket.

"How can God burn them if we bury them in the ground
and they rot like when we buried the dead cow?"

"He don't burn their bodies. He burns their souls."

It was always confusing.

"What does a soul look like?" I asked.

"You can't see a soul. It's a spirit."

"If you can't see it, how do you know we got one?"

I wanted to know about death, but no one could tell me
about it. Death was the Great Mystery, the Big Dread, the
Passing Over into . . . Into *what?* There had to be *something.*
Years later I argued, "There is no purpose to life, no logic,
if a person comes from nowhere, lives a life so brief that it
is like a light bulb that burns out the minute you turn on
the electricity, and then checks back out into nowhere. From
nothing to nothing? What's the purpose?"

My friend Crystal laughed. "What if we checked out and

then we found out our purpose for life—and we had missed it?"

Ultimately no one could save himself or anyone else from death.

Death got us all.

We all ended up in that goddamned bucket.

War was death. Maybe that was why war intrigued me so. In war, you looked at death, and you felt and tasted it and were abhorred and fascinated by it, and you dreaded it and played with it and taunted it. War was a glimpse into the Beyond. I often thought of death as the ultimate windmill. Don Quixote jousted with death.

We all jousted with death.

Outside the city of San Salvador stood a tall cliff that locals sometimes referred to as the Charnel Wall. A narrow road ran along the top next to the edge. Government death squads, rebel assassins, and occasionally wife killers and other murderers drove along the road in the dead of night and hurled corpses off the cliff. Always the silent-winged birds of death, *pelotes,* sailed overhead in high wide circles, gradually losing altitude until they landed stiff-legged and stiff-necked and shambled forward to feast like ghoulish undertakers.

"If there is someone disappeared, go first to the foot of the cliff," I was told. "We have sometimes found as many as five bodies there after an exceptional night."

Sweating, I watched the *pelotes,* the buzzards, sailing slow and patient in a white-hot sky. I clambered down a precarious footpath cut into the cliff to the rocks and short growth below. I detected dried blood, black and crusted, smearing the stones. Scraps of bloody clothing lay strewn about.

The place smelled of death. But *old* death. Rot and corruption.

Five or six men and a weeping woman stood around last night's harvest—a young brown man in khaki trousers and no shirt. The wound in his throat gaped like a great, red, smiling second mouth without lips. His body was battered and torn from his flight off the high cliff's edge.

"*Quién es?*" I asked. "Who is he?"

"A victim." The speaker looked at me. "You are an American, a gringo?"

"*Sí.*"

"Leave. You are not welcome even in this place of death."

Throughout Latin America, not just in El Salvador, war was a struggle to control minds, hearts, souls, and bodies. Everyone was considered a combatant, from contra commander Colonel Enrique Bermudez to the two-year-old child at Palmerola abandoned to starve to death by fleeing refugees. Life was cheap. Rebels planted bombs in churches and opened fire on crowded buses. A baby or a grandmother or a cripple became an acceptable combat casualty and the subject of counterpropaganda. Government and rebels alike commonly used assassination as a weapon in the strange shadow wars.

In Honduras, Oscar Puerto of the Honduran Committee for the Defense of Human Rights showed me a plastic bag he kept filled with the charred clothing of missing people. "My little bag of horrors," he called it. "The military has great power to 'disappear' people however it chooses."

So many assassinations occurred that the clearing of corpses from the streets became almost a street sweeper's chore. One story related how a man shot and killed a common burglar who was breaking into his house. Afraid to call the police and report it, the man and his wife loaded the body into the trunk of their car and drove into the countryside. They were parked in the dark along a secluded road, struggling to get the corpse out of the trunk, when they saw headlights approaching. They hurriedly tossed the dead man into the ditch and sped away.

It terrified them when the oncoming car stopped in the same location they had just left; they thought their crime had been discovered. However, their fears were partially allayed when they happened across a small news story a few days later about how *two* murder victims were discovered alongside the lonely country road.

I thought of the assassinations and the government *escua-*

drillas muertas the afternoon I had an appointment with President Duarte at the Presidential Palace in San Salvador. Arriving early, I bought a *helado,* an ice cream, from a street vendor and waited outside the palace gates. Although I noticed the palace guards in their Nazi *Guardia* uniforms looking suspiciously at me, I thought little of it until two of them broke through the gates and came my way.

Without uttering a single word, they grabbed my arms, ignoring my protests, and hustled me through a back gate, across a wide drive, and through a rear basement door. I found myself thinking with sudden chilling terror that if they took away my identification I'd be just another unidentified corpse found at the foot of the Charnel Wall.

53

Was this how the "Disappeared" disappeared?

At the bottom of a flight of stairs I found myself thrown into a bare gray room furnished only by a straight-backed chair and a metal desk like the one I used when I was a homicide cop. There were no windows. The two Nazi goons stood at the door until the flat-faced major behind the desk waved them out. Their place was immediately taken by two plain-clothesmen armed with MAC-10 submachine guns. Something about the size of a grapefruit got stuck in my throat.

"Qué pasa? No hago nada," I protested as soon as I could speak.

"Bad Spanish. Bad," the major clucked. He held up a finger to silence me. He wrote something on a pad, then pretended to read a document. I knew the routine: make the suspect nervous.

It worked.

I cast glances at the plainclothesmen. One wore jeans and a belt buckle that said "U.S. Army Special Forces." The major's chair squeaking drew my attention back to him. He seemed to be studying me from behind sleepy eyelids.

"What were you doing?" he demanded suddenly, snapping his words.

"Waiting."

"You could find yourself waiting at the foot of a cliff."

This was no time to be a wise ass, but I had had time for my anger to build. The more contact I had with government—*any* government—the more I disliked and distrusted it.

"Los pelotes," I ventured evenly, "do not like the taste of American flesh."

The major returned the announcement with a cruel smile. "They *love* the taste."

"They have tasted before?"

"Perhaps."

Asshole.

"You're a saboteur or an assassin," the major accused.

"I'm a journalist. I have an appointment with the president. You can check."

"We will."

He took my military press pass and handed it to one of the MAC-10 hard cases, who turned and left. I hoped Duarte's secretary spelled my name correctly. How easy it would be for a lone scribbler to vanish.

"Into the basement by one door, out at night by another. Is that the way it works?" I taunted.

"Don't press your luck, gringo."

Duarte's secretary knew how to spell. The hard case came back. The major returned my press pass. I breathed a sign of relief.

"We cannot be too cautious," the major said. "There are many in this country who would like to see our president dead."

"Then I suppose it's better to kill one or two on suspicion than to take a chance, eh?"

His face reddened.

*   *   *

President José Napoleón Duarte had two bodyguards who sat on either side of him with their hands resting on machine pistols inside their suit coats. Duarte was a solid-looking man with the look of the Indian in his dark eyes. The interview I had with him found its way into newspapers back in the States and helped form some pieces I did for Time-Life books. My photo of him in *Modern Warfare* showed a tired face drawn and gray from the endless war; perhaps already he endured the pain of the cancer that would shortly kill him.

"We will win this war," he said. "If we win, we demonstrate that there is a way out for democracy. The United States will have a real example for the world. It will have real friends."

It sounded like more Cold War talk to me. He had to say it, because that was what politicians said. I thought of James F. Dunnigan's book *How to Make War*. Dunnigan wrote:

> Even though leaders know how bad the situation is, they preach optimism. Otherwise they could be replaced by less pessimistic politicians. Wars acquire a life of their own and just keep going. . . .
>
> Nobody wins, but this is often forgotten. Wars are easy to start, expensive to continue, and difficult to stop. Wars often begin when someone feels that victory is assured. Wars end when one or both sides are devastated, demoralized, or, rarely, suddenly enlightened by the absurdity of it all.

54

Lieutenant Camino, the gentle one of the Salvadoran Fourth Brigade with whom I had patrolled at the time of the Battle of the One Dead Chicken, who had killed a guerrilla with his bare hands, whose rifle, he said, was not his friend. I heard about him maybe a year after our time together in the Chalatenango.

"He was my friend," I said.

Margie said, "You have so many friends."

"I have no wealth. I own little. My friends are my wealth."

"They take advantage of you."

"They give more than they ever take."

It was before Desert Storm, before that nastiness. Before Paris. Kathy had divorced me after I was reported missing in El Salvador, after I was a national finalist to go into space with NASA's Journalist in Space project. I guess she couldn't take so much excitement. And now Margie. Margie was not yet my wife. I enveloped her in my arms. I held her as close as I could. There was so much dying, but *we* were alive. My heart matched the beat of this beautiful woman's heart.

"We fit," I said. "Do you have any idea how I adore you?"

"I love you too."

I really believed she cared for me.

"Camino, I think, had three kids," I said. "How fleeting it all is. How we waste life on trivialities. By the time we understand what is important in life, life is over and we have wasted much of it on what is not important."

Margie looked at me, puzzled. I'm not sure she ever understood me. I held a rose, one of the red ones that I loved most of all. I saw so many things in it—people and places and lives—that tears came to my eyes. I never forgot how, at the little fair in La Palma, Camino posed for my camera with his basket of flowers but always refused to pose with his rifle.

Lieutenant Camino, I heard, had died when the guerrillas attacked Colonel Ochoa's Fourth Brigade headquarters at El Paraíso. I remembered from my time there the rusted barbed wire, the neglected guard towers, the sense of general carelessness and inattention that had settled over the brigade headquarters.

"The guerrillas are not strong enough to attack a combat headquarters," Colonel Ochoa had assured me. "When we want to fight, we go outside the wire. Otherwise we are safe inside our compound. Was it not the same in Vietnam?"

In the *beginning* it was that way in Vietnam.

I contacted my friend Vasconcelos in El Salvador to ask him about Camino's death.

"El Paraíso was much more fierce than our battle, Cholla," Vasconcelos said. "I was not there when it happened, but I have heard that it was at that battle that Teniente Camino fell. I heard that he died a hero."

"His widow and orphans will be happy that he died a hero."

Vasconcelos paused for a long time. *"Sí,"* he whispered presently.

It had been near 2:00 A.M. in the month of April, I was told, when mortar fire suddenly erupted from the hills above the Fourth Brigade headquarters. Explosions inside the garrison splintered buildings and sowed confusion among soldiers thrown abruptly from their bunks. Minutes later about two hundred uniformed guerrillas with satchel charges, grenades, and automatic weapons hacked their way through the defensive wire perimeter. Illuminated by burning buildings and accompanied by the fierce crackle of machine-gun fire, the battle raged at close quarters for nearly two hours before dawn absorbed the guerrillas back into the countryside.

"It was such confusion," said a survivor. "It was dark, and the wounded were screaming, and we didn't know what was happening."

Wisps of smoke still crawled from the carnage when General Adolfo Blandon, commander of Salvadoran forces, arrived at the garrison a few hours later. Soldiers poking among the charred debris stuffed the dead into body bags supplied through U.S. aid. Rebel forces suffered ten dead to government forces' sixty-nine. Among the casualties was U.S. Army Staff Sergeant Gregory Fronius, a Green Beret adviser. Although five American soldiers had been assassinated by terrorists in El Salvador, Fronius was the first to die in combat.

"I heard the rifle of Teniente Camino was empty in his hands when they found him," Vasconcelos said. "There were three dead enemy lying in front of him."

El rifle no es mi amigo.

55

In Honduras during the wet season the road from Cifuentes to Las Trojes stuck to your boots in heavy clumps of mud. During the dry season it caked in your throat. An occasional vehicle traveling fast between the bristling guns of the Honduran Sixth Battalion on one side of the road and the Sandinistas on the other kicked up a dust trail that settled in Nicaragua.

During the mid to late 1980s, Las Trojes near the end of the road was a frontier town where *hombres* carried pistols thrust into their belts and contras from the camps in the hills beyond trickled down to trade American-supplied food for cigarettes. Uprooted by the border fighting, the *desplazados*—the displaced persons—haunted the wide unpaved street of the frontier village with fear and wariness in their eyes. In these parts, the thin strip of ruts that ran along the

Honduran-Nicaraguan border between Cifuentes and Las Trojes was known as the most dangerous seventeen kilometers in the world. In these parts, the road was called *El Camino de los Muertos*—the Road of the Dead.

Until recently, Nicaraguan Sandinistas had wandered in and out of Honduras chasing the contra rebels who, with U.S. assistance, had been waging war against Daniel Ortega's communist government for over six years. In 1986, however, at U.S. urging, Honduras had clamped down on its borders to prevent Sandinistas chasing the contras on Honduran soil. Honduras's providing the contras a base of operations from which to launch attacks was viewed by Nicaragua as an act of war. During more than sixty major border incidents in 1986 alone, Sandinistas mounted attacks against Honduran soldiers along the border as well as against contras. In each of the months of March and November, Nicaragua hurled at least a full battalion across the border. Bloody clashes between the two nations along *El Camino de los Muertos* left more than two hundred casualties on all sides.

Driving a rented four-wheel-drive Mitsubishi with a *Time* stringer from Tegucigalpa as passenger, I stopped at the soldiers' roadblock in Cifuentes. A sign warned: *Peligroso! Danger!*

"Yeah," said Ring, the *Time* stringer.

The last time he had run the road to Las Trojes, he spent the night in jail for trying to reach the contra camps. The Honduran and U.S. governments did not want the contra presence played up in the American press.

A *teniente*—a lieutenant—at the roadblock looked the Mitsubishi over. It was white.

"A good target," he decided.

We entered the frontier to pass between the armed outposts of enemies facing each other across the road. I grinned and dug the accelerator into the floor. The automobile shot along the gauntlet where dying was as common as wild banana trees. Ring, the *Time* stringer, glassed the Sandinista positions.

"Any signs?" I asked, driving hard.

"Just the usual. If they were massing, they wouldn't do it so we could see them."

We had picked up rumors in Tegoose that the Sandinistas were preparing another cross-border invasion. That was why we were bound for Las Trojes. I wanted to witness the next battle.

"You'll get your balls shot off," my friend Llave had warned before he caught the flight out of Tegoose. Llave—Keith Laub—and I had just completed an assignment together in Honduras for an international security agency.

"Maybe Danny Ortega will get *his* shot off," I countered.

Llave grinned. "Don't even whisper it. The FBI is listening."

In Tulsa, the FBI had arrested two men involved in a conspiracy to assassinate Nicaraguan dictator Daniel Ortega. Before their arrest, the conspirators had called Llave late one night, and they had called me, recruiting.

"You're ex–Special Forces?" a husky voice had demanded from the telephone receiver.

"Who wants to know?"

"I hear you do special jobs in Latin America for a price."

"I'm a journalist, not a mercenary."

A snigger on the other end. "Yeah. Right."

"Who gave you my name?"

"We have contacts."

"What do you want?"

"A couple of your Special Forces buddies are in," the voice said. The caller sounded drunk. "They said you could be trusted. You speak Spanish. We want you to take us to Nicaragua. It's worth a quarter million to you."

"Why?"

"Let's say that it would be a major blow to communism if a certain person were ... eliminated."

"Who?"

"Ortega."

I blinked in astonishment. What kind of fool called virtual strangers on the telephone to recruit for an assassination of

219

a foreign head of state? Obviously a drunk one, but more than drunk.

"We have high-powered backing in the government," the drunk said. "Can you do it?"

I could have done it. "No," I said, and I hung up.

After the conspirators were arrested, an FBI agent looked at me in my living room. He had eyes blue enough to cut diamonds. Our gazes locked.

"We know you, Sasser," he said. "If you had been in on it, Danny Ortega would have been dead before we found out about it."

I wondered what kind of files the government kept on people like me.

The CIA and the FBI had their noses and their clumsy hands stuck into everything in or about Central America.

If a free-lance American mercenary tried anything in another country, his government sent him to prison. If the same mercenary took a contract with the CIA and did the same thing, he was okay as long as nothing got fucked up. If it did get fucked up, though, he was on his own. That was part of the contract.

Take Eugene Hasenfus.

A Sandinista soldier armed with a Soviet-made surface-to-air missile called a *flecha* shot down a C-123 cargo plane flying over Nicaragua. Three Americans, including the pilot, died in the air explosion that ripped the right side out of the airplane. Hasenfus, an ex-Marine from Wisconsin, parachuted into the jungle. Sandinistas captured him early the next morning hiding in an abandoned hut. The CIA issued a statement through the U.S. State Department that he was a mercenary acting on his own and had no connection with the U.S. government.

I felt my stomach churning with disgust.

In El Salvador at the Llopango military airfield, I had watched unmarked "sterile" C-123 cargo planes scuttling in and out. Reminded me of Air America in Vietnam. The aircraft were loaded in secrecy and kept guarded at an isolated corner of the airfield. I learned through sources—hang around the bars, find a gringo and pump him—that the flights had made at least one hundred successful resupply airdrops to contras inside Nicaragua during the three months before Hasenfus's plane went down.

Do whatever you want until you're caught, then deny it like hell. That was a standard motto for *all* governments.

Ring and I passed the place in a deep valley next to a stream where two American journalists had died after their vehicle struck a Czech-made mine set on the road by Sandinistas. Not far away Sandinistas had ambushed two Honduran buses in separate incidents, killing a conductor and wounding two passengers. A little farther along *El Camino de los Muertos,* Nicaraguan soldiers had pinned down a TV camera crew for more than an hour.

We came upon the wreck of a Mercedes truck the Sandinistas had rocketed for hauling supplies to the contras. Burned down to naked metal, it sat hollow and abandoned, rammed into a three-strand barbed-wire fence that separated the two countries. I concealed the Mitsubishi behind a bank of earth beside the road to protect it from a similar fate and got out to look at the truck. About four hundred yards away across a field of waist-high grass Sandinistas behind sandbags craned their necks.

"They'll shoot you," Ring cautioned.

"They couldn't hit me at this distance."

I photographed the rocketed truck; we continued on to Las Trojes.

In Las Trojes the local eatery was a whitewashed adobe building on a rut-ribbed side street. It had two rooms and a kitchen where an emaciated woman and her daughter tended a wood-burning cookstove. A red dog wandered in and stretched out underneath the long table as Ring and I devoured rice, *plátanos,* and refried beans wrapped in thick tortillas.

The village *jefe,* a man named Andrés Martinez, dropped a bag of coffee beans in the front room and joined us at the table. He was a big olive-skinned man with short curly black hair and an ancient .38 revolver stuck in his back pocket.

As always, talk soon centered on the Sandinistas and the contras.

"It is we Hondurans who are paying the price for their war," Martinez said, wrapping frijoles in a tortilla and cramming the bundle into his mouth. "We don't have anything to do with it. We're afraid, but what can we do? We have to stay and live. What I see is bad. We should be free to walk along our border, but if anyone sticks his head out, he gets shot. Why does our army have to machine-gun the Sandinistas on the road? They are making a conflict. If our army continues to give help to the contras, thousands of Hondurans will die. Everybody believes the Nicaraguans will invade us someday, but all we can do is run.

"The contras are not going to win. They are campesinos who were born to raise corn, not to fight. They don't have the desire to be guerrillas. Each time the Sandinistas cross the border, the contras fall back deeper into Honduras. They are not really committed. All contra leaders have U.S. green cards so they can go to the United States when the war goes too badly."

I finished my last tortilla and rose from the table. The red dog followed me outside where a team of oxen drew a wooden-wheeled cart down the dusty street toward a soldier sentry brandishing an automatic rifle. An odd, sad juxtaposition of the modern with the ancient.

Andrés Martinez came and hoisted his bag of coffee beans onto his shoulder.

"The Hondurans who must flee their homes blame the contras," he said. "If not for them, people would be happy harvesting their coffee."

People everywhere, that was all they wanted, to harvest their coffee or plant their rice. . . .

Down the street from the eatery, Emma Mendoza ran the general store. She said, "If you stay, you will see more fighting. People die of fear here, like it says in the Bible. A friend of mine was having soup with egg when the Sandinistas came. She died of fright like it says in the Bible."

Ring returned to Tegoose. I stayed on in Las Trojes to visit the UN refugee camp at Jacaleapa and wait for the border fighting to resume.

56

The UN refugee camp in Jacaleapa. It said everything about this war and about all wars. It was one of forty such camps in Honduras to which more than two hundred thousand people out of a Nicaraguan population of three million had already fled. The UN rep in Tegoose gave me the figures: 200,000 refugees, among them 10,500 Miskita Indians had defied "collective resettlement" and fled en masse to Honduras ahead of blazing Sandinista mortars, rocket-propelled grenades, and tank guns; 20,000 Nicaraguans were fighting with the contras; 9,000 had been executed inside Nicaragua or were being held as political prisoners. But statistics were cold, hard, meaningless. Reality came in seeing the crowded UN camps composed of rough clapboard shacks and unhappy lean-tos among which ragged children with haunted eyes scrambled in the silent purpose of little ones robbed of childhood.

I walked through the gate of the high fences at Jacaleapa and halted, stunned. My nose was assailed by the stench of the rows of crude hole-in-the-ground outhouses in the center of camp and the slightly less offensive odor of pigs and chickens wandering in and out of doorless huts. Everywhere black eyes stared out of a sea of brown faces.

"These and the thousands of dead and dying and wounded are the victims of man's folly for war," said the UN rep. "They have nowhere to go, these thousands of refugees. Your country and the Russians make war through the little peoples, and then the little peoples are left without homes and fathers, and no one will take them and give them homes. Some of these children were born in this camp."

223

A young mother of five stood wearily in the opening of her poor hut and gazed in the direction of Nicaragua, less than twenty miles away. Tears brimmed her eyes. One of her small skinny daughters clutched my hand.

"I love you," she said in English. "I love you."

Something caught in my throat. After a moment, I replied, "I love you too, *niña linda.*"

"My husband was a contra," the little girl's mother explained. "He was killed by the Sandinistas two years ago. Because of it, the government in Nicaragua would not let me take a job and would not let me have food for my children. One night my neighbors and I took our children and crossed the frontier. Many of us are fleeing. In my country, life grows dark."

For the next year or so after I returned to the United States, I collected clothing and toys and other things for the five children of the dead contra. The oldest daughter was about eleven. She liked most of all a photo portrait I did of her. Then my letters started being returned unopened.

"Where are they?" I inquired of United Nations representatives.

"They are gone."

"Where?"

"They are gone."

57

Soldiers near Las Trojes along the border marked by *El Camino de los Muertos* lived in sandbagged trenches, like rats. At one of the Honduran outposts near the rocketed Mercedes truck, a soldier clambered out of his trench. I climbed out behind him. I stretched and looked around. Dawn separated earth from sky in one of those glorious translucent displays when you know you want to live forever.

I remembered summer mornings back in the hills when dew still touched the blades of grass and made your bare feet cold. I remembered Paw scratching himself and going out into the yard to take a leak with Buster the dog before he ambled off to the horse lot to grain Jude and Nig prior to starting the day's work. He stood there with the colors of the dawn painted on his rough old face. He farted and pissed on the grass, looking thoroughly contented with himself and the world.

"There ain't nothing like a good first piss in the morning," he groaned.

I stood next to him and peed too.

Now the Honduran soldier slung his M16 and, still yawning and stretching, slid down to the road and stood there and unbuttoned his fly. On the other side of the road were Nicaragua and the Sandinistas.

A single rifle shot cracked from inside Nicaragua. The kid in the road was dead by the time we reached him. He was seventeen years old. At five-thirty we carried his corpse to the outpost at Cifuentes and laid it out on a wooden bench. The other soldiers came to look at him. They were kids too, as I had been when I first started learning war. They stood and looked at the body. Then they looked at a cur with the mange as it trotted down the road between the wild banana trees.

"Tonight," vowed a sergeant, "we have sharpshooters who will sneak into Nicaragua and seek revenge."

One death required an enemy death in return. It was mostly that kind of war along the road, a personal war of revenge and counter-revenge. Still, it seemed unfair to shoot a kid answering a call of nature. An inglorious way to die.

It was the night after the boy had died in the dust of the road while taking a leak. To the right flank of the trench outpost, out of the valley where the journalists had died, flashed an explosion that strobed like lightning across the dark sky and, a few moments later, made the ground rumble. Shaken from sleep, I crowded into the trench with the Hondurans as the sudden rattle of machine-gun and small arms fire rocked the valley further. Excited Spanish crackled from the radio; the outpost next to us was being attacked.

"Sandinistas are coming across the border in force!" exclaimed one of the six soldiers manning my outpost.

I stood in the trench behind the sandbags shoulder to shoulder with the boy soldiers. They fumbled with their weapons. I *felt* the kid next to me trembling as we listened to the fierce battle beyond the neighboring rise. Tracers buzzed red or blue-green into the night sky. Grenades flash-popped against the horizon.

"Keep a sharp eye," the young sergeant said. "We will be next."

"Ojalo que no, por Dios."

"Do not call in God's name," said another. "God does not listen to soldiers."

The Sandinistas probed the outpost, then withdrew. A tense silence replaced the recent sounds of battle. I listened to the singing and chirping of crickets and tree frogs along a tiny brook that meandered out of the hills behind us. It squeezed through a pipe underneath the dirt road, then arrowed out as it cut through the enemy's wide plain of grasses in front of us.

Eyes strained for movement. Nerves stretched so tight they could have been played like guitar strings. Two Hondurans whispered to each other and pointed at stray breezes riffling the grass. One was convinced it announced an enemy advance. I heard the click of his rifle safety to auto.

My heart pounded against the wall of the trench. It beat in my ears like down-and-dirty rap with a double-time cadence. Stare at a shadow, any shadow, long enough and it turned into a man.

"Be prepared to flee, *periodista*," the Honduran sergeant whispered in my ear. "It is foolish for only six soldiers to be here. The Sandinistas will overrun us the first minute."

"They are coming," someone muttered in a voice strung like tight wire. "They are out there."

The sergeant moved quickly. "It is shadows," he said. "Do not fire at shadows."

"I *see* them."

"You see nothing, understand? Nothing. Yet."

An hour passed so slowly it was as if the minutes were being excavated one by one. Thoughts of sleep were gone. I strained my eyes against the terrifying night. Although home was only a rented apartment filled with books in Tulsa, I suddenly felt acutely homesick. I even thought of Sharon. It had been thirty years since our last and only real kiss playing spin the bottle at the creek.

Other thoughts raced through my head as if they were competing to get their moments before it was too late: the Oklahoma hills where I was a kid; books I had not yet read or written; places I had not seen; things that needed doing; somewhere out there, maybe, a lovely warm woman to hold me against darkness such as that out there now so real with danger.

"Life is love, laughter, and tangerine roses," the girl Nancy used to say. She was tall and willowy with great dark eyes and black hair. "Move in with me, sweet Cholla."

"I can't. Not yet."

Kathy had just divorced me. The hurt was too fresh.

Suddenly a warning yelp snatched my thoughts back from their wanderings. My pulse tripped to double time. A burst from an M16 shredded the night, accompanied by its muzzle flickering flame.

"They are coming!"

I saw nothing in the darkness in that instant before the entire outpost of six soldiers opened up with a fusillade that streamed tracers across the road and cut through grass like a scythe. I thought I heard boots crunching on the road. But by then panic had set in. Screaming and firing back over their shoulders, the Hondurans scrambled out the back side of the trench and bolted toward a distant tree line on top of the hill where the sergeant had established an alternate defensive position.

Not to be left behind, I joined the confusion of shadows in the night. Running, *running.* Muzzle fire blossoms. Rifles banging on full automatic. Yelling and screaming.

The soldiers were shooting at anything that moved and at some things that did not move. At each other. At *me.*

I completed a forty-second dash across a rising field to the tree line. With adrenaline coursing through my veins, it was as if my feet never even touched the ground. I raced blindly through the darkness, hoping to avoid flying bullets. I was so *goddamned* scared. I knew the Sandinistas were hot behind me, gaining ground. I had myopic vision. I could have run through a pride of lions and never seen them unless I bumped into one. I threw back my head. My arms pumped.

It wasn't terribly heroic.

Wham!

One moment I was running as if the Holy Roller devil from the hills was hot on my ass; the next moment that ass met ground with a shock that jarred my brain stem. A huge fist had delivered a right cross out of the sky. Either that or Mad Dog's Bigfoot had caught me in the teeth with a front kick. I grabbed my face; it went instantly numb.

Oh, my God! They've shot off my face!

I gagged on blood, retched. Fingers touched mangled flesh and mustache dripping with blood and teeth barely hanging from gums. Frantic, I explored my lower jaw until satisfied that most of it remained. Then I stumbled to my feet and continued my wild flight to the top of the hill. Later, when I had time to reflect on it, I decided a ricocheting bullet had glanced off me. Either that or a chipped-off rock or something from all the lead flying.

Sandinista fire or "friendly fire," whichever, I endured a painful and fearful night holed up in a second trench. We waited for the Sandinistas, but they did not come. At daybreak, a young Honduran soldier stood up and gazed downhill back over our route of flight. Seeing no signs of the enemy, he managed a grin. He looked at me. I groaned pitifully.

"We cannot plow with tanks, cultivate with rifles—and no one can eat bullets," he quipped, and grinned some more.

58

Ahead in the street darkness of Tegoose stood a policeman clad in cheap forest green and tan. Fortunately he was looking at something downstreet. I almost blundered into him, racked as I was with chills and fever. Spotting him at the last moment, I stumbled into the nearest alley and ran in a shambling, laboring shuffle until exhaustion and illness forced me to stop and catch my breath.

It wouldn't do for the Honduran police to catch me. No telling how long they might keep me while I tried to explain all the blood. I could be held in-country for weeks, months even, while the Honduran government and the U.S. embassy worked through red tape.

Fuck that. I wanted to go home.

Latin American cities are almost always dark. It was easy

to slip through the city in shadow. Trying to remember directions, I came at last to Ana's familiar street. I recognized her home—a pleasant little pastel adobe jammed close to the street with a courtyard in back. It sat in the dark with no lamp in the window. I shot glances to right and left, then rapped on the door.

Please. Please be home.

I knocked again, desperately.

A sleepy female voice. *"Quién es?"*

"Es Carlo, Ana. Tengo daño."

"What?"

"I have difficulty talking. I am wounded. Ana? Ana, it is me. Carlos."

The door flew open. Ana stood there with her dark hair flying and her face pale in the thin silver moonlight. Ana's family was Castillian, Old Spain. Light olive skin, eyes gray rather than dark. Her face clouded with sudden dread when she saw the blood on my khaki shirt.

"I'm hurt, Ana. I didn't know anywhere else to go."

She grabbed me, hugged me, blood and filth and all. "Are the police looking for you?"

"I don't think so."

Ana could get me out of the country. She had worked for a travel agency. That was how we had met on one of my previous trips to Tegucigalpa. We dated whenever I was in-country. It was she who had given Llave his nickname when I introduced them.

"Ana, this is my friend Keith. Keith Laub."

She misunderstood. "Oh. Key," she said. "Key. Like *llave.*"

Llave was Spanish for "key." Laub became Llave.

Pulling me into her house, Ana started to strip me, feeling for injuries, cooing little things all the while and touching me with her fingertips as though to reassure herself that I wasn't some apparition dropped in out of a night dream.

"I thought the Bigfoot had caught up with me," I mumbled through pain.

"Bigfoot?"

"I thought I was dying."

"You cannot die, Carlos. I want to keep you."

"It felt like dying."

I lay morose and withdrawn between Ana's cool sheets, recuperating enough to leave the country. My lips were shredded. I had lost teeth and weight. I looked into the mirror to shave and saw a face bloated and turned hideous in shades of green and red and purple.

"I love that face even as it is," Ana said.

"It is hard to love such a face even when it is normal," I said, mumbling as if through sausages.

"You are a beautiful man where it counts most—inside," Ana said. "I see that in you when you let me."

"Ana ... ?"

"*Qué tu quieres, chico?*"

"Nothing. I want nothing."

"We all must want something in order to get it."

What did I want? Years ago, with Dianne, I had said, "I envy all the ordinary people—the laborers and office workers and others who have their days the same day after day. There must be a great satisfaction in looking forward to a weekly paycheck and Monday Night Football, to coming home tired after work every night to the little woman and kids and parking your car in your own two-car garage. People like that must be very content."

"What drives you, for God's sake?" Dianne had cried.

I laughed. I quoted from *Don Quixote:* " 'So many were the grievances he intended to rectify, the wrongs he resolved to set right, the harms he meant to redress, the abuses he would reform ...' "

"What?"

I laughed again. "Nothing. The ramblings of a fool."

And Ana ... Ana looked at me lying in bed laboring over *Don Quixote* in its original Spanish.

"You are a strange man," Ana said.

I lay between the cool sheets. This was the first time I had been wounded in combat, if you didn't count the time the pimp stabbed me in the back when I was a cop working prostitution. Outside Ana's bedroom window grew a lime tree. Its thin limbs scratched against the window when there was a breeze. Scratching like the dry bones of a corpse risen in the sun.

It was sobering. I could have died along the road called *El Camino de los Muertos.*

"Listen," I coaxed Ana. I read Don Quixote's epitaph:

> Here lies the noble fearless knight,
> Whose valor rose to such a height;
> When death at last had struck him down,
> His was the victory and renown.
> He reck'd the world of little prize,
> And was a bugbear in men's eyes;
> But had the fortune in his age
> To live a fool and die a sage.

I looked up and laughed wryly.
To live a fool and die a sage.

PART 3

Put the guns into our hands and we will use
them. Give us the slogans and we will turn them
into realities. Sing the battle hymns and we will
take them up where you left off. Not one not ten
not ten thousand not a million not ten millions
not a hundred millions but a billion two billions
of us all the people of the world we will have
the slogans and we will have the hymns and we
will have the guns and we will use them.
—Dalton Trumbo

59

George Bush and Saddam Hussein. They were in all the newspapers, magazines, and on TV in 1990. Posturing, looking tough, rattling sabers, squaring up, facing off, and daring each other. The way they talked, you swore they were about to go for each other's throats in personal combat.

Which, of course, they weren't. They had soldiers to do that for them. Let the fighting cocks get in the ring and rip each other's throats out to prove how tough the handlers were.

Saddam dug in his Republican Guard and stockpiled his Scud missiles. Bush activated the Reserves and National Guard and massed nearly a half million American troops in Saudi Arabia. Even before the war began it was costing one billion dollars a day.

In the Dammam Harbor floated a Japanese ship with 70,000 refrigerated berths ready to receive American corpses. Body bags—"human remains pouches," 16,000 of them—were shipped to Saudi; Secretary of Defense Richard Cheney said such arrangements were an "unfortunate part of preparing when you deploy a force this size." Some generals were predicting 100,000 American casualties.

And the folks back home in the United States were in a war fever. Yellow ribbons and "Support Our Troops" banners flew everywhere. Stores sold out of American flags. Everyone seemed so proud to be a kick-ass American and part of a winning team.

"The war?" said a man in Georgia. "Oh, we're for it. We're very stable here, very patriotic. We're for it for patriotic reasons. There was one little demonstration against it—a couple of old hippies."

A National Guard general whose wife wouldn't let him go to Vietnam saw his opportunity.

"We had a compliment paid to us by some Regular Army officers at Fort Dix," he said. "They were two colonels and old friends of mine, both former members of the division. They said if they had to go to battle again, they'd rather go with us than with any other unit, active or reserve. That, gentlemen, is a big compliment coming from those two. I told them we were ready to go. If they'll get us a war, we'll make them proud of us."

"Fucked up," Mad Dog Carson said.

If the United Nations led by the U.S. attacked, Saddam warned, it would be "the mother of all battles."

"I obviously cannot say when a ground operation might commence," returned George Bush. "What I can say is our preparations are on schedule. . . . There are no negotiations. The goals have been set. There will be no concessions—not going to give."

The combat veterans, all middle-aged now, were forgotten in the heat of a fresh military challenge. Shorty Adcock, who had run SOG missions with the Fifth Special Forces Group during the Vietnam War, lost his job at the post office and went on pension with post-Vietnam stress syndrome. Mad Dog Carson who had fought with the 173d Airborne in Vietnam said his wife knew he was crazy, too, although he really wasn't. Shooting off his left nut was an accident, but he was still applying for a pension. Mother Norman rubbed his wound where the muscle used to be in his arm and wouldn't talk about Iraq and the preparations for war. All he said was "How quickly we forget."

"We are a stupid people!" Mad Dog exclaimed. "We're deluding ourselves if we think this shit has anything to do with God, country, and Mom's apple pie. It's over oil and big business as usual.

"Wait until sons and husbands start coming home in body bags and all fucked up like vegetables, without arms and legs and dicks and stuff. See how we like trading lives for cheap oil then."

Crazy Craig Roberts, the ex-Marine, had personal reasons to remember war too.

"Remember," he said, "when we were told that if we didn't stop the commies in Saigon we'd be stopping them in Chicago? Now we're told that Saddam is another Hitler whose next step is the conquering of the world.

"The world is full of petty tyrants like Saddam. Are we going to fight them all? The more we use our military, the easier it is. Fuck talking, fuck diplomacy. Let's just go kick ass. Pretty soon we're no better than they are."

Mad Dog stepped in again.

"Our government tells us what to do and we jump to do it—go to war, pay more taxes, give up our guns. Now that Russia is collapsing, we don't have an enemy outside the gates anymore. We have to find a new enemy to take our minds off government and politicians and how they're fucking over all of us at home. If the politicians and lawyers aren't careful, the next war is going to be right here in the United States of America. There's a revolution coming."

At Duke University, my son David was about to graduate from medical school on a U.S. Air Force scholarship. He said there was talk that in the event of a long war the new doctors might be sent to the front. It would give them experience in treating battlefield trauma.

"They won't send a son to the front if the father is already there," I quickly countered.

Legislation was being introduced to prevent immediate family members from being sent to the same combat zone. "Losing one member of a family is a real tragedy," explained Wisconsin Representative Toby Roth. "Losing more than one, especially when we could have acted in time to prevent it, is too great a sacrifice for any family."

My other son, Michael, the libertarian: "They can do anything to us we can't stop them from doing."

Michael and I, we talked into the night, debated, before I volunteered for active duty.

"Don't go to this one, Dad," he pleaded. "You're being

used. The United States doesn't support countries because they're democracies, but instead because of what they have to offer business. Our leaders know that war is not simply good for the economy, but that war and a huge standing army are necessary to our entire economic system."

Michael was the philosophical son, the intellectual. He questioned everything. "Just like you, Dad," he said.

"Read the newspapers," he challenged, "and see how intertwined the civilian work force is with military contracts. War is money and money is war. The military means jobs. War means jobs, and that's all most people think of is their job, even if it means turning out warplanes and tanks and guns so people can kill each other. Our big money-making prospect in this country is manufacturing and selling weapons. If you go to Iraq, you'll be fighting U.S. weapons *with* U.S. weapons."

Michael had tears in his eyes.

"Don't go, Dad," he pleaded. "You've been to enough wars. You've earned the right to stay home. Why don't you marry Margie? You need a home."

60

From the Tulsa *World:*

With Fourth-of-July pageantry, several thousand McDonnell Douglas workers and their families turned out for a rally to push the sale of 72 F-15 fighter jets to Saudi Arabia that could salvage their jobs.

Free American flags, live country music and words of support from top government and McDonnell

Douglas officials highlighted the event, held in a building near the company's flight ramp. . . .

A somber mood among workers, however, shadowed the revelry.

"I have two sons this plant helped raise. If something doesn't happen, I'm quite sure I'll lose my job," said Frankie Taylor, line foreman and 17-year employee of the company. . . .

A flag-waving crowd erupted in cheers as Governor David Walters called for federal legislators to "cut the political bull" and approve the $5 billion sale.

"It's just not fair" to close the plant after years of service to the government, [Owen Bieber, president of the International United Auto Workers Union] said. "That's not the way you treat human beings."

For many small and minority-owned businesses that depend upon McDonnell Douglas and other local aeronautical companies, danger lurks closer to home, said Gussie Jennings, a McDonnell Douglas socioeconomic advocate.

"Everything has dried up. Those businesses are already hurting," said Jennings, as she corralled employees to sign a banner emblazoned with "F-15—U.S. Jobs Now." The banner will be sent to President Bush to make the workers' message seem more personal, she said.

"I have no idea what's going to happen. There will be a lot of bankruptcies and a lot of people on the street."

About 750 of the company's 2,000 employees build the rear fuselage of the F-15—about one-third of the aircraft. Officials say 40,000 jobs around the country are in jeopardy.

61

When Colonel Thames assumed command of my U.S. Army Reserve Forces school a year before Desert Storm, he arrived with creases as sharp as folded paper. Sergeant Major Taylor went to him.

"Master Sergeant Sasser is the best instructor in the school system," Taylor said, "but he's not much of a garrison trooper. He's blunt, sloppy in military appearance, sometimes disrespectful—but if we ever go to war, he's the man you want to go to war with."

"Sasser," replied Thames, "will shape up like everyone else—or he'll get out."

I had no tolerance for military absurdities or petty abuses of power. I never learned to keep quiet when, for example, three officers conducting an in-ranks personnel inspection climbed down a grunt's throat for wearing his first aid pouch upside down on his LBE—and two of the officers were wearing theirs wrong. Or when generals and colonels became so preoccupied with details that they issued orders that officers would personally line up their troops and measure each one's uniform with a ruler to determine that the distance between the seam of the shoulder and the unit patch was correct. An eighth of an inch off the regulations and the patch had to be ripped off and resewn.

One afternoon at final formation, Colonel Alexander arrived carrying a cardboard box. Alexander was so short I sometimes referred to him as Colonel Smurf.

"The general wants everyone in his Army Reserve Command to have one of these and use it appropriately," he announced.

240

He handed out little sewing kits containing a thimble and thread and needles.

I stared.

"You've got to be shitting me!" I blurted out from ranks. "A *combat* sewing kit?"

"Goddammit, Sergeant Sasser!" Alexander shot back, exasperated. "He's the *general*. What the general wants, the general gets."

"Even if he's a goddamned idiot? Measuring patches, handing out sewing kits, checking mustaches for one hair too long ... What's happening to this man's army?"

The general and his combat sewing kits rapidly became a laughingstock in the enlisted ranks; if there was one thing an enlisted man spotted faster than a chow line, it was chickenshit.

Thames kept watching me. I taught combat tactics.

"I didn't realize Sasser was *that* good," he remarked to Sergeant Major Taylor.

Taylor grinned. "Hide him when the general comes around, then break him out if there's a war."

After the Desert Storm buildup began, the commanding general of the 122d Army Reserve Command telephoned Colonel Thames.

"We have a military police company that's about to be activated for the war and shipped overseas. It has a few problems. We need a strong first sergeant to whip it into shape. How about Master Sergeant Sasser?"

I doubt if Thames recognized the irony when he answered, "He's your man. He's the best we have. He's not much of a garrison trooper, but if we're going to war he's the type of man to go to war with."

I laughed when I heard about it. I had already determined to go, one way or another. Not long before, I'd received a call from the Ohio-based international security agency for which Llave and I had done work in Central America. I was just completing a summer of training troops at Fort Chaffee. I left my dusty field jeep parked in front of the head shed, dusted off my camouflage BDUs, and flung my helmet into a corner next to the operations sergeant's desk.

"The caller said it was urgent," he said.

I picked up the receiver. "Yeah?"

"This is Jim. How fast can you be ready to travel?"

"Give me twenty-four hours."

"I've already talked to Keith Laub. We have a client who has some people trapped by Saddam in Iraq. We may have to go in and bring 'em out. The pay's good."

"We'd better hurry. I think the army's wanting me too. One more war."

"You can't stay away from them, can you?"

The client's people escaped before the air war began. I found myself first sergeant for a Louisiana Army Reserve MP company.

"This company has the reputation for being the worst company not only in the reserve system but in the entire U.S. Army as well."

My eyes rolled back. The speaker was one of my new platoon sergeants, a black man who resembled the boxer George Foreman, only smaller. I looked around the armory in Hammond, Louisiana. It was a bustle of activity as soldiers—some with little apparent incentive or motivation, a few of whom were crying or trying to hang on to wives and sweethearts and the like, most of whom had the demeanor of convicts—piled up squad tents and boxes of boots and cartons of MOPP gear and other equipment. I had arrived by airplane an hour before; the company was moving out the next morning to its activation site at Fort Polk, Louisiana.

Going to war.

The company commander, Captain Gregory Powell, was a young black policeman from New Orleans. He had gone through college playing in a band. In spite of the fact that he was a cop and had grown up ghetto poor, he wore such an air of naïveté and innocence that I had to resist the urge to sit him on my knee and explain to him the facts of life.

The three lieutenant platoon leaders were shake-and-bakers, ninety-day wonders out of Officer Candidate School. And the platoon sergeants—I watched them with growing apprehension.

This was the leadership for 122 soldiers, 21 of whom were females. "Fuck off," I overheard one of the soldiers tell his platoon sergeant.

I looked away. I took a deep breath. A *few* problems?

The company rated a police escort out of town to its assembly point at Fort Polk. American flags lined the streets. Little kids waved their arms off. People cheered. Yellow ribbons gaily fluttered and banners snapped at their tethers.

At the company's first staff meeting, one of the lieutenants asked innocently, "What about Top here? How do we discipline him if he needs it?"

I could be a hard-looking son of a bitch. I trapped the lieutenant's eye with a gaze that I tried to turn into a laser. The lieutenant's mouth froze wide, in mid-sentence. He fidgeted. My eyes shifted slowly to each of the other two lieutenants, to the captain, while the silence expanded like smoke from a smoke grenade. When I had their undivided attention, I emitted my best Mad Dog growl.

"Listen closely. First of all, no goddamned boot lieutenant is going to discipline me. That had better be clear right now. I work directly with the commander. The commander *commands,* but the first sergeant *runs* the outfit. You lieutenants command your platoons, but your platoon sergeants run the platoons, and they are going to answer to me. You don't do anything without checking either with me or with the commander. Do we all understand now how this company is going to be run?"

"Well, now, uh, Top . . . we didn't mean anything."

I settled back. "Just so it's understood. We have a long way to go. We have three weeks at Fort Polk to uptrain the company, get it range and NBC qualified, resupplied, and skyed up. We're going to war, and we're going as soldiers if I have to drag every ragbag in the outfit through hell and back."

And soon thereafter, on Armed Forces Radio, President Bush proclaimed, "Just two hours ago, allied air forces began an attack on military targets in Iraq and Kuwait. These attacks continue as I speak."

62

From *How to Make War* by James F. Dunnigan:

Another problem of military leaders, especially in peacetime, is their tendency to prefer hardware over less tangible items like training and creating effective troops. Hardware you can see and feel. The troops? The goal is often to have the troops smartly turned out. Never mind that effective armies often look like a bunch of bandits. Perfectly aligned and attired formations of soldiers are easier to perceive than their ability to inflict devastation upon the enemy. . . .

The habits and customs of war are bizarre to a nation at peace. The armed forces must maintain these attitudes blindly between wars. They can do this only by establishing generation after generation of soldiers who will accept certain practices blindly and faithfully. . . .

Armies are [large], expensive to maintain, and there is a great deal of pressure to keep costs down. Army leaders have to rock the boat to weed out officers who may be ineffective in wartime. Making waves is dangerous in any large organization, so the incompetents tend to remain.

63

It was a cold rainy day in January 1991 at Fort Polk when my MPs moved into wooden World War II barracks across the street from a graves registration outfit bound for the Sandbox. Uptraining started with PT at four o'clock the next morning. My days for the next three weeks ended with staff meetings near midnight.

Like the rest of America, the post had caught war fever. Tanks and tracks and other vehicles and big guns all freshly painted desert camouflage were loaded onto railway flatcars for shipment to airheads. Ranges rattled and rumbled with gunfire from daybreak to day's end. Troops marched geared out in bulky anti-NBC MOPP suits and gas masks, preparing against Saddam's expected nuclear, biological, and chemical attacks. They—*we*—looked formidable and impersonal, almost like piggish robots from Future Wars 2020. Excited and self-important young troops in brown desert battle dress uniform rushed about as cocky as the gamecocks I used to raise back in the hills.

"We are going to kick ass!" they shouted. "Yes! Yes!"

Two of my female soldiers came to me: "We're pregnant, Top. We can't go."

I sent them to the hospital infirmary. They weren't pregnant.

"We don't want to go."

"You have no choice."

A third female soldier requested intervention from her congressman; she said she was a single mother and had to stay home to care for her four-year-old daughter.

"Why did you enlist in the reserves in the first place?" I asked her. "You always knew you could be called up."

"I never thought we ever would, though. I wanted the army to help pay for college. I can't go to war. I'm a *woman.*"

It rained; we did PT. The sun blazed down; we marched in MOPP gear. It frosted; our fingers froze on the triggers of M16s and .45 caliber pistols. It grew dark; we practiced security procedures and patrolling.

"If we go to this war," I lectured, "I want to keep you alive. I don't want any of you killed because you weren't ready."

And then, one morning when I reviewed the troops, *my* troops, I realized with an unexpected surge of emotion that I loved this ragtag outfit; it was *my* ragtag outfit. It had shaped up very nicely after having been described as "the worst company in the entire U.S. Army." Devil Troop Brigade, our higher command, complimented Powell and me for having led the company through uptraining and deployment procedures in record time; we were in and out and ready for deployment faster than any other reserve company to date.

Starner, the supply sergeant, said, "Top, we never had anybody to take charge and make us do it before. You worked a miracle. This company's got its pride back."

Before the company skyed up for overseas movement, I held Margie desperately in my arms. She drove to Fort Polk to see me off. In a Leesville motel we made love into the night, then slept naked, spoon-style. I kept waking and drawing her closer; I couldn't get close enough. It was as if I wanted to absorb every beautiful inch of her through the pores of my skin until we were one and I could take her with me. We had to face it. There were no real assurances in these uncertain times that we would ever see each other again.

I had met Margie at a cowboy barn dance in Afton, near Tulsa, about a year after I returned to Oklahoma from being wounded in Honduras. I think I loved her the moment I

246

saw her sitting at a table with friends—the saucy tip of her nose, the smile that reminded me of Elizabeth Montgomery on the old *Bewitched* TV sitcom, the way she filled out her jeans, the thick dark hair. She was French, with all the beauty and qualities I liked best in French women.

I walked over in my cowboy boots and, to her obvious surprise, simply lifted her out of her chair and carried her in my arms onto the dance floor. Since then, for over four years, we had been together almost constantly. I trusted her and loved her totally, like no other woman I had ever met. She was a divorced registered nurse, with four kids, and only thirty-one years old, but I knew, I *knew*, finally, this was the woman with whom I wanted to spend the rest of my life.

"The only way I'll go to another war," I promised her, "is if the United States is involved."

Now we talked of being married when I returned from Desert Storm.

"I *have* to go," I explained. "It's my duty. I took an oath."

Maybe it really wasn't altogether that simple. Maybe it was also the idea of being caught up in a grand adventure, of leading troops into combat. Maybe, even though I was almost fifty years old, I still had a lot of Don Quixote left in me. Saddam was wrong to invade Kuwait; somebody had to kick his ass, clip his windmill.

"It looks like the company's being shipped to Germany first," I explained to Margie. "Everything changes when the ground war starts. If it continues, I'm sure we'll be shipped to the war zone."

We had been watching the bombing of Baghdad on CNN. Much later I found myself in the war zone, but for now I trained my MPs for law-and-order and anti-terrorist missions in Germany.

"You will wait for me?" I asked Margie.

"Of course I will."

"Leaving you is tearing out my heart. I've never loved a woman like I love you. After this war, we'll have the rest of our lives."

I carried photographs of her in my breast pocket. I knew

no bullet would ever penetrate them. They were my luck, my talisman.

"Tell me, Margie," I insisted.

"I love you very much."

"And you will wait?"

"Why shouldn't I? I don't want any man except you."

God help me, I believed her.

Desert Storm was to be another of those major turning points that occur in every man's life. The real war, at least for me, I soon discovered, was not waged in Iraq and Kuwait but instead in the halls of power at Eighth Infantry Division headquarters in Germany, at a WW II Nazi concentration camp called Dachau, and deep inside my own being where sets of beliefs and values had been built and reinforced over more than two decades of military service.

64

A city of huge tents had been erected at Alexandria Air Force Base to accommodate troops on overseas movement. In one of them, the USO set up a long table containing peanut butter and jelly sandwiches and Kool-Aid. My troops were fully combat-armed and laden with MOPP suits and gas masks, as per orders; we were informed that our airplane could be diverted in-flight to Southwest Asia. They sniffed around at the skimpy fare before seeking places to play cards or nap.

Word was passed down that some general had arrived. Ten minutes before his appearance, REMFs—rear echelon motherfuckers—lugged in silver trays laden with ham and cheese, roast beef, hors d'oeuvres, and chips and dips. They uncovered raw cut vegetables and iced down several cases of soft drinks. It looked great, only there wasn't nearly enough to go around.

"Don't eat it yet," the REMFs scolded, fighting back soldiers from the table. "Wait until the general leaves."

The general breezed in with boots spit-shined by his enlisted valet. He wore his wide black belt of command over desert camouflage as if he might really be going into the war zone, which he wasn't. He looked over the spread.

"They feeding you soldiers well?" he boomed.

No one said anything. An aide stepped forward so briskly that someone muttered he looked as if he had a MRE ration stuffed up his ass. "Sir, General, sir. Look what we've done for them."

Some grunt made the sound of lips smacking on bare ass. The aide blushed.

"Yes," the general said, ignoring the smacking lips. He sampled the food to show the troops that if it was good enough for a general it was good enough for them. "Yes. Nothing's too good for our fighting men and women. Carry on."

He breezed on out again. A minute later there wasn't anything remaining on the table except more peanut butter.

In the troop belly of the jet C-141 transport, it was so cold our breathing made balloons. Soldiers piled on top of each other like puppies seeking warmth as the airplane reached altitude. I hunched down inside myself. I could just hear Mad Dog: "I don't *need* this shit."

When the C-141 refueled in New Jersey, I glanced out one of the small round windows and then stared in open amazement. War was a gluttonous consumer. Hundreds of tons, *thousands* of tons, of crated war matériel waiting for transport to Saudi literally overwhelmed the airfield. It was like an urban slum with alleys and streets cutting between tenements of crated supplies prepared to be thrown into the desert maw. No wonder war meant jobs.

A long, cold time later, the plane touched down again. I looked out and saw snow, not sand. Frankfurt, Germany, where my MP company would be attached directly to the Eighth Infantry Division.

Ordinarily a line company of troops fell underneath a battalion. MPs in Germany, however, were odd ducks who fell directly under Division, commanded by a general. The in-place MP company at Rose Barracks caserne in Bad Kreuz-nach, along with my company, came under the control of the general's representative—the division provost marshal, a tall black colonel named Hackett. Hackett's immediate staff consisted of a major who was his deputy provost and a staff sergeant major.

Blinking in the bright dawn reflected off snow, I stepped onto the airfield and looked around. Standing near the nose of the aircraft were two soldiers bundled up in fur-collared parkas and soft winter caps. The officer, a major, was thin with a haughty face like a blade. The other was tall and lanky with a perpetual sneer and a bad complexion, as if he'd had acne or something thirty years ago when he was a kid and had never quite forgiven the world for it. With a brusqueness as cold as the winter's air, they introduced themselves as Major Schuetz and Sergeant Major Coker, Colonel Hackett's staff.

When I thrust out my hand to shake the major's, he looked at me as if I had offered him a dog turd. Proper officers, his expression conveyed, never shook hands with enlisted men, not even first sergeants.

"First Sergeant," he said, and his upper lip lifted in obvious distaste. "I want this ... these *people* unloaded with all their gear in fifteen minutes. Do you think you're capable of handling that?"

He sniffed.

And late that night the fire drill alarm sounded in the barracks an hour after my weary soldiers had crawled into their bunks. They had been traveling straight for over twenty-four hours. They had come from relatively warm Louisiana, and now they found themselves standing, coughing, in the snow of Germany.

"First Sergeant, we didn't plan it that way," Sergeant Major Coker protested.

He grinned. "We really didn't," he insisted.

"Top," Captain Powell muttered aside, "do you get the feeling we're not exactly being met with open arms?"

65

One year back in the hills when times were particularly hard, Dad and Paw had a lapse of pride and signed up to receive what they called "gimpy groceries"—government surplus commodities doled out to the poor—cheese, powdered milk, beans, rice. Once a month county officials opened up the maintenance barn, and the poor flocked in carrying their gunnysacks.

Having to accept charity embarrassed Dad. It embarrassed him further because he had to sign his name and he couldn't read. Dad gave me the gunnysack and ordered me to go get the gimpy groceries. He let me out of the car in town. I wadded the sack up real tight and hid it underneath my arm and padded down side streets and through alleys until I arrived at the barn.

"Come on, come on," the officials shouted. "All of you. Get over there and line up."

"Don't touch me," I protested. "Don't push."

"Kid, just do what you're told if you want the government to help you."

"The government don't have to push me around."

"The government'll do what it damn well pleases."

Finally Mom threw up her hands. "That's enough. We won't be humbled by taking charity. If we let 'em rob us of our spirit so we can get some beans, even if we ain't got a pot to pee in or a window to throw it out of, then we ain't no more than pigs in a pen being slopped."

That always stuck with me. If you got the beans but lost your spirit, your pride, the best part of you, then the beans weren't worth it. At Rose Barracks in Bad Kreuznach, it

251

became immediately apparent that in order to get the beans I was going to have to swallow my pride. The provost marshal's staff—Major Schuetz and his ever-present sidekick, Sergeant Major Coker—sent over a cadre of NCOs from our sister MP company, the Eighth Division War Boars. The staff under Schuetz and Coker took over, thrusting the company commander and the first sergeant helplessly aside. Powell stood and blinked with me as Coker and the Eighth Division MPs planned our training, conducted the PT tests, and issued orders to the platoons.

The Eighth MPs, the War Boars, were commanded by a hefty female captain whom my MPs quickly dubbed the She-Boar. All of her platoon leaders were, by some luck of the draw, only a fraction of her stature; to my MPs they became the Boarlets.

The She-Boar confided to Powell and me that Major Schuetz and the sergeant major had both been passed over for command slots. That was why they were on staff duty. "Their careers are at a dead end," she said. "But don't be fooled. If they want to run the MPs, you have to let them do it. They have the backing of Colonel Hackett and the general. You can't fight that."

We were having coffee in the chow hall.

"It's wrong," I protested. "This is *our* company, the captain's and mine. We're capable of running it, and that's what we're going to do."

The She-Boar seemed to choose her words carefully. In the political world of officers, you always spoke in guarded terms.

"Here under the flag," she said, and it was clearly a warning, "everyone likes you—and no one likes you."

Powell and I exchanged puzzled looks.

"I live by a simple rule," I said. "I abuse no one, and I will not be abused."

For two days I watched with disgust as the tyrant wearing the sergeant major's stripes bullied and cajoled his own Eighth MP NCOs, often shouting at them and berating them in the presence of other enlisted men.

He would not treat my soldiers that way; he would not run my company.

"Sergeant Major Coker," I protested. "Look. *I* run this company. You give us the mission and we'll do it, but don't go over my head to my troops."

He exploded, his bad complexion mottling with the flush of blood to his face. "This is bullshit, First Sergeant!" he shouted. "This is all bullshit!"

"Sergeant Major, I want us to get along. We have to work together. Let's talk...."

"I don't want to talk to you. You'll do what I say."

He stormed off. One of my platoon leaders was a cartoonist. A cartoon appeared on the bulletin board depicting Major Schuetz as a ferret, Sergeant Major Coker as a coyote, Captain Powell as a rooster, and me as a badger. The badger was pissing on the coyote's desk while the ferret had the rooster in its mouth. From then on, Major Schuetz became known as the Ferret, Sergeant Major Coker as the Coyote.

I assembled the War Boar MPs assigned by Coker to my company.

"Listen carefully," I began. "I am first sergeant of this MP company. You are advisers. You *advise* my captain and me. You give no orders to my people without going through me. Is there anything about this you don't understand?"

"But the sergeant major says—"

"I don't give a damn what the sergeant major says. He doesn't run my company."

The sergeants flashed wide grins. "Awww *right!*"

"Nobody's had the guts to stand up to them before now," said one of them. "Everybody's afraid."

That afternoon as I walked across to Eighth Division headquarters, two young soldiers I had never seen before grinned and gave me clenched-fist salutes of victory. Suddenly, everywhere I went it was happening. Clenched fists and grins. From sergeants and privates alike, even from some officers. I had a strange feeling that there was much about the situation at Rose Barracks that I didn't know.

The Ferret and the Coyote drew the battle lines. When Powell and I strode into the PMO's office for the next staff meeting, Major Schuetz pointed for us to go back out the door. *"Nix nein, nix nein,"* he simpered, crossing his skinny legs like a woman and flapping his wrists. "Wait in the hallway. We'll let you know when to come in."

The sergeant major crooked his finger at Sergeant Dodd, the clerk who had shown us in. Glowering, he led the sergeant into another room.

When Dodd escaped, his face resembled chalk. He looked away from Powell and me and hurried down the hallway. I followed. Dodd stepped around a corner.

"What happened in there, Dodd?"

"Sergeant major chewed my ass out for not leaving you and Captain Powell waiting in the hallway. You don't know that man, Top. He's mean if you get on his bad side—and you're on his bad side. I overheard him and the major saying they were going to get you and Captain Powell relieved of command. They hate reservists. They'd make my life miserable if they even thought I was talking to you."

From up the hallway I heard the Coyote howling: "Dodd? Dodd?"

"You're being paged," I said, grinning.

"Top, please stay around the corner here so he doesn't see you until I'm gone. Please? Everybody on post respects you, but that man could destroy me. All I'm trying to do is get my twenty in."

I looked at him, surprised. "You actually hate the army," I said. "Dodd, you've lost the best part of yourself, son, trying to get the beans."

He frowned, then hurried off meekly, like a dog responding to its master's call.

At the staff meeting, the Coyote was still angry. "Sir," he said to Colonel Hackett as soon as everyone was seated. "I wish you'd make it clear to First Sergeant Sasser that he's to do what I tell him."

"Wait a minute," I interrupted. "My problem with him is his going directly to my people over the heads of the commander and myself—"

"I'm talking!" the Coyote snapped.

"That's your problem. You talk, but you don't listen."

The She-Boar tapped my leg frantically underneath the table, urging me to shut up. Powell stared grimly at his hands.

"I demand respect for my rank," Sergeant Major Coker shrieked.

"I demand the same respect for myself and my soldiers."

"Hold it. Hold it," Colonel Hackett interceded. "You two get together afterward and settle this. But, Sergeant Major, First Sergeant Sasser *is* the first sergeant. You go through him from now on for anything you need from the company."

The Coyote glared armed missiles. The Ferret pursed his thin lips, crossed his skinny legs, limp-wristed his hands across his knees. He shook his head and rolled his eyes.

"Nix nein, nix nein," he simpered, looking at me as if I might have been something that stuck to his shoes.

God damn, Sasser, I thought. You're making wonderful enemies.

A high-ranking division staff officer telephoned that he wanted to see me in private. We met in a basement office where we wouldn't be noticed. The officer looked me over carefully. Then he smiled suddenly and extended his hand.

"You're going to need an ally," he said. "It's all over post that you don't take shit from anyone, no matter what his rank. The word's out that you're an undercover, a head hunter assigned to investigate corruption. You haven't even seen past the surface of it yet. Now, I want to warn you as a friend: this place is political like nothing you've ever seen. They'll get you now. One way or another, they'll get you. Watch your back at all times."

I had been in Germany for three days. The ground war in Iraq had not yet begun, but the troops were lining up for the ground war at Rose Barracks.

66

Snow fell in the vineyard on the other side of the security fence that enclosed the hospital caserne. Wearing BDUs, field jacket, and gloves, venturing out tentatively into the morning darkness like a groundhog making a mistake about the arrival of spring, I emerged from the hospital basement where I lived with Starner my supply sergeant and my platoon sergeants. I lifted my face to catch the snowflakes melting on it.

The hospital, its floors stacked five high, covered about ten acres. Light shining from some of the windows cast bright squares on the fallen snow. I dreaded the start of the ground war in Iraq. The hospital was preparing to receive thousands of casualties—young men without limbs, men burned and maimed and ripped and shredded by the horrible machines and explosives of modern warfare.

In Vietnam I had visited a battalion aid station. Sometimes, even these years later, I awoke smelling decayed blood and flesh.

"I was in Vietnam for three weeks," a veteran friend once told me. "I was hit. I've been in this wheelchair since then. I've been without legs in this wheelchair for twenty-two years, four months, two weeks, three days, nine hours, and ... thirty-one minutes."

When he came home without legs, his fiancée broke their engagement and married a teacher with a deferment and a whole body.

The hospital lay a mile away from Rose Barracks.

"I'll get transportation for you and your sergeants and officers," the Coyote had promised me. The bachelor officers' quarters where Powell and the platoon leaders lived was just around the corner from the hospital. I never saw a vehicle until I wrangled a van myself from the motor pool.

"It's against army regulations to keep the van and use it for personal transportation," the sergeant major warned.

"What do we—the company commander and the first sergeant—have to do? Walk everywhere?"

He shrugged.

One afternoon the Coyote and the Ferret caught me parking the van to let my sergeants and officers do their grocery shopping at the commissary.

"I told you it's against regulations to use a government vehicle like this," Sergeant Major Coker snapped.

"What would you suggest?" I demanded in exasperation. "You've billeted the company leadership a mile away from the rest of the company and away from the commissary, the post exchange, the movies, the chow hall—everything."

"Nix nein, nix nein," chimed in Major Schuetz, wagging a skinny finger. *"Nix nein* on government transportation."

Although as a kid I had roamed the Ozarks and the Cooksons, sleeping underneath the stars with no one for company except a few hounds, I had never felt so completely alone as now. I wasn't even sure I could trust Captain Powell. I thought him a good man but perhaps not strong. He was often eccentric.

One of his favorite habits was to sit in a stall of the enlisted men's latrine so he could eavesdrop on what the soldiers were saying about him. "Top, we have to keep our finger on the pulse—i.e., *listen* to them talking."

That was a part of Powell's speech pattern—"i.e.," generally used inappropriately.

"But in the *latrine?*"

One afternoon he fell asleep on the throne. The next day there was a sign on the toilet stall door: "Cap'n Powell slept here."

Like most junior officers, Powell seemed intimidated by all the heavy brass at division headquarters. The Ferret drew him aside for lectures.

"Captain Powell, *you* are the commander, not your first

sergeant. *Nix nein, nix nein.* The first sergeant is *enlisted.* You must take charge of that company. Understand, Captain Powell? I've overheard division staff talking about it."

"Top, I have other considerations to think about," Powell reasoned. "I'm an officer. They can ruin my career—i.e., just like that." He snapped his fingers. "If they relieve me of command, they'll put Major Schuetz in command. That's just what he wants. He'll get rid of you, too. They'll really screw with the company then."

"They're trying to divide and conquer," I replied. "As long as I'm first sergeant, I'll *be* first sergeant."

I watched the officers at division headquarters. I had always been one of the grunts, with a grunt's perspective until now, when for the first time I was obtaining a raw insider's look at the higher mechanics of military power. I started calling the Eighth Division headquarters building "the Castle." It reminded me of a king's court, with all the squires and earls and dukes jockeying for favor in the king's eyes and trying to knock everyone else out of favor. Everyone fawned over the next higher rank and stepped on the lower.

The high-ranking staff officer, my secret ally at division headquarters whom I mentally referred to as Deep Throat, said, "The military with its rigid structure is despotic by nature and necessity. It distrusts democracy where the little people have a say in how they're governed. The military elite looks upon you as defying everything they stand for. You're upsetting the equilibrium by not playing all their little games. That's unforgivable. It's especially unforgivable from an enlisted man. You've got guts, something sorely lacking at staff level, and they're jealous."

"Maybe I'm not real smart. I just do what I think is right."

Deep Throat looked at me. *"They* don't," he said.

Each day introduced a different battle in a continuing war. I almost preferred the heated rattle of small arms fire over the colder silence of psychological warfare and its little skirmishes of deceit and maneuver. Although not quite sure of the rules of engagement, I found myself a quick study.

When the Ferret scheduled the post chaplain, a colonel,

to speak to my company on Friday morning, my platoon sergeants came to me. "Top, if our people aren't at Finance on Friday morning to get advance pay, some of them won't have money to eat on until Monday."

I rang the Coyote. He spluttered, "First Sergeant, we don't ask a colonel to change his schedule for you. You have your company in that theater Friday morning. Understand?"

I dialed the chaplain and explained things to him. "First Sergeant, you're thinking about your soldiers when you ask me to change my schedule. The soldiers are the most important part of the army. Many of us forget that these days. Of course I'll change my schedule. Friday afternoon is fine."

That sent Sergeant Major Coker into a rage. "First sergeant, you went over my head!"

"What my people need comes first."

The chaplain was a tall black man with gray hair. He nodded formally at the staff brass when he arrived at the theater. Then he spotted me. He grinned and marched directly to me, hand outstretched.

"First Sergeant," he said later, "you and I are going to be friends."

My company went on the road, patrolling Bad Kreuznach, Mainz, and Baumholder as military policemen. Some of them worked the Castle door or the caserne gates. From PMO headquarters, Sergeant Dodd kept me informed of staff activities. Every time the Ferret and the Coyote left their offices, Dodd grabbed his telephone.

"Top, Code Red. They're on their way."

Every day it was: "First Sergeant, that man you got on the door. Get him off. He needs a haircut."

Every day. The Coyote: "First Sergeant, your Sergeant Triguero is at it again."

"Yes?"

"He's issuing parking tickets to all the cars at division headquarters. He gave the division sergeant major a ticket. He gave the commanding *general's* car a ticket."

"Let me see if I understand you correctly, Sergeant Major. If a lowly enlisted man parks his car in a No Parking zone, he deserves a ticket? But my MPs are to make an exception for the higher ranks?"

"It's just not *done*. You don't give the *general* a parking ticket."

"My MPs do if his car is in violation."

"I want something done with Triguero."

"I'll write him a letter of commendation for being diligent on the job."

The phone slammed in my ear.

The Ferret called Powell. Powell came into the orderly room. "The Ferret called to say he's disapproving Triguero's request to remain on active duty after Desert Storm."

Every day.

In the rarefied air of the upper military structure, staff and general officers were accustomed to blind obedience from underlings. Maybe the air up there did something to their judgment. If it did, it was a common contagion. Every one above major seemed to be afflicted with the disease.

Okay, it was part of my job to place an MP shift to guarding the general's house and family when terrorists made anonymous telephone calls threatening him. I thought little of alerting a squad to surround the officers' club, the Nahe, to protect a women's function hosted by the general's wife. But I blinked in disbelief when I learned that low-ranking enlisted men in Heidelberg were assigned twenty-four-hour duty guarding a *tree*. Night and day, standing in rain and snow, guarding an ash—the general's tree—planted to commemorate some forgotten military event. Terrorists had threatened to cut it down.

"The tree is extremely important to the general," I was informed.

Okay. A tree. But then there was the one general who parked his staff car outside his headquarters door and assigned a sergeant to make sure everyone saluted it. Any enlisted man who failed to salute the general's wife inside the car, or his poodle, or the unoccupied car itself was dragged to his commanding officer and brought up on charges.

The general went so far as to order a star painted on his bus. An MP rode on the bus. The bus drove about post until someone failed to salute the star. The MP jumped off and placed the offender under arrest. At the end of the day, and even sometimes in the middle of the night, the general broke out the offender's entire unit and held the soldiers to in-rank attention while he lectured them on the protocol of saluting officers, especially general officers—and apparently anything the general touched.

Division in Germany held a change-of-command ceremony on the green in front of the Castle. The division band played stirring marches while bored soldiers stood at attention and parade rest. Colonels and generals vying for the limelight delivered windbag speeches to each other and to the bored soldiers.

My MPs who worked the night shift were sleeping in their barracks on the other side of the green. The martial music awoke them. Three of them in T-shirts and shorts staggered sleepily to their third-floor window to see what was going on.

Immediately after the ceremony ended, my MP stationed at the headquarters door telephoned. "Heads up, Top. I just got the word. The general's wife saw some of our guys in their T-shirts looking out the window. The general's pissed off."

The Ferret summoned Captain Powell to his office. Powell grabbed his hat and flew toward the door.

"You look awfully pale for a black man," I said.

"Our MPs have really done it this time."

Powell looked grim when he returned. "I don't have much ass left—i.e., it's chewed down to the bone. The Ferret says we're to punish them."

"For looking out the window of their own house in the middle of the day? That's no violation of any regulation that I know of."

"They embarrassed the general's wife. We have to punish them."

I dug in.

"Captain, we are not going to punish our guys. Either you

261

tell that to those cocksuckers in the Castle—or I will. Our guys have done nothing to be punished for."

"Top, see, what we can do is, i.e., we can. *tell* them we've punished them, but we don't really have to do it."

"Captain Powell, no. No."

The Coyote called me every day for a week. "The general wants them punished."

"No."

Finally I learned that Colonel Hackett had supposedly told the general that the offenders who embarrassed his wife had been severely dealt with.

As Mad Dog or Call would have said: Fucked up.

In the German winter before the spring came, I closed my eyes outside the hospital basement where I lived and let the snowflakes touch my cheeks like gentle kisses. If I were at home, Margie and I would probably be in Colorado skiing. We went every year. We would ski hard during the day, and then, when the night came, we would hibernate to the little log cabin in South Fork, strip, and hold each other while snow piled high around the eaves and whispered at the frozen windows.

I missed her. It was like a part of me was missing.

"I live for your letters," I wrote her. "A first sergeant is in the middle; he can have no friends."

Starner came out of the basement into the snowfall. "Morning, Top. It gets lonely at the top, doesn't it?"

The company clerk collected mail and distributed it. I looked for Margie's handwriting.

"Sorry, Top."

Every day: "Sorry, Top."

At Easter I received a card. It held a color photo inside of Margie sitting on the lap of a great pink Easter Bunny. "Bad news," she had written jokingly underneath the Easter greeting. "I got caught fooling around with the Easter Bunny."

I laughed at her joke. She was so cute.

Maybe I shouldn't have laughed.

When spring came and the cherry trees blossomed along

the river that ran through Bad Münster in the valley below, Starner and I took long walks along the river and then up into the little German town for dinner. There was also a trail that rose steeply into the mountains east of town. Jogging it, I sometimes came upon wild boar and squirrels with tufted ears and fallow deer. The trail snaked high through forest for several miles and ended at an old castle ruin from the thirteenth century. I sat on the crumbling walls alone and watched the valley turn red from sunset.

It was still winter, though, when the first American died in the air war. He was a thirty-three-year-old pilot who left behind a three-year-old daughter and a one-year-old son. Then other people died down there in the sand. But here, at Rose Barracks, the hijinks continued.

"Trust no one while you're here," Deep Throat warned. "Don't even trust me."

It was going to be a long war.

67

Running a company as first sergeant was difficult enough under the best circumstances; dealing with the Ferret and the Coyote compounded problems. They smacked their lips and rubbed their hands with glee when my female MPs started killing the rabbit. They had a hot issue over which I had little control, but at the same time one that made Powell and me look bad.

"First Sergeant, how many women in your company are pregnant this week?" Sergeant Major Coker smirked. "What are you doing about it?"

What could I do about it? Issue corks instead of condoms?

"We could use a cork," admitted one of my platoon sergeants. "Specialist Nader has gone through every swinging jock in the Second Platoon and is starting all over again. I don't have soldiers. I have a pack of dogs in heat, and they're all starting to fight over the bitch."

He grinned. I groaned.

"The army don't have camp followers anymore," he concluded. "We don't need 'em. We recruit 'em and bring 'em with us."

Ten of my twenty-one females got pregnant within the first six months. Rumors about who was or wasn't sleeping with whom, where, and how many times reminded me of some kind of bizarre juxtaposition of *M*A*S*H* and *The Love Boat.*

I had been to wars, spent much of my military life as a tough sergeant in combat outfits. I had shot it out with Central American guerrillas, parachuted out of airplanes and crashed in them, gone to Vietnam twice. I'd been wounded in combat. Had it all come down to this—refereeing a bunch of women in uniform, half of whom were pregnant?

Old sergeants like me used to stand ramrod straight up in front of a formation and bellow, "All right, men. Sound off like you got a pair."

Not anymore. It took bigger balls to face the strong political lobby that kept pushing to put women in foxholes than it did to stand up before an enemy. On each officer's and NCO's fitness and evaluation report was a block to be marked on whether or not he supported equal opportunity. The career of any soldier who did not at least pay lip service to women's rights in the military, including the right to accompany men into combat, received the kiss of death. Since lifers lived by their fitness and evaluation reports, they routinely lied about the activities of women or exaggerated their feats. It was political correctness enforced—and to hell with any truth.

"In Saudi Arabia," said Randy Pruitt, a reporter for *Stars & Stripes,* "it's understood that any journalist who releases anything negative or derogatory about military females will be blackballed."

A female soldier named Cindi was asked in a network

news interview: "And what's your job? What are you doing over here?"

"I'm the camp whore," the woman shot back with more honesty perhaps than the American public was deemed prepared to accept. The footage was censored.

Elsewhere in Saudi, the army quickly squelched a report about a woman NCO who earned $10,000 in just a few weeks engaging in the world's oldest profession. Army investigators quietly shipped her home.

A few cable stations did run an edited piece about the "Love Boat," a navy ship in the Gulf that had to set sail for home port because so many of its female crew members apparently suffered from a combination of morning sickness and seasickness.

When the Desert Storm call-up began, the press exploded with headlines about women and photos of cute rifle-toting blondes from Texas and buxom warrior brunettes from California. "Nanny Wears Combat Boots," the headline blazed. "Papa Stays Home with Junior While Mommy Defends the Nation." Women, who made up less than 10 percent of forces called up for the Gulf War, received 60 percent of the news coverage. You would have thought they were going to fight the whole war themselves.

"It fucking makes me nauseous," grumbled Llave, who had been called up to train troops on heavy weapons at Fort Hood, Texas.

But what else could you say?

At Rose Barracks in Germany, Supply Sergeant Starner lugged in three Hefty bags of condoms and dumped them on my orderly room floor. They were now standard issue in the army. On patrols in the jungles, we had stretched rubbers over M16 muzzles to keep out rain, mud, and dust. But even if my MP company was sent to the Sandbox, we wouldn't be doing *that* much patrolling.

"The company that screws together stays together, First Sergeant," Starner quipped. "Make sure you tell our soldiers to keep fornication within the company. No use raising the morale of some other outfit."

It quickly became apparent that my MPs would be burning far more rubber than gunpowder. With men and women billeted in adjacent rooms on the same floor, the action started immediately.

"They're up there fucking like minks!" my platoon sergeants exclaimed.

Even my female NCOs were doing it. A platoon sergeant caught Sergeant Samuels in the hallway with two of her male subordinates. One had his palm thrust down between her legs while the other had both hands up underneath her battle dress uniform, cupping her breasts.

"Goddammit," I fumed. "These are men she might have to lead in combat. The only place she can lead them now is to the nearest little Arab tent with a bed in it."

I dropped my head into waiting hands. The army accepted there was nothing you could really do about pregnancies except issue rubbers and maternity battle dress. Pregnant women waddled about every post garbed out in combat boots and maternity camouflage. Charlie Signal Company on the floor below my MPs had a female six feet tall who wore size ten boots. She was so pregnant she needed help to get out of her chair at the chow hall.

"How'd that beast ever get pregnant?" Starner wondered. "It makes you believe in the virgin birth."

"You can't discriminate against them even if they get pregnant," the Coyote said with his built-in smirk. "But I want it stopped."

How could you run an army when your soldiers kept turning up pregnant and couldn't work or fight?

Upstairs in the barracks I sat on the edge of the bed while Specialist Norwood gripped my hand and sobbed softly, waiting for an ambulance. She was having a miscarriage. Norwood, an enlisted woman, had become pregnant by one of my platoon lieutenants. I stared at the wall, a little confused by it all. The feminization of the American military. A kinder, gentler military. Tough combat sergeants settling female spats and handling miscarriages.

Article 134 of the Uniform Code of Military Justice stated that the maximum penalty for fraternization between enlisted and officer included a punitive discharge and two years' confinement.

"We're going to be married, Top," the lieutenant protested.

"L.T., goddammit, I told you. I *told* you ... not in the army you're not. Couldn't you have just waited until we were out of here?"

"We're in love. We may be here in Germany, or in Saudi or someplace, for another year."

A miscarriage was something that couldn't be hidden from the Castle. Colonel Hackett, the provost, assigned the fraternization investigation to the Ferret.

"He is stupid," Hackett said of the lieutenant. The implication was clear: the rest of us were stupid too. "Captain Powell, can't you control your officers? Your company cannot leave Germany until every legal problem is settled."

The Ferret snickered and crossed his legs. "Your company could be here for *years.*"

68

Deep Throat seemed to think I was CID undercover investigating corruption. I did nothing either to encourage or to discourage the misconception. It played some minor part, I believed, in keeping the Ferret and the Coyote at bay.

"Those two are very small fry when you consider everything else," Deep Throat said.

He said that cover-ups, bribery, abuse of power, and a general air of debauchery had created an atmosphere of decay at Eighth Infantry Division flag headquarters. Officers casually terrorized soldiers, who were conditioned to passively accept tyranny. Everyone at staff, he said, knew how the chief of staff, a full-bird colonel and a heavy drinker, had chased a sergeant through headquarters shouting obscenities at him, of how the same colonel had arrived on post drunk and had ripped the door off the guard shack in a rage. The gate guard was warned to keep his mouth shut after the staff duty officer hustled the colonel off-post and back to his quarters.

"Everything has a double standard—one for the enlisted and lower-ranking officers, another for the staff officers," Deep Throat said. "The corruption starts at the top and bleeds down. It's common knowledge that some officers' wives prostitute out of the downtown bars and that certain officers are involved in graft and shakedowns. Other military people are making a lot of money dealing drugs. Drugs are cheap and easy to get from the Turkish section of the city."

He had details, he said. Names. Places. It would blow the lid off U.S. Army commands in Europe.

"Then why haven't you gone higher up with all this?" I asked.

"This is *division* headquarters!" he exclaimed. "This is a general. How much higher could I go?"

"Go to V Corps."

"First Sergeant, this kind of atmosphere is prevalent in all high-ranking headquarters. Do you think it would really do any good? My own head would roll. I'd be shipped out of here tomorrow. Everything is pure politics among officers at division level and higher. It's worse here than it is in Congress. They try to bring each other down in internal fighting, but no one dares squeal on anyone else because no one's ass is clean. See what I mean?"

"Why are you telling me all this?"

Deep Throat shook his head, as though to clear it. "Because," he continued, "you're showing you're not afraid to fight the system."

A military magazine called *The Pathfinder* had run an article about me, the journalist who volunteered, the week after I arrived in Germany. *Stars & Stripes* would soon publish a full-page feature on the first sergeant who published books.

"I don't think you realize how much they fear you," Deep Throat said. "Rather, how much they fear what you are—a journalist. You have the power to expose, and exposure is deadly to those who have something to hide."

Yeah?

I remembered a quote from Cervantes: "The lance has never blunted the pen, nor the pen the lance."

I was a grunt, a common soldier. True, I had been a homicide detective, and I saw myself as a middling reporter and journalist. But I wrote about the common people—grunts at war, cops in the streets, the little people, the ordinary. Deep Throat was asking for investigative reporting of institutionalized corruption. I was a soldier in uniform, not an officer, and not even a journalist as long as I wore army green. I had little access to the upper ranks. One wrong step on my part and army brass would be down on me like a pile of cow shit splatting on a flat rock.

The Coyote and the Ferret were simply looking for an excuse.

"Look at this," Deep Throat said one morning, slapping a copy of *Stars & Stripes* down on the desk in front of me.

The story had already hit the rumor mills.

A young War Boar MP on patrol had come upon a vehicle with an expired license plate parked in the officers' housing section. Standard operating procedure called for the MP to confiscate the plate. The MP was doing just that when Colonel Hackett, the division provost and highest-ranking law enforcement officer in the division, stormed angrily from his quarters and snatched the license plate out of the MP's hands.

"Do you know who I am?" he demanded.

The MP was about twenty years old. He apparently did not understand the politics of rank and privilege. He went to his higher headquarters, seeking backing. When he failed to find it there, he turned to the press.

"Give this a little while to work out," Deep Throat said to me. "This is only a petty example of the hijinks in court.

Can you guess who's going to end up on the short end of this stick?"

"Would you say the MP?"

"They're after you too, First Sergeant. You'd better learn how to cover your own ass."

Not long after that, while the license plate incident was still working itself out, one of my own young MPs came to me nervously lighting one cigarette off the butt of another.

"Top, what am I going to do?"

"Was it a violation?" I asked.

"Yes, but ... but he's the chief of staff."

"Tell me about it."

"I was on routine patrol," he said, automatically lapsing into policese, "when I observed a yellow Mercedes with a USAREUR license plate pull into an unlighted area off of Bolheim Strasse and stop. I went around the block. When I came back, I observed the same vehicle still parked with the headlights off. I pulled up in front of the vehicle. I observed one white male sitting upright in the driver's seat. As I pulled up, a white female suddenly sat up, like she had had her face in his lap."

I laughed. "He was getting a blow job in an alley? Like a common enlisted man?"

"That was what was happening, Top. I proceeded to call in the vehicle description and plate number to the MP station. The driver attempted to leave, but I blocked him with my vehicle. The desk sergeant informed me that the Mercedes was registered to the chief of staff. I confirmed the colonel's identity and told him politely that it was unlawful to occupy a USAREUR-plated vehicle in an unlighted area. He said he was unaware of this and that he would move."

"Make me a detailed report," I said.

I kept laughing. I sent the colonel a copy of the report and kept the original. In addition to being the scourge of the ordinary enlisted men, the chief of staff also had a reputation for tearing up officers and senior enlisted during periodical briefings.

"Humma, humma," he would say, impatient. "Get on

with it. Fuck, get this goddamned shit on. What are you, an idiot?"

During my next briefing, he asked two or three polite questions about my company. Then I sat down.

Deep Throat winked slyly at me from the briefing room. "You're learning how to play hardball, First Sergeant," he said, grinning.

69

One afternoon a sergeant from the other MP company crossed the parking lot to intercept me. He made our meeting seem to occur by chance. "First Sergeant, can we meet tonight? It's important."

He named a bar that most soldiers avoided because of the Turks. It was near a small city park in Bad Kreuznach that had been taken over by dope dealers and users. Turks had attacked a GI there with knives and carved him up pretty good.

I agreed to rendezvous. The MP worked plainclothes investigations and undercover narcotics. I had enough problems simply taking care of my own company and protecting it from the Coyote, but the tone of the MP's voice and the way his eyes narrowed and shifted intrigued me. I could never resist the promise of a new windmill.

"Top, be careful going anywhere alone," Deep Throat cautioned. "I don't want to alarm you, but try to keep someone with you at all times."

I blinked. The man appeared to be dead serious.

"They may think you know a lot more than you actually do," he said.

After pretending to retire to my quarters at the hospital

for the night, I called a cab and let no one know when I was leaving or where I was going. The taxi let me off at the Bahnhof, the train station. I slipped down side streets and doubled back on my trail to make sure I wasn't followed. The streets lay dark. My footfalls echoed.

Now who was paranoid?

It was the middle of the week, and the bar near the Turkish slums was almost unoccupied. In civilian clothing, the MP and I took our beers to a corner table. It began to rain against the window. I sat with my back to the wall, looking out. An old habit from when I was a cop.

"Working undercover like I have, you come up with a lot of shit," the MP opened. He shifted in his chair to get more comfortable with the .45 automatic carried in his belt underneath his shirt. "But I think you're already getting a pretty good idea of how things work here. Top, I've got too close to something or somebody. Somebody big."

Why couldn't I have been sent straight to Saudi and the war? I knew how to fight that kind of war.

"This is how it works," the MP continued. "If an enlisted man gets hot and starts posing a threat, he's shipped out of Europe to keep him quiet. They call it a 'career move.' Take the kid who tried to confiscate the PMO's expired license plate. They're transferring him. He's an example to any other enlisted man who thinks he can buck the system. But before they transfer him, they're going to court-martial him for stealing a pair of binoculars from the commanding general's staff car."

"Did he do it?"

The MP shrugged. "I don't know. Maybe. Maybe not. But doesn't it seem strange that he's being court-martialed for it so soon after his confrontation with the provost?"

Mad Dog had a word for such things: "Fucked up."

"I've filed two complaints with the inspector general, and I've asked for a congressional investigation of the PMO and the Eighth Division army community," my companion went on. "What do I get because of it? I'm going to be transferred. A simple and effective way to keep enlisted men in their place is to court-martial them or transfer them."

We sipped beer. We watched rain on the dark window crawling like worms in a rotted carcass. I felt as if the worms were crawling on me.

"Top, I've learned that V Corps is sending down its own provost marshal and CID team to conduct an investigation. I'm going to be called to give a statement. Colonel Hackett's going to be called, I hear, as well as the chief of staff, the deputy provost marshals in the various communities, and of course Major Schuetz and Sergeant Major Coker. But I can tell you now, before they even get here, that a few enlisted men will get screwed but the investigation won't even touch captains or above. That's the way things are always handled. Screw the enlisted; cover up for the officers and their precious careers."

I kept staring out the window into the streets black from a cold drizzle. An MP van cruised by. I recognized one of my MPs at the wheel. How had I gotten mixed up in the middle of all this? What could I do about it?

"Top, I can give you names, dates, times, locations—drug deals, prostitution rings, misappropriation of government funds. Corruption. The goddamn system is rotting out from underneath us—in politics, in the military. Our fucking *system!*"

He thrust his body across the table toward me, jarring our beers and sloshing them. His eyes burned.

"I tried through the IG. I tried through Congress. What happens? They get rid of the squeaking hinge. Now I'm coming to you. *Somebody* has to do something. I understand there's not a lot you can do right now. But later you can. You can write about it. Let everybody know what's happening before it's too late."

" 'Evil loves the darkness and hates the light,' " I murmured.

"Yes. *Yes.* Will you do it?"

We probed each other's eyes across the table. This, I thought, was a young man of courage and idealism. I raised my glass. We clinked glasses.

70

I contacted Randy Pruitt, my reporter friend with *Stars & Stripes*. Although *Stars & Stripes* received its funding from the Department of Defense, or some branch of the U.S. government, it was civilian-run and had some autonomy.

"We can't step on too many big toes" was how Pruitt explained it, "but we can step on them around the edges."

"I've got a real fight going on down here, Randy. I'm in a corner, partner. There's some things I want the press to know. Just in case."

"Just in case what?"

"I don't know if I'm paranoid or what."

"How about lunch? Today?"

Pruitt used his press pass to get through security at Rose Barracks. I met him. Across the street from the gate a handful of German antiwar protesters with signs and paint-whitened faces marched silently back and forth. Twice so far the Ferret and the Coyote had alerted my MPs against the protesters. MPs in helmets and battle gear stood at the barricades and watched.

"They may charge the barricades," the Coyote had warned.

I scoffed. "All ten of them?"

Pruitt's was a welcome friendly face. A man I knew I could trust. We had been friends for at least ten years, since he reported for the Tulsa *World* and even before. Our friendship dated back to my marriage with Kathy. He had the journalist's quick, inquiring wit, the natural skeptic's irreverent distrust of government and power, and he had this wonderful bush of unruly steel-gray hair and a full beard also flecked with gray. The sight of him was a welcome change. I had had enough of uniformity, of that particular military mind-set which itself bore the stern and unforgiving constraints of a GI haircut. High and tight with no room to grow.

"This whole place is crazy, Randy. It's right out of a loony bin, out of *Mad* magazine."

"Let's get off-post so we can talk."

Pruitt and his wife, Bernadette, also a journalist, lived in a small German community near Frankfurt. I had met Bernadette a few years before, when she interviewed me for a news article about my journalist-in-space selection. The Pruitts' apartment was small and decorated with Persian rugs and other exotic works of art. They were connoisseurs of wine. We sipped wine, went out for schnitzel, and then walked the quiet, narrow streets of the German village.

"Randy, for the first time in my life I'm actually ashamed of being a part of the U.S. military."

I told him everything. About Deep Throat, the warnings, the MP in the bar, my continuing struggle with the provost marshal's staff, the rumored V Corps investigation.

Pruitt, it turned out, was having his own struggle with the military—over freedom of the press. During Vietnam, the press had received free run, with the result that it brought the full bloody impact of the war into American homes nightly. General Schwarzkopf and the other military leaders in the Gulf were determined that that wouldn't happen with *their* war. Americans would receive the story the military wanted them to receive.

Pruitt had just returned from assignment in the Gulf.

It was an odd war.

U.S. B-52 Stratofortresses from Saudi Arabia flew daily missions against Saddam's Republican Guard forces, which were dug in along the Iraq-Kuwait border. A single B-52 could deliver 60,000 pounds of bombs. It was like Nixon's B-52 carpet-bombing of Vietnam a generation before. The earth trembled for miles around after a run. Clouds of dust rolled across the horizon. Desert winds picked up the dust and whipped it against troop tent cities studded all over Saudi.

Iraqi Scud missiles streaked across the skies toward Riyadh in Saudi, and they streaked against Israel, even though Israel remained neutral. U.S. Patriot missiles streaked back, bringing down most of the Scuds before they struck targets.

A few miles outside Riyadh, an American platoon leader and one of his squad leaders came upon an ailing camel lying in a ditch next to the road. The squad leader was a country boy from Georgia who knew livestock. He got out of the jeep and started to put the camel out of its misery.

The lieutenant grabbed his arm. "We'd better not. The ragheads value camels. It could cause an incident."

The lieutenant made his report. Captains and then majors and finally colonels drove out to look at the sick camel. While General "Stormin' Norman" Schwarzkopf and his staff planned for the coming ground war, while President Bush and Saddam bumped verbal heads, while hospitals and graves units prepared for the terrible onslaught of expected dead and wounded, a staff of high-ranking officers pondered the fate of an ill camel lying in a ditch.

After a week of debate, the officers decided they should shoot the camel. A colonel gallantly led a little convoy of officers and NCOs to the site. The colonel got out to oversee the proper disposal of the animal. A captain volunteer drew his 9mm pistol.

The camel suddenly lifted its head and looked around. Then it got up and slowly lumbered off into the desert. The speechless combat soldiers watched.

"No one will say a word of this to the press," the colonel said, frowning and looking around.

It was an odd war.

One of the largest single units in the Gulf came under the title of Public Information. Each evening representatives of the various networks, wires, and news publications submitted their requests to military Public Information on what they would like to see or whom they wanted to interview. The next morning, military PIOs went down the list approving and disapproving. Journalists with approved requests were escorted in small groups on their missions.

"You were briefed on which questions you could ask and which you could not," Pruitt said. "They picked the people you could talk to; those people were carefully selected and briefed on what they could say before you ever got there. They wouldn't allow you to walk through a camp talking to soldiers at will."

In Riyadh, a colonel of the type whose head shrunk and whose neck thickened when he put on a uniform stood before a group of newsmen waiting placidly for their interview requests to be approved.

"We want the war to be a positive experience for the folks back home," he announced. "This is a good war, a just war. The people don't need to see our young people maimed and hurting. They don't want to hear the bitchers and complainers. They want heroes, and we're here to show them heroes, because that's what our young men and women are—heroes. You people have a duty to all Americans to portray this war accurately as a struggle of good against evil."

"The press surrendered and rolled over like beaten curs," Pruitt said. "We accepted the rigid controls put on us by the White House and the Pentagon. There wasn't much else we could do. If you tried to go outside the limits imposed by the military PIOs, you were blackballed and left sitting in Riyadh or wherever. The other newsmen were escorted out, but if you were blackballed you sat behind on your butt without a chance in hell of getting a story."

"You can rot here as far as we're concerned," a PIO snarled at a journalist who attempted to circumvent military controls. "You'll never talk to one of our soldiers. You can spend the war right here in this tent."

Pruitt and I talked late into the German night. We sipped more wine and looked at each other across his dining room table.

"Dwight Eisenhower once said that an informed public is necessary to win wars," Pruitt said. "Maybe that was true during the Second World War when the cause was just—if there can ever be a just cause for the annihilation of millions of people. But since then the military and the press have been at each other's throats. War is less acceptable when people see behind the propaganda. I can understand how you might be viewed as a threat. You're in the military, and at the same time you're a writer. Those illusions that make men go to war? The illusions you talk about?"

"I have few illusions left."

"That's why you're so dangerous."

71

I visited Dachau in Germany with my company supply sergeant, Starner. A huge mocking inscription over the concentration camp had greeted arriving prisoners:

> There is one road to freedom.
> Its milestones are:
> Obedience—diligence—honesty—
> Order—cleanliness—temperance—
> Truthfulness—sacrifice and love
> Of one's country.

i looked at Starner. "Words are powerful things," I said. "How could the Nazis say that and then burn people in the next building?"

Paw might have had an answer. From him I learned to question everything, never to accept anything on face value.

"If the guvment tells you something, anything at all," he had said, "look it in the mouth like you'd look a cheap horse in the mouth. 'Cause if it ain't an outright lie, then it's slanted so that you can't tell it from an outright lie.

That's politicians and that's lawyers, and they put the green scum on good ponds."

Even as a kid I wanted to know *why* people did the things they did. I was always searching behind the words and deeds for motives. "Mom?" I asked once after a neighbor in the hills caught his wife in a motel with another man and shot them both. "Why did he do it? Now she's dead and he's spending the rest of his life in the pen and the kids are orphans."

"People have got two sides to them," she replied, after considering it. "They got the side that tells them to get up early and go milk the cows and go to work and the like. That's the day side that everybody sees. But then," she said, "there's the side that just behaves, and lots of times you don't know why it behaves the way it does. That's the night side."

In the distance beyond the concentration camp loomed the German Alps. In the foreground loomed with even greater, darker presence the ovens of Dachau. The chimneys were long cold, but the stench remained of all the poor bastards—32,000 of them—who were stuffed into the furnaces at this first of Hitler's concentration camps. The bad air seemed to turn the German sky to the blue of a corpse.

I stood there before the low brick building, staring through tears. I actually *felt* the suffering; I had that kind of imagination. I walked near the ovens. They were innocuous-looking now, something like the clay baker's ovens I had admired in Central America and elsewhere. Only these ovens had baked different loaves.

A Nazi doctor named Rascher had conducted cooling experiments on prisoners at Dachau. The helpless victims were garbed in pilot flight suits, then submerged in tanks of ice water. Rascher explained in a letter to Himmler that his experiments called for lowering his subjects' body temperature "within a period of nine to fourteen hours to between 27 and 29 degrees centigrade."

He begged Heinrich Himmler for a transfer to the death camp at Auschwitz where, he said, "large scale experiments can be conducted on the re-warming of persons who have been subjected to extreme cooling in the open air. Auschwitz is more suitable from every point of view as it is colder there and the camp itself is much larger, thereby attracting less attention to the test persons, who tend to scream when freezing."

It struck me with the impact of an exploding 105mm howitzer round: The military under whatever uniform had its night side. The difference between military experiments conducted on unwitting U.S. soldiers and the experiments the Nazis conducted on prisoners was merely a matter of selection and degree. In fact, a number of the scientists who performed tests on American servicemen at Edgewood Arsenal in Maryland were former Nazi Germans.

U.S. soldiers, some seven thousand of them between 1955 and 1975, were used in government testing of nuclear radiation, mustard gas, LSD, and other chemical and biological agents. Some were towed on a barge out to sea and ordered to look at the mushroom blast of a 15-megaton hydrogen bomb exploded in the South Pacific. They were then instructed to swim in waters contaminated with radioactive fallout. Others who believed they had volunteered to test military protective clothing were placed in sealed chambers and exposed to LSD and to gases they later learned were poisonous. Threatened with disciplinary action, they were sworn to secrecy. The army later conceded that any records of the experiments were sloppily kept or intentionally destroyed by army researchers.

Many of these American servicemen later developed common conditions and illnesses including cancers, mental disorders, and respiratory diseases. One of them, James B. Stanley, sued the United States for dosing him with hallucinatory LSD without his knowledge during the testing of anti-chemical clothing and equipment.

The Supreme Court ruled in favor of the government. Justice Scalia said, "Questioning the military's decision could disrupt the entire military regime."

I knew a captain who had been MI—Military Intelligence—in Vietnam. His job was to interrogate enemy prisoners of war.

"Did you really kill them like that?" I asked him one night.

"My sergeant did it."

"You *ordered* him to do it?"

"We had an understanding."

"So you're in a helicopter, flying at three thousand feet with five Vietnamese—"

"VC. They were Vietcong."

"This was sanctioned?"

"Officers looked the other way. They knew we were saving American lives."

"An American life is worth more than a gook's?"

"Exactly."

The captain's lips thinned. After Vietnam he lived on a hill outside the city. He erected a flagpole and constructed a kind of little memorial to Vietnam in his front yard. He always flew a giant American flag. At night a floodlamp bathed Old Glory in white light.

"Tell me about the VC," I coaxed.

"If you just questioned the gooks, they sat there like possums or they lied to you," he explained. "But they didn't lie—not the way we did it. We took up five gooks, or three or however many we had, in the chopper...."

When the helicopter reached altitude, the captain nodded curtly at his sergeant. The VC sat bound on the floor. The sergeant went slowly down the line, tossing the gooks out of the chopper one by one. The wind as they fell tumbling through the air ripped their screams from their throats.

"I never actually killed one myself," the captain said.

"The sergeant did it for you."

"He pushed them out. All except the last one. We saved the last one. I interrogated him while the chopper hovered at three thousand feet. He always talked. Always."

"What did you do with him afterward?"

"Pushed him out too. We couldn't leave anyone to talk about it."

"Saving American lives?"

"Yes."

* * *

281

At Dachau I stood in front of the ovens and thought about the night side of the military. An old woman stopped next to me and dabbed at her eyes with a pink handkerchief as she wept. A German man old enough to have served *der Führer* swept his gaze past the ovens, too quickly. He looked at the woman, not directly, but he looked at her.

"We in the town did not know what was going on here," he said. "None of us did. We were shocked when we found out."

She turned on him. "You *knew!*" she cried. "We *all* knew, but we pretended we did not know."

He looked away. "Yes," he admitted in a voice so small that it might not have been.

"We ignored it when the military gained power over our hearts," she said, "and when our minds donned the uniforms of national conformity. We pretended that Adolf Hitler and all his military knew what was good for us. We gave up choices and responsibility to the state. In return, the state burned some of us."

The old man turned and silently walked away, head lowered. I watched him slowly cross the great quadrangle where the prisoner barracks had been. He trailed along the wire and the wall and the ditch over which no prisoner back then dared venture on pain of death. He left the memorial with his head still lowered.

"Are you okay, Top?" Starner asked.

"Dianne, my first wife, was Jewish," I replied. "That makes my sons Jewish. In different times they could have ended up here."

I thought of the captain who had pushed the VC from the chopper, of my platoon sergeant who had participated in the rape and murder of a female prisoner, of Lieutenant Calley at My Lai, of the American major in El Salvador who had condoned the execution of prisoners. . . .

How far did it go, this night side? How far would military men go in obeying and following orders? What would they do to save American lives or to keep their jobs or in the name of "Obedience, diligence, honesty, order, cleanliness, temperance, truthfulness, sacrifice and love of one's country?"

How far?

"It took someone like Hitler to issue the orders," I said, "but it took officers all along the chain of command to follow those orders without question."

I looked at Starner. I looked away. I had been in uniform for twenty-four years and more.

"Starner, are we Americans developing that kind of mentality?"

72

The V Corps provost marshal's staff drove up in mysterious vans with camouflage curtains covering the windows. They were majors and light colonels and stern-faced, self-important men in civilian clothing—CID agents, lawyers, legal experts. Colonel Hackett rushed over from the Castle, followed by the Ferret and the Coyote, sniffing hard after him. They looked nervous. A crowd gathered in my orderly office in the basement of Charlie Signal Company.

The sergeant major from V Corps glanced around at my clerks' computers and typewriters and office files and reference materials.

"First Sergeant," he snapped, "the V Corps provost marshal will arrive here in fifteen minutes. Colonel Hopwood does not like to wait. You have fifteen minutes to get all this shit out of here."

That was the Coyote's opening. He stepped forward briskly. "Colonel Hackett, sir, I ordered First Sergeant Sasser to clear the offices—"

I exploded. "That's a goddamned lie, Sergeant Major. All

you told me was to take everything off my desk and lock the desk drawers."

Thirty minutes later everything needed to administratively sustain a company of 122 soldiers was piled outside in the hallway. Soldiers rushed in to repaint the scaling walls of the two rooms the company had been assigned in the basement. They began scrubbing and cleaning and moving in new furniture more appropriate for a colonel and his staff. A sign went up on the door: V Corps Provost Marshal. No Admittance.

My MP in the bar had been right. It appeared V Corps was preparing for a major investigation.

When I handed over the keys to the offices to Colonel Hopwood, he curled his lips, and his hand shot back as from a hot stove.

"Do you know who I am?" he snapped.

"Yes."

"Yes, *sir.*"

I waited. Why was it, I wondered, that the moment an officer put on his uniform his head shrunk three sizes, his neck enlarged, and his IQ dropped twenty points? I almost laughed aloud at the little man sitting there behind my former desk like a Napoleon or a Caesar. He reminded me of Ross Perot, the shrimp of a Texan who later ran for president. Same size, same prunish head, as if headhunters maybe had started to shrink it but quit before they finished. The features were pinched, mean.

Powell and I stood before his desk. I forced Hopwood's eyes to clash with mine. His shifted first, quickly. Something I saw in his eyes surprised me. I saw the soul of a little man who might have been selling hardware or used cars on the outside. But in the army he had *power.*

"Colonels do not handle *keys,*" Hopwood lectured, sniffing. "Give them to my major."

Before Hopwood arrived, his major had taken me aside and apologized: "First Sergeant, I'm really sorry about all this. The colonel can be an asshole sometimes."

The asshole now rocked forward in his new swivel chair

and clasped his hands in front of him on the desk. He stared at Captain Powell. He wasted no time.

"One more incident like the shooting barrel," he said, "and I'm going to relieve you and your first sergeant."

So far, everyone in the chain of command except the general himself had threatened to relieve us. The shooting barrel incident had been nothing, really, an accident. It was just another reason for the brass to fuck with us.

Shooting barrels were kept outside MP headquarters. They were open barrels filled with sand. To prevent injuries in case of an accidental weapons discharge while loading for duty or unloading after duty, MPs pointed their .45 pistols at the sand. A female MP had accidentally fired a round into the barrel.

"The forty-fives are difficult for our females to handle, sir—i.e., their hands are too small," Powell explained.

Accidental discharges like that were not uncommon. The MP detachment assigned to Hopwood's own V Corps had riddled their barrel and even discharged a round through the floorboard of a patrol vehicle. That didn't count; it counted only if the MP was a reservist belonging to my company.

"Punish her as an example, Captain Powell," Hopwood ordered. "Give her at least an Article Fifteen."

"It was an *accident*, sir."

"Captain Powell, you're awfully close to being relieved."

"Yes, sir." Powell's words snapped.

I saw that in a quite casual way Hopwood was enjoying making us squirm. I had a way of grinning at the most inappropriate time. I grinned as I visualized reaching across the desk and slowly throttling Ross Perot.

Hopwood swept a glance past me. Then the tone of his voice softened. He leaned back in his chair. "Do you know what we're doing here?" he asked conversationally.

I thought it a curious question to be asking us.

"I suppose it has something to do with the license plate incident with Colonel Hackett," I guessed.

"It has nothing to do with that."

I tried again. "You're investigating charges of corruption within the community?"

His eyebrows rose. His face reddened. "What corruption?" he demanded. "What are you talking about?"

That was when I knew the MP in the bar had been right. This investigation was going nowhere. I let the silence hang. Colonel Hopwood fiddled with a pencil. He shuffled some papers.

"I've heard all about you, First Sergeant," he said presently. His eyes still wouldn't hold mine. "You're the writer." He hesitated. "Are you going to write about your experiences here?"

He seemed as self-conscious of my being a journalist as everyone else at the caserne. The *Stars & Stripes* article about me had really set the brass talking. Even the commanding general of the Eighth Division had made a point of meeting me at a reception held at the Nahe Officers' Club honoring German chiefs of police for their antiterrorist support of Desert Storm. He charged up and vigorously wrung my hand. A hush fell. Eyebrows rose all over the ballroom.

The general introduced me around, speaking loudly enough so that everyone heard. "First Sergeant Sasser," he boomed, smiling, "is the most famous MP in Europe."

The Ferret and the Coyote had stood together whispering, their drinks frozen halfway to their lips.

"Look at their faces," Powell had whispered, "i.e., they'd kill you if they could get away with it."

Deep Throat had grinned broadly, enjoying it.

"You got them worried," he'd said.

Colonel Hopwood looked worried now. "Are you," he repeated, "going to write about your experiences?"

"Maybe."

"The investigation V Corps is conducting here is strictly confidential," he said pointedly.

More like a cover-up, I thought. I had turned cynical. Whatever corruption existed in the provost marshal's office and at headquarters would probably be "exposed" by charging a few low-ranking enlisted men with crimes and shifting around and transferring officers through "career moves." That was the way it was done in the military.

"You're dismissed, First Sergeant," Hopwood said.

* * *

Evicted from our own offices, Captain Powell and I moved MP headquarters across the parking lot to the War Boars' copy room. The room was about the size of a large walk-in closet. The She-Boar offered Powell and me the back half of it. There was no telephone. We shared a single battered desk. I sank wearily into a chair with the back support broken off. Twine held the legs of Powell's chair together.

We looked at each other and burst into bitter laughter.

"We can't go much farther down than this," Powell said. "The next stop is the Dipsy Dumpster."

He stopped laughing. He reached out his hand and gripped mine. "Top, we're in this together."

73

Saddam Hussein's "mother of all battles," the bloody ground war he had predicted, turned out to be the One Hundred Hour War. Far from extracting the large numbers of American casualties some generals expected, combat by first reports took only 144 U.S. KIAs—killed in action—and 339 WIAs—wounded in action. The war ended while I was still trying to arrange to have my company shipped out of Germany to the war in Iraq. The end of the war meant my mission was essentially completed. The company remained in Germany on its law-and-order mission.

My thoughts turned from war to home and Margie. We had been separated for five months when she flew to Germany in May to marry me. Captain Powell's fiancée, Monique, also flew over. We intended to make it a double wedding.

We married in Denmark when the cherry trees were blossoming. The four of us clasped hands, laughing and hugging each other. It rained a little and we all carried matching pink umbrellas and the Danes were a friendly people who smiled on us.

On our honeymoon in Paris, Powell suddenly shouted from the hallway of the hotel, "Top! Top! Get out here quick. Help me carry Monique across the threshold."

Monique was pregnant. On her honeymoon two roaring laughing men carried her across her threshold.

"Top, you two were drunk as skunks," Monique protested. "You couldn't even have carried Margie, and look how tiny she is."

"Margie," I said, "all I want to do is come home to you. That's what I'm living for—you and the kids and the home we'll build."

I had grown to love her four kids too.

However much I had loved other wives and other women in between wives, I felt my heart and soul consumed by Margie. I could never get enough of her. I slept with her tight in my arms and in my thoughts and in my heart.

"It just shows all over how much you two love each other," Monique cried.

We all have our dark sides, our night souls, and we are all prone to self-destruction.

"When?" Margie asked. "When will you come home? I've missed you so."

"The war's over. I can't understand why we're being held here now. It's been almost six months."

Colonel Hackett couldn't, or wouldn't, give me a straight answer on when I might expect to take my MPs back to Louisiana.

"You could be here until October or even next January," he kept saying.

"Why? I need to give my people a definite date of deactivation, something to look forward to. They need to get home to their families and jobs."

"It's not up to us," Hackett said.

"Who's it up to?"

"The Pentagon."

"The Pentagon is keeping one MP company in Germany for no reason? The war is over. Desert Storm has ended."

"We don't question orders. We just follow them. Like you should," Hackett said.

The Coyote smirked.

"You have no right to question anything," he scolded. "Better get used to being here. You could be here for a long time. Your company still has legal problems."

I had one soldier AWOL, who took emergency leave home and refused to return, and then there was the ongoing fraternization investigation between my lieutenant and his enlisted girlfriend. While V Corps investigated the provost marshal's office on what I assumed to be serious corruption charges, the PMO in turn investigated my company because an enlisted woman and an officer had fallen in love.

"*Nix nein, nix nein* on going home," said the Ferret, crossing his legs and his limp wrists. He looked as if he had indigestion but enjoyed having it.

Since the war in Iraq had ended without the expected deluge of casualties arriving at the hospital in whose basement my sergeants and I lived, the hospital became all but abandoned again. My sergeants and I lived in the basement like rats.

Colonel Hopwood's V Corps investigation also ended with few casualties. Nothing much happened except that a lot of people *might* have run scared for a few weeks. Some lower-ranking officers at the MP stations were shifted around a little; four low-ranking enlisted men were eventually court-martialed and ended up at Fort Leavenworth army prison for drug, AWOL, and theft offenses. I heard that the MP who had confronted Colonel Hackett was one of them.

"See?" cried the MP from the bar as he packed his gear for transfer. "It's a cover-up. Enlisted men take the rap for the corruption at the top."

"Margie," I said wearily before she flew home, "I'm so tired from fighting them. I just want to come home to you and start our married life together."

Once, years ago, after Kathy, my second wife, and I divorced, I rode my motorcycle back to the hills that I had roamed as a kid. It was as if the rope that tied my life together had been tethered there and had broken, leaving me adrift without purpose or direction. I had to find the break and repair it.

Alone, skinny from sorrow, I found the old sandstone foundation from the three-room shack where Mom had built me my first desk and where I had often huddled underneath the tarp by the brook when it rained. Out on Drake's Prairie, all that remained of Paw's old farm was the storm cellar. It had caved in partially. I found the concrete slab from above the cellar door. "Henry Sasser," it said, "September 17, 1947." I remembered when Paw had finished the cellar and carefully written his name in the wet cement.

In the weeds I picked up a piece of weathered siding from the old house. Holding it, closing my eyes, I almost saw the old man again in his patched bib overalls with the brown stains of his snuff dribbling in the skin seams at the corners of his mouth.

There was an old joke men told about how they wanted to die at ninety, shot in the saddle by a jealous husband. Paw was living with his thirty-six-year-old barfly girlfriend when her ex-boyfriend broke into the house and beat Paw senseless. Paw was ninety-three years old, and he was drunk. He died from the beating.

"You old scoundrel," I said to Paw's simple tombstone at the Sallisaw cemetery.

I looked—and everything was much smaller than I remembered, everyone so much older. Sadly, I found that wherever I went, weeds grew where grass had once grown. Was that what they meant when they said you could never go home again?

I kicked up my motorcycle and left the hills behind.

I so wanted a home that I could keep, a woman to keep who would love me just because I was me. Was that too much to ask?

"Come home soon," Margie said when she left Europe. "I'll be waiting."

74

Shooting wars begin and end, but the paper war of bureaucrats continues forever, amen.

I sent Enlisted Evaluation Reports over to the Castle; the Coyote returned them for corrections. One time there was a period missing at the end of a sentence. Another time there was an extra space between sentences. They came back three times in one afternoon, twice the next day, four times the third day.

"First Sergeant, you're in the *real* army now," sneered the Coyote.

I stuffed the reports in my desk and left them there until the deadline date. The Coyote rang my phone off the desk.

"Where are the EERs?"

"Beg your pardon, Sergeant Major?"

"The Enlisted Evaluations? The major and the colonel are on my ass."

"Oh? I left them with you, Sergeant Major. That's the last I've seen of them."

Came a long pause.

"First Sergeant, they *have* to be here today."

"I'll look around and see if I kept copies."

Powell laughed until tears came to his eyes when I pulled the originals out of my desk and sent them over.

Everything the company generated had to be funneled through higher headquarters for approval. I delivered a letter to Division addressed to the transportation office. The Ferret returned the letter seven times for minor corrections. My clerk burst into tears. Tossing the letter into the wastebasket, I telephoned Transportation.

"I can't seem to get a letter to you," I explained. "Can we handle this over the telephone?"

"Of course. You could have scribbled me a note on the back of an envelope."

I kicked the wastebasket across the room.

The Desert Storm war ended; the war at Rose Barracks continued.

"Top, you look so tired," my clerk said.

Yeah.

I jogged the trail on the mountain above Bad Münster and came to the castle ruins and found my place on the wall. I watched the red haze of sunset over the valley and the little town below along the river. Over in Baumholder, another reserve MP company from New York was threatening open revolt against regular army treatment. In Texas, most of an entire reserve company called up for Desert Storm had rebelled at the contemptuous treatment and simply walked away. You couldn't have a war if soldiers did that. The army eventually court-martialed many of the reservists and sent them to Fort Leavenworth prison.

It was the same story everywhere.

"The regular army treats us like second-class citizens," Starner mused. "They have their jobs to think of. If part-time reservists can do the job as well as full-timers, people are going to start asking why we should pay so many full-timers. Regular army has a big stake in making sure reservists look bad."

Deep Throat agreed. "Your company has taken a load of petty shit here," he said, "but you've done a better job than most regular army MPs. That has caused a lot of jealousy and resentment."

"They keep threatening to relieve Powell and me. Why don't they?"

"You've done your job and done it well. Second, you're very high-profile. If they do anything at all to you now, there may be questions asked all the way to the Pentagon. This division can't stand any close scrutiny. Third, they don't have the guts. The army has turned into a bunch of paper shufflers and ass kissers. Managers, not warrior leaders.

When we go to war, we need to go to war with men like you. Instead, we've created an officer corps of ticket punchers. The war was just a game to them, a way to advance their careers—and it ended too quickly."

Combat command time made officers' careers bloom. "Without it," said a frustrated infantry captain, "you are outta here. We *needed* that war, and it ended before most of us could get into it. War is the only way to season troops. You have to blood them. If only it had lasted for six months. Was that too much to ask? Combat decorations look good in your file."

The Gulf War was the only game in town. You couldn't keep training a football team without using it sooner or later. Fewer than 150 American lives had been lost in combat. The toll would have been much higher had most officers had their way.

Deep Throat looked at me. "Top, what do you hear about a date for sending your company home?"

"Division won't give me a date. I don't understand it."

Every day I watched my company's morale sink lower. Only about 10 percent of my soldiers were actually needed. The rest hung around waiting to go home.

"What do you know about the Kurds?" Deep Throat asked me.

I knew the Kurds had links to resistance groups rebelling against Saddam. The United States sent a task force to the Turkish-Iraqi border to protect fleeing Kurds from reprisal.

"Top, Division has had an air date for over a month to ship your company home."

I blinked, stunned.

"The way I understand it," said Deep Throat, "is that Colonel Hopwood, the V Corps provost, is bucking for his star. He's politicking to get Department of Army to send him and his corps MPs to Turkey in support of the Kurdish relief effort. That means he has to have MPs to replace his here in Germany."

"*My* MPs!"

"You could be here for another year or longer."

"So it's *not* the Pentagon holding us! It's Division officers playing politics—and my soldiers are pawns for them."

Colonel Hopwood, the prune-faced Perot of the U.S. Army.

I sat on my castle wall.

"Top, we have to do *something,*" Powell said.

75

My daily afternoon run from the hospital basement where I lived up into the mountains above Bad Münster always ended at the castle ruins set on their rock pinnacle. From the castle wall I looked straight down into the little river two hundred feet below. Birch and aspen grew on the banks. Beyond the river lay a park where Germans strolled in couples and in families. Bad Münster, the town beyond, tiered out into mountains and vineyards.

As I watched the sunset, I missed taking long walks at this time of the afternoon with Margie and the children. She lived in Small Town, America. Flags flew. Yellow ribbons decorated half the shade trees in town.

I inhaled a long deep breath. You could look directly at the sun where it turned red just before it dropped behind the mountain.

I pondered.

Over the years I had been willing to fight the military and the government for what I believed to be right and just. I truly believed that if you were right, you had to win. You had to. I had won years ago when I was in Special Forces and the group commander attempted to kick me out for insulting the American ambassador to Liberia in the *Soldier of Fortune* article; I had won the Goat Lab Revolt at Fort

Bragg when the medical commander would have subjected my men to double jeopardy over the I.V. testing.

But would even Don Quixote, that foolish knight, possess the courage to take on the entire U.S. Army? Would he dare dispute the authority of the army to use its soldiers as it deemed fit? Would even he question government's motive and structure and legitimacy? Would he fight back out of moral principle if it meant he might also destroy himself?

Would even Don Quixote challenge these windmills?

Yet Captain Powell was right. We had to do *something*.

I climbed slowly down from the wall. A man, Paw used to say, must *always* be a man. I jogged the long trail back to the basement at the hospital caserne. It was downhill most of the way. I jogged faster until, for the last mile, I was sprinting.

Colonel Hopwood was not going to use my company to win his star. Fuck him. I was going to take my company and go home. Our job was over.

I broke out a stack of paper. I began to write: "Dear Mr. President . . ."

76

President George Bush
The White House
1600 Pennsylvania Ave. N.W.
Washington, D.C. 20500

Dear Mr. President:

The Minuteman, the reserve soldier, in American society has a long tradition stretching back to the Revolutionary War. When the bugle sounded, he dropped his plow and rallied to the call. When the emergency ended, he immediately hung up his rifle and returned to the plow. He had fields to till.

As a veteran of some twenty-four years in the military, first sergeant of a Military Police Company (U.S. Army Reserve) activated to Germany in support of Desert Storm, and a published author some of whose books have been recommended reading at West Point, war colleges, and other military schools, I carefully considered the role of the American reserve soldier before deciding that I could not remain silent in the face of gross waste and abuse extending far beyond a company of 122 young Americans ten thousand miles from home.

All that is required for injustice to prevail is that good men do nothing. . . .

The letter that followed, six pages long, highlighted high-jinks at the Castle. It ended this way:

If the war had continued, my men and women . . . would have proudly served without complaint. Even now they serve, feeling as they do that they are not really needed and not really wanted other than to satisfy some uncertain requirement that has nothing to do with Desert Storm.

Mr. President, congressmen, and political representatives who receive this letter, if we would retain this great well of Minutemen to serve in another time of crisis, it is mandatory that they be treated as the first-class citizens they truly are. They were rushed away from homes and families and lives when there was a need; now there is a personal need for them to be rushed back home.

Mr. President, the Minutemen have their fields to till.

Charles W. Sasser
1SG, MP, USA
APO New York 09111–2111

77

I thought of the human ovens, the dead skies over Dachau. I drew my jacket close to ward off chills that had nothing to do with the weather.

"Top, you did what was right, what you had to do," Starner said.

"Yes," I said. I felt like talking, working out thoughts that must have lain dormant for years waiting for the right time. Seeds that were now sprouting. "Starner, our young men are fed illusions of glory and honor and selfless service. God, country, and Mom's apple pie. Because of these illusions, each generation of young men marches off to kill and to die. The machine grinds up their flesh, but first it grinds up their souls. We are systematically brutalized to accept regimentation and war, even to love war as a necessary condition of democracy. We become vehicles of destruction on command."

I kept thinking of the human ovens.

"This first round in Iraq is only the prelude to the biggest bloodbath since the Second World War. The generals think they have a mandate for the use of military force now because of the popularity of this war back home. They see that the end of the Cold War and the cutback in the military is eroding their power and their career opportunities. They're not going to let that happen. They need wars; the economy needs wars. The generals will start wars."

The Pentagon was already planning for the post–Cold War era, envisioning separate scenarios in which the United States might become involved in foreign wars—in Panama, the Baltics, the Persian Gulf region again, Korea, and Philippines, and combinations of these.

Games. Deadly games.

I remembered Uncle James: "Folks like them can't stand to see anybody that ain't got saddle sores and that ain't got his wings clipped."

"Starner, in the name of obedience, order, sacrifice, and love of one's country, I truly believe our American military would burn 'wetbacks' or 'ragheads' or Muslims or 'dinks' or anyone else our leaders designated as enemies. It saddens me, but as time passes I see fewer and fewer differences in the mentality of American leadership today and that of Hitler fifty years ago."

"The world is getting so fucked up," Mad Dog would say later. "Join us," he said. "We're not going off to foreign lands again to fight for oil and power and get killed so politicians can prove how tough they are. Our government has become abusive of its own people. It's taxing us to poverty, it's taking away our guns so we can't resist, and it's passing hundreds of new laws every year to control us like a bunch of sheep. The sons of bitches in Congress are arrogant and corrupt. This ain't a democracy no more. Some of us ain't going to stand for it much longer. The next fighting I'm going to do is right here in the United States."

Another antigovernment "survivalist" showed me stockpiles of ammunition, weapons, combat uniforms, and foodstuffs, enough to supply a platoon of irregulars. His group had also bought a large tract of wilderness surrounded by even larger expanses of swamp and mountains owned by the government.

"It would take a brigade to dig us out of here," he assured me. "By the time they did, there would be hundreds of freedom fighters all over America fighting to regain liberties politicians and lawyers are taking away from us. One twelve-man team of ex–Special Forces could tie up a thousand soldiers for months."

He glanced about. "Do you still have sources in Central America?" he asked, voice lowered. "We need to find a new source of supply for M203 grenade launchers. Right now we're paying one hundred twenty-five dollars just for a single grenade."

In addition to the twenty thousand Americans whom FBI agents working internal sedition have targeted as involved in some form of direct antigovernment or revolutionary activities, there are perhaps another ten times that number supporting them indirectly or tacitly.

"Join us, Sasser," Mad Dog said. "The government is leaving us no choice but to resist."

After I'd finished my letter calling for a presidential investigation, Captain Powell and I met to discuss possible consequences. We sat in an army van in the gathering darkness of the storm in front of the BOQ.

Dark clouds boiled above the valley of Bad Münster. Neat little German cottages in dress-right-dress rows lined the street in front of us. The German culture was so lockstep, so organized, so obedient to authority. Even televisions had to be registered with government. I had watched Germans in the middle of a rainy night wait for a red light to change rather than jaywalk against the signal. I always suspected they organized sex and counted cadence.

No wonder the Ferret adored Germany. The Ferret and his smirking *"Nix nein, nix nein."*

"The letter. It's the right thing to do, Top," Powell said, his voice grave. "They've proved we can't depend on them. Now we have to do things for ourselves."

"I'm sending the letter in my name, Captain. You're an officer; it could destroy your career. What can they do to me? Send me to Vietnam? I want you to disassociate yourself from me, Captain."

A look of hurt surprise crossed his dark face.

"Top, are we friends or what?"

"That's why I'm offering you a way out."

"I've been around you too long, Top. I couldn't look at myself in the mirror again if I let you stand up alone. I'm a cop; you were a cop. What kind of man would I be if we shared an armed robbery call and, i.e., I let you go in after the robber by yourself?"

Wind picked up fallen leaves off the lawn of the BOQ and sent them thrashing down the middle of the street.

"Partner," I said, "here comes the storm."

78

"When I took the oath to my country," Colonel Hackett said, "I swore to give up my life if necessary in obeying the orders of my superiors. If I'm ordered to take a hill and I know that I and all my men are going to die, I'm still sworn to obey and lead us to our death."

It was late at night. We had been talking for hours. Powell dozed next to me, sitting up on the colonel's sofa.

I leaned toward the big colonel. "How far does that go—following orders?" I demanded. "If your superiors told you in advance that it was a suicide mission and that it served no real purpose, would you still go?"

"I am sworn to obey."

"Blindly?"

"The oath doesn't set those kinds of conditions."

"If your superiors ordered you to burn Jews, would you burn Jews?"

"The orders must be legal and moral," he countered.

"In 1943, Hitler's officers apparently believed their orders were legal and moral. Do our officers today know where to draw the line? Do they care? Or is career the only thing that matters? The difference between us and other animals is that God gave us reasoning power so that we do not blindly follow orders to self-destruction or the destruction of others. He gave us the ability to make choices for ourselves—although I'm sure the military would like to take away that ability."

A look of indecision, of almost raw anguish, flickered over Hackett's dark features. I almost felt sorry for him; he was conditioned to follow orders, not to question. He concealed his feelings quickly and fell back upon his authority.

"First Sergeant, your letter has made life very difficult for the military," he announced. "Your letter has tainted the career of one general and maybe even up to a three-star general. Do you realize what you've done?"

"Completely. Colonel, one way or another, I'm taking my people home."

He pointed a trembling finger at me. "We don't want to keep anyone here who doesn't want to be here. We don't want you here now. You've embarrassed us enough. We're kicking you and that bunch of misfits out of Europe."

"How about the legal problems—the fraternization investigation and all that?"

"It's over. We just want you out of here. The general ordered me to give you an air date. We've had to suck it up to do it, but we're going to do it. You have a lot to get ready before then. It's all up to you."

"My company will be on that airplane. Will that be all, Colonel?"

I awoke Powell. He grinned, embarrassed. We started for the door.

"First Sergeant?" Hackett said. His voice softened. "You're intelligent and articulate. I have to like and respect you for having the courage of your convictions. It looks like you won."

"Yes," I said.

"First Sergeant, when you write that book I hope you'll remember ol' Colonel Hackett kindly."

Colonel Hackett recommended Captain Powell for the Army Commendation Medal; Powell in turn recommended me for it. Powell received his medal; I didn't.

"Nix nein, nix nein," simpered the Ferret. "I can tell you right now I'm going to disapprove it."

"Why?" Captain Powell demanded.

"What has Sasser done to deserve it?"

Powell started listing: "He came to the company cold and prepared it for war deployment in record time. He led the company through retraining twice—i.e., for two separate missions. He oversaw the day-to-day activities of the company under trying conditions. He personally taught leadership to NCOs and to the officers. He has organized redeployment home. He has earned the respect of every member of the company. He's the best first sergeant we've ever had."

"You haven't seen many first sergeants, then."

Snigger. Snigger.

Deep Throat explained it: word had come down from the general; I was a rebel.

Powell marked my Enlisted Evaluation "Excellent" in every category. Colonel Hackett declined to sign it.

I looked at him. His big hands hung alongside his uniform seams like those of a fast-growing schoolboy wearing last year's shirt. I knew he wanted to sign, but he still had his career to consider. One word from the general and he would have found himself looking for a job in civilian life.

"You don't have to sign it, Colonel," I said gently. I wanted to pat his arm. "None of you here judge me—and I certainly don't judge myself—by little ribbons and pieces of paper. I judge myself by much higher standards. I have to look at myself in the mirror every morning."

"First Sergeant . . ."

Speechless, he shook my hand hard. The Ferret and the Coyote turned their backs.

At the Frankfurt airport, Colonel Hopwood the Ross Perot look-alike strutted back and forth. He had his MPs search Stateside-bound MPs for drugs and contraband.

"He looks pissed off," Powell said.

"It's his last chance to fuck with us," I said, then laughed. "Apparently things didn't work out the way he planned them."

As our cheering troops boarded the big Pan Am airliner,

going home first class to bands and speeches and yellow ribbons and all that, Powell and I slapped palms and gripped hands.

"We kicked some ass!" he shouted.

I was too weary to respond. I looked out the window at Hopwood. He stared hard back at the airplane. I flipped him the bird—fuck him—as the airplane began taxiing.

Germany soon disappeared beneath the wing. I fell immediately asleep. . . .

79

From Bruno Bettelheim's Foreword to *Auschwitz* by Dr. Miklos Nyiszli:

Years before Hitler sent millions to the gas chambers, Freud insisted that human life is one long struggle against what he called the death instinct, and that we all must learn to keep these destructive strivings within bounds lest they send us to our destruction. The twentieth century did away with ancient barriers that once prevented our destructive tendencies from running rampant, both in ourselves and in society. State, family, church, society, all were put to question, and found wanting. So their power to restrain or channel our destructive tendencies were weakened. The re-evaluation of all values which Nietzsche predicted would be required of Western man, were he to survive in the modern machine age, has not yet been achieved. The old means of controlling the death instinct have lost much of their hold, and the new, higher morality that should replace them is not yet achieved. In this interregnum between an old and new social organization—between man's obsolete inner organization and the new structure not yet achieved—little is left to restrain man's destructive tendencies. In this age, then, only man's personal ability to control his own death instinct can protect him when the destructive forces of others, as in the Hitler state, run rampant.

Afterword

"I've been having an affair," Margie said.

It was my first day home. She had seen him, slept with him, just a few nights before. I felt like a frag grenade with the pin pulled. Overcome with shock and grief and pain, I grabbed myself and rocked and moaned. I wanted to scream with rage, hurl myself into walls, jump in front of a truck.

I whimpered like a beaten dog.

"It didn't mean anything," Margie said. "It was just physical."

That was supposed to make me feel better?

I grabbed my pack and rode my bicycle furiously north in the July heat. I rode for days. Sometimes it rained, but mostly there was the burning sun, like in Saudi. Each day I rode myself to exhaustion; one day across Oklahoma and Missouri was like the day before and like the day after. I rode, panting, sweating, burning underneath the sun. I got off the bicycle and broke bottles, smashed them and stomped them with my heels until they were glistening dust. I collapsed alongside the highway and held my head in my arms, and out came great pathetic sobs and mewlings.

"Where you going?" people sometimes asked.

"I'm a veteran," I said, as if that should explain everything.

"So where you going?"

"I don't know. I went to war. When I came home I found my new wife was sleeping around. Where would you go?"

They wouldn't look at me after that. "I don't know," they said.

AFTERWORD

Later, much later, after the nightmares dwindled, I took still another ride back to the land of my roots, to where I could still see. Paw in his old felt hat walking out to feed the pigs, where I could still hear his voice down in the pasture cussing ol' Jude the mule. Where Mom had built me a desk to help feed my dreams of becoming a writer. Where Mr. Mullins had introduced me to Don Quixote.

I had found strength there in those hills when I was a poor kid roaming the mountains and picking cotton. I could always find it there again when I needed it. The toughest trees, Paw always said, grew in rocky soil.

Besides, Don Quixote never gave up.

There would always be new windmills to joust.